Federalism and Nationalism

The Struggle for Republican Rights in the USSR

Federalism and Nationalism

The Struggle for Republican Rights in the USSR

Gregory Gleason

with a Foreword by John N. Hazard

Westview Press
BOULDER, SAN FRANCISCO, & LONDON

Westview Special Studies on the Soviet Union and Eastern Europe

Copyright © 1990 by Westview Press, Inc.

Published in 1990 in the United States of America by Westview Press, Inc., 5500 Central Avenue, Boulder, Colorado 80301, and in the United Kingdom by Westview Press, Inc., 13 Brunswick Centre, London WC1N 1AF, England

Library of Congress Cataloging-in-Publication Data
Gleason, Gregory.
   Federalism and nationalism : the struggle for republican rights in
the USSR / Gregory Gleason, with a foreword by John N. Hazard.
     p.   cm. — (Westview special studies on the Soviet Union and
Eastern Europe)
   Bibliography: p.
   Includes index.
   ISBN 0-8133-7552-5
   1. Federal government—Soviet Union. 2. Regionalism—Soviet
Union—Republics. 3. Nationalism—Soviet Union—Republics.
I. Title. II. Series.
JN6520.S8G54   1990
321.02′0947—dc19   88-4970
                                                                                          CIP

Printed and bound in the United States of America

⦿   The paper used in this publication meets the requirements of the American National
     Standard for Permanence of Paper for Printed Library Materials Z39.48-1984.

10   9   8   7   6   5   4   3   2   1

Contents

Foreword

Ethnic unrest is sweeping the Soviet Union. As a result, some now believe that the Communist Party will eventually be forced to consent to a dissolution of the federation. What has caused this unrest, which seemed to have developed suddenly after Mikhail S. Gorbachev was named General Secretary in 1985? What outcome can be expected—suppression by forceful means, accommodation through compromise, or secession of disaffected ethnic groups?

In this book, Gregory Gleason explores the causes of the unrest and speculates on the possible future direction of national movements. His unconventional thesis is that although Lenin and Stalin were centrists in their thinking, they could not administer their enormous country without enlisting minority peoples in the process. In so doing, they created a basis for the emergence of nationalist bureaucracies, which, by adopting self-protective and self-promotive strategies, actually augmented the *de jure* federalism proclaimed by the constitution.

Time, Professor Gleason maintains, has reinforced the cleavages. Peoples in the republics have sought to defend themselves against the bureaucratic centralism sponsored by Stalin by strengthening their own nationalist bureaucracies. The center has had to compromise with this developing force, and the result has been the emergence of what Gleason calls a "political contract." Although Stalin expected that he could eventually replace this contract as an economic union created interdependence of peoples and as the Communist Party induced proud peoples to transfer their ethnic loyalties to a class-oriented Soviet Union, he failed. His attempts to unify the diverse ethnic populations were thwarted by the political institutions of the federal structure, the administrative bureaucracies controlled by the leaders of ethnic groups, the national cadres, and even career incentives for the communists of the national republics. In short, Stalin's own creations, designed not only to pacify the national groups but to administer efficiently what the center at its distance could not administer through its cadres, became the instruments of his undoing. Although his ruthless tactics cowed minorities into acquiescence during his lifetime, his successors were incapable of maintaining the terms of the "contract." Finally, Gorbachev's unleashing of

vii

the forces of *glasnost* released minority peoples from fear. They raised their voices, took courage, and began to demand recognition of the sovereignty declared by the constitution but suppressed in practice.

Professor Gleason's thesis is attractive, and it appears to be supported by the evidence as minority leaders exploit opportunities afforded by Gorbachev to speak their minds. Some of these leaders are even ridiculing Stalin's explanations of his federal structures, asking why some peoples are accorded higher status in terms of rights and representation in the legislature than others who are less numerous. They reject as irrelevant Stalin's argument that the highest designation in the federation's hierarchy—union republic—can be granted only to people living on Soviet frontiers. Stalin argued that a republic should border the capitalist world so that secession would be geographically feasible, yet all knew that Stalin on several occasions had declared that his Communist Party would oppose secession under any circumstances. With such opposition, secessionary movements were unrealistic.

Outside analysts, and even those within the Soviet Union, speculate on Stalin's reasons for attempting to press peoples with long, distinguished histories of independence into a single mold so as to create a seemingly homogenized people to be known as "Soviet." Why should officials at the center in many cases attempt to dictate the administration of centrally established policies in outlying regions of which they know nothing? Was Stalin moved by a conception of Marxism that required all peoples to shed their ethnic loyalties for a universal class loyalty as prescribed by the Communist Manifesto of 1848? Or was Stalin more likely moved by his estimate of what was necessary to govern a large area populated by peoples who had struggled with each other over the centuries? Was the Marxist doctrine of "class unity" merely a convenient way of explaining repression of ethnic demands for recognition in a manner presumably acceptable to regional leaders imbued with "revolutionary" zeal?

Professor Gleason indicates that the center finally realized how great was the peril created by reliance upon national bureaucrats to direct the administration of their respective republics in the name of the center. He cites as evidence the center's actions in Central Asia when the Kazakhs took to the streets to protest the ousting of their republic's leader, whose personal corruption had become notorious: An ethnic Russian, rather than a Kazakh, was placed in the seat of local power.

The Kazakh unrest led to unrest among other minority peoples. Finally, in 1989, the Communist Party of the Soviet Union felt itself compelled to redefine the relationship between the republics and the center. A constitutional drafting committee was formed, and the Party's Central Committee held a meeting to consider possible remedies for the problem of newly emerging centrifugal forces.

The prospect of unity seems dim, as cries for the center's recognition of sovereignty and even for secession resound in the streets. Even indigenous communists have felt themselves compelled to join the general public in what are called "national fronts," although these groups support nationalist aspirations and nothing is said of the "class" unity of all peoples. Some fear that the stage is being set for open, perhaps even armed, conflict. The immediate enemy is not the center but workers imported from other republics to staff the new factories planned by the center; the ultimate enemy may be troops sent by the center to quell the conflict.

Professor Gleason's study and conclusions come at a time when the complexity of the problems facing Soviet leadership needs to be known by a larger public in the United States than the professional Sovietologists. It is becoming commonplace among the political commentators of the U.S. media to declare that a splintered Soviet Union could, or probably would, upset the balance of forces throughout the world. No thinking American can ignore the likelihood that such a change would be unsettling to many peoples. Professor Gleason's analysis prepares the reader to follow the interplay between center and minority peoples in the Soviet Union with a truer understanding of the issues.

John N. Hazard
Columbia University

An Explanatory Note

In an effort to do justice to Soviet political discourse, this book takes some liberties with established Western usage. A few expressions in particular may cause the reader some initial pause. One may ask, for instance, Is not the expression used repeatedly in this book, "national federalism," needlessly confusing? Are not, indeed, "national" and "federal" governments one and the same thing? In Western societies, of course, we do think of "national" as applying to the central or federal government. But in multinational states such as the USSR the word national typically refers to one or another of the constituent "nations," or national groups. Thus the term national is used in Soviet political discourse to apply to ethnic groups, whether Russian, Armenian, Uzbek, or any of the other 100-odd "nations," "nationalities," and "peoples" recognized in Soviet official sources. The citizens of the USSR, Russian and minority alike, speak of national history and traditions, national republics, national soviets, national literatures and languages, national leaders, national heroes, and so on. Following this Soviet usage, in this book the term "national" refers specifically to the constituent groups of the USSR, not to the central government.

The researcher working on federal relations in the USSR inevitably encounters materials in a variety of languages. Systems of transliteration from the various languages differ widely. One way of avoiding ambiguity in reference to individuals, place names, etc., is to transliterate all materials from the vernacular languages of the national minorities in the Russianized form. Thus one would use "Azerbaidzhan" rather than the more felicitous "Azerbaijan." While this is not meant to imply a value orientation on the part of the researcher, it unfortunately imparts an imprimatur of legitimacy to the Russianized version. Reacting to such conventions, a vocal group of Western scholars has adopted a conscious practice of avoiding any implied sanction of political legitimacy in its discourse about certain Soviet borderland regions. Among some researchers one finds avoidance of the expression "Soviet nationalities" since it tends to accord a measure of privilege to the center. Similarly, one finds reference to life "in Ukraine" rather than "in the Ukraine" to avoiding giving sanction to the idea that the Ukraine is a constituent territory. (We would not say "in the Russia.") These are not merely semantic issues. However, I see no way of resolving this other than to state simply and straightforwardly as a matter of principle that the "union-centric" language and transliteration conventions adopted in this book imply no intentional pro-centric bias of my own.

Transliterations from the Russian follow the Library of Congress system except in rare cases where conventional or idiomatic use recommends a phonetic variant (e.g., as in the case of Yakovlev instead of Iakovlev). As a rule, I have omitted the Russian soft sign in words such as "glasnost" since these have become familiar to most readers. I have retained the full transliterated form in the notes at the end of each chapter, however. For the purpose of maintaining consistency of reference, quotes from Lenin come from the most complete Russian language compilation of his works, *Polnoe sobranie sochinenii*. Translations are my own.

Gregory Gleason

Acknowledgments

Even in a culture as individualistic as ours, scholarship of any form is invariably a collaborative enterprise. During the preparation of this study I have benefited from the assistance of a number of institutions and individuals. I am especially grateful to the Kennan Institute for Advanced Russian Studies of the Wilson Center, under whose auspices the research for this book was begun. The University of Illinois Summer Russian Research Laboratory made research materials available to me. The staff of the Center for International Research of the United States Bureau of the Census offered valuable assistance regarding statistical material. The Research Allocations Committee of the University of New Mexico provided me with assistance in the revision of the manuscript. The final version of the manuscript was completed while I was a U.S. State Department Title VIII Visiting Researcher at the Hoover Institution.

I have benefited from the encouragement, advice, criticism, and data offered in a spirit of *tovarishchestvo* by a number of scholars and analysts, many of whose names appear in the footnotes. Enrique Baloyra, Ralph Clem, John Cunningham, Kenneth Gray, Alexander McIntire, Jr., and Mohiaddin Mesbahi offered particular support and encouragement at a critical point in this project. Paul Goble expeditiously read the manuscript repeatedly, sending me back to the drawing board on each occasion with valuable criticism. University of New Mexico graduate students Ross Miller, Paulius Narbutas, and Andrea Philliber cheerfully proofed and "pere-proofed" more drafts than anyone cares to recall. Debby Knotts-Callahan transformed a morass of data into graceful tables and also produced the map. I am particularly grateful to Rebecca Ritke of Westview Press for her encouragement and patience. Barbara Gleason was the Rock of Gibraltar during numerous storms. I am grateful for the contributions of all these institutions and people. The views and interpretations expressed here are my own.

G. G.

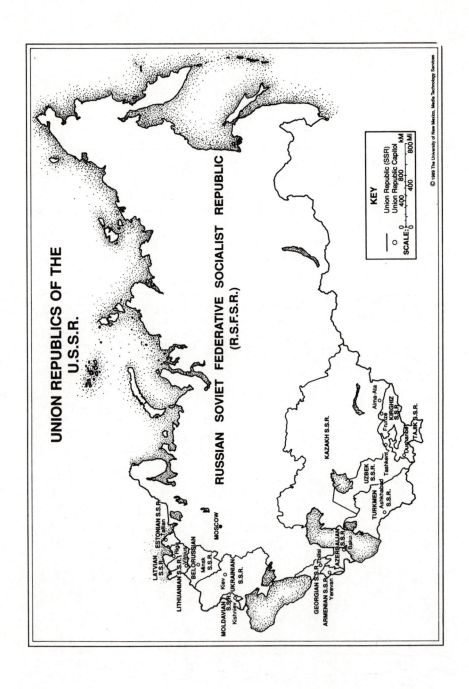

UNION REPUBLICS OF THE
U.S.S.R.

RUSSIAN SOVIET FEDERATIVE SOCIALIST REPUBLIC
(R.S.F.S.R.)

KEY
— Union Republic (SSR)
○ Union Republic Capitol

SCALE: 0   400   800   kM
        0   400   800 Mi

© 1989 The University of New Mexico, Media Technology Services

KAZAKH S.S.R.

Alma-Ata ○
KIRGHIZ S.S.R.
Frunze ○
TAJIK S.S.R.
Dushambe ○

UZBEK
S.S.R.
Tashkent ○
TURKMEN
S.S.R.
Ashkhabad ○

AZERBAIJAN
S.S.R.
Baku ○

LATVIAN S.S.R.
ESTONIAN S.S.R.
Tallin ○
Riga ○
LITHUANIAN S.S.R.
Vilnius ○
BELORUSSIAN
S.S.R.
Minsk ○
MOSCOW ○
MOLDAVIAN
S.S.R.
Kishinev ○
UKRAINIAN
S.S.R.
Kiev ○
GEORGIAN S.S.R.
Tbilisi ○
ARMENIAN S.S.R.
Yerevan ○

1

A Question of Federalism

Marxists will never under any circumstances advocate . . . the federal principle.
—Lenin

Early in 1988, nationalist-inspired demonstrations in the Armenian and Azerbaidzhan republics of the USSR erupted in violence. The protests marked only the most recent in a series of long-simmering irredentist disputes over the relationship between ethnographic and administrative divisions in the area. Facing the most serious constitutional challenge since the consolidation of political power in the USSR, the Presidium of the USSR Supreme Soviet on March 23, 1988, adopted a decree condemning local efforts to "recarve national-administrative boundaries" or to "resolve complicated national-territorial issues through pressure on state authorities."[1] Some eight months later the USSR Supreme Soviet Presidium responded to a yet more explicit challenge from another of the 15 constituent republics of the USSR. On November 16, 1988, an extraordinary session of the Supreme Soviet of the Estonian republic approved changes in the Estonian Constitution. The amendments declared the right of the republic to veto all-union legislation passed in Moscow and claimed political and economic sovereignty over the land, natural resources, industry, banks, and capital of the territory within the Estonian republic.[2]

The constitutional challenges in the USSR were unexpected by Western public opinion. Long accustomed to thinking of the constitutional guarantees of republican "independence" and "sovereignty" as radiating "a sense of legerdemain and make-believe," Western audiences thought of the coopted political institutions of the Soviet borderland republics as dutifully if grudgingly following the dictates of Moscow officials.[3] Yet, in virtually all the borderland national republics of the USSR, disputes of territory and jurisdiction have complicated the lives of Soviet leaders for decades. The sensitivity of the boundaries continues to make the open discussion of some aspects of minority rights a violation of "Leninist nationality policy" and, indeed, a challenge to the Soviet socialist system itself. The outbreaks of violence over the national-territorial boundaries are testimony to the fact that the issue of "national statehood" is as important now as it was when the federal principle was adopted seven decades ago.

The national-territorial delimitation of boundaries in the USSR is far more important than a question of mere lines on the political map. It is the key question of Soviet-style federalism. As the Soviet Constitution adopted in 1977 observes, "the Union of Soviet Socialist Republics is a unified, [*edinyi*] federal, multinational state formed on the principle of socialist federalism."[4] Soviet usage in this instance takes exception with prevailing usage in the West. Western constitutional theory regards "federative systems" and "unitary systems" as polar opposites. The idea of a "unified federalism," as apparently contradictory as it is on the surface, poses yet deeper questions for understanding the Soviet system, the nature of communism and, indeed, for comparative political theory itself. How are we to comprehend the idea of a federal system under the conditions of a socialist economy with a monoparty political system? What are the implications of socialist federalism for political development within the USSR? These are the two questions this book seeks to answer.

Federalism and Nationalism

History attests to a variety of claims to political legitimacy. Divine authority, heredity, personal charisma, prestige, wealth, power, knowledge, to name but a few, have been used as a basis for claims to political authority. In the Western legal tradition the most influential and enduring claim to political authority, however, has been property. In the European political tradition, rights of private property came to imply entitlements and privileges of political position. The enfranchisement of landed nobility eventually resulted in institutionalized forms of political participation. Through the years of European political development, *Estates general* gradually acquired deliberative as well as consultative functions. The history of Western legal and parliamentary institutions cannot be separated from the history of private property.

By way of contrast, private property did not serve historically as a foundation for the participation of the nobility in the affairs of the Russian state. The institution of private property was only weakly developed in the Russian legal tradition. Corresponding political rights of representation and participation were similarly underdeveloped. At the advent of the Soviet period, a sense of the "naturalness" of territorial representation did not exist, at least not to the extent that it did in the West. The property-oriented, territorial principle of political organization, moreover, was antagonistic to Marxist communalism. The confluence of these historical and ideological factors made it easy for the Bolsheviks to deny individual rights, the rights of localist parties, and the rights of territorial governments. Yet the popular appeal of nationalism was sufficiently strong to make it hazardous for the Bolsheviks to abandon the potential political constituencies that nationalism provided. The Bolsheviks reasoned that only by combining the popular sentiments of nationalism with the attenuated political institutions of territorial federalism could they harness prevailing political forces to the service of socialism.

This then became the root compromise of Soviet socialist federalism. The Soviet constituent republics were first formed on the basis of a hybrid "national-territorial" principle. The principle entailed a recognition of the "national statehood" of the constituent republics. As we will see in the subsequent chapters of this book, the rights of these constitutionally recognized political groups were severely circumscribed in practice. The fact remains, however, that the national groups' territorially based claim to political recognition was enshrined in the instrumental language of the regime. Promises often made, even when abandoned, are not lightly forgotten. So it was with the rights of republics in the USSR. The recognition of national-territorial status endured despite the centralizing influence of the planned economic apparatus and the politically centralizing influence of the monoparty state.

Far from withering as Lenin anticipated, the administrative institutions of the national republics over the years of Soviet power gradually developed a sense of proprietary bureaucratic self-interest. In the republics the administrative organizations of government and party became to a large extent the "captives" of the national ethos of their namesake populations. These organizations have not had political "independence" in any meaningful sense of that expression. Nor have they become, except in a few extreme cases, a staging ground for nationalist diversions and secessionist movements. But, as the following pages of this book argue, considered cumulatively, the self-protective and self-promotive strategies which the national bureaucracies have pursued have had the effect of augmenting the *de jure* federalism proclaimed in the Soviet constitutional order.

The proprietary attitudes and self-promotive strategies were directed largely by the local elites, the local intelligentsia, and indigenous bureaucrats. Compounding these efforts on the part of the national communities were larger changes taking place in the sociopolitical environment. These changes reinforced bureaucratic segmentation along national-territorial lines. These changes included: (1) the growth of corporatist constraints exercised through bureaucracies; (2) the continued importance of collective styles of leadership; (3) the scientific-technical revolution; (4) shifting economic constraints; (5) shifting demographic forces; and (6) the tenacity and resilience of cultural loyalties and ethnic identities. The strategies of the national political and administrative elites, in combination with these shifting environmental factors, gave decision-making a federal character. More important, each of these factors was dynamic. Movement in each category over recent years was in the direction of further reinforcing the segmental cleavages. Bureaucratic centralism—the processes by which the hierarchical, compartmentalized, and self-interested constellation of central economic and political organs attempted to implement decrees issued from the "heights"—had the effect of creating a form of federalism. This federalism was based not in legal guarantees but in the divergence of interests between central administrative institutions and the subordinate branches in the national federal republics. The republics responded to the logic of this situation by creating narrow, segmented, and insular "national bureaucracies." Bureaucratic centralism, ironically, created and sustained bureaucratic nationalism.

But does this form of bureaucratized nationalism create a structure that can be considered a federalism? The nature of socialist "national federalism," to be sure, is circumscribed. Beyond the formal and largely meaningless guarantees of the constitution, national federalism does not have legal sanctions to defend it. It does not have a political culture equating the claim to property with a right of representation. Unlike the pluralist systems, in which a dynamic balance of competing interests restrains, regulates, and stabilizes, national federalism does not have internal self-stabilizing mechanisms. National federalism possesses none of the consociational innovations developed in consensual systems of "power-sharing" among ethno-religious blocs subject to an explicit compact.

Not only does national federalism not have these institutional defenses, but the evidence is overwhelming that the central Soviet government has uniformly sought to preempt the development of any such forums for bargaining, deliberation, and conflict regulation. Not without warrant, the center has seen such institutions as threatening. The center's rationale has been that submitting to deliberation of demands would be perceived as legitimizing attacks on the system. Rather than mollifying demands, this would surely invite further, more disparate and, perhaps, unmanageable demands.

What then accounts for the resilience of national federalism? Two factors are important. One is simply that central *direction* of the economy cannot be equated, under the circumstances of Soviet socialism, with central *control* of the economy. For decades informed voices have been pointing out that "practice shows that large territories are practically not administered."[5] Gorbachev himself has referred to "individuals and territories that for years were outside government control."[6] As Donna Bahry has summarized it: "the proliferation of central controls has led to an erosion of control."[7]

The second factor is the relationship between ethnic identity and representation. This relationship is focused on the institutions of "national statehood." The following chapters explore the relationship between the nationality question and federalism, focusing on the influence of multinationality on the federal structure. The arguments put forward will show that national federalism, like all federal arrangements, constitutes a form of political contract. It is not a contract among equals, but as Hobbes pointed out long ago, even the highway brigand offers his victim a choice: your money or your life. A choice, any choice, implies a contract. The demands of the central government and the demands for recognition of regional ethnic collectivities have led to a series of compromises between the regions and the center. What are the terms of this contract?

On the part of the center, the contract has meant principally two things. First, the regime recognized the national-territorial principle and enshrined it in the instrumental language of the Soviet Constitution. Second, for several decades the regime continued to formally recognize this situation although, through legerdemain and prevarication, the formal guarantees were ignored in practice or circumvented by means of artful ideological reinterpretation. In sum, the federal structures were adopted by the center to placate national sentiment, were adapted to contain it, and were designed to eventually destroy it.

From the perspective of the peripheries, the contract meant many different things. For some national groups it meant protection from larger neighbors. For some individuals it meant personal advancement. For many groups and individuals it no doubt meant an opportunity to participate in the "great experiment" of socialism. But with this compact, as with any tactical alliance for limited means, the passage of time took a toll. The original motivations of the parties gradually lost their vitality. The motivations and intentions proved ephemeral. What endured were political institutions, administrative bureaucracies, national cadres, and the career incentives of the leaders in the national republics. These are the things which today linger on.

Republican Rights and Perestroika

Nearly seven decades removed from the original compromise, in a setting only remotely resembling the original situation, Gorbachev appeared with plans for "radically restructuring" the economy and, in larger compass, the entire system of Soviet socialism. Gorbachev came to power in a situation of unprecedented public consensus in favor of change. Unlike the reformist coalitions which supported Khrushchev and Brezhnev in their early tenures, the consensus for change which Gorbachev inherited united both political and economic interests. Gorbachev quickly gained the support of the military as well as those who identified with the interests of the consumer sectors, agriculture, commerce, and the intelligentsia. The rhetoric of his "new thinking" in foreign policy spoke to the deep concerns of Soviet citizens regarding the hostility of Western countries, especially the United States. Gorbachev came to power at a time when socio-occupational mobility had been postponed for an entire generation as a result of Brezhnev's status-quo policy of "cadres stability." Gorbachev's proposals for change promised to dismantle the oligopolistic powers over socio-occupational advancement that the Brezhnev personnel policies had produced.

Gorbachev's proposals for radical restructuring were initially met with skepticism from the Soviet public. But the skepticism was not so profound that it overcame citizens' hopes that the new policies *might* work. In Gorbachev's first two years he reached out to the citizenry of the Soviet Union offering prospects for change in their daily lives. His policies promised prosperity, consumer goods, reduced international tensions, increased openness in culture and the arts, more public voice and representation in public decision making, and an increased likelihood that socially valuable work would result in personal advancement. For all the comprehensiveness of the Gorbachev platform, one critical question of Soviet society did not occupy a position on the Gorbachev agenda. This was the nationality problem. Gorbachev's pronouncements on nationality policy were rare and unexceptional. He appeared to have adopted the posture of a savvy Western politician: avoiding entanglements in disputes where there was no clear public relations gain to be made. Any substantive statements on nationality affairs were certain to gain him as many enemies as supporters. If one judges only from his declarative statements, the early Gorbachev seemed almost oblivious to the problems of multinationalism.[8]

The events of Alma-Ata in December 1986, the demonstrations by Tatar nationalists in Moscow in 1987, the revelations regarding the "Cotton Affair" in Uzbekistan, the Armenian imbroglio, and the "Estonian Clause" changed this situation. By the end of 1988, the year of "firsts" in the USSR, there was an unprecedented amount of candid discussion of nationality relations.[9] Under the circumstances of increasingly strident demands for national recognition and republican rights, Gorbachev's indifference became impossible to maintain. While equivocation and vacillation could hardly be said to be characteristic attributes of Gorbachev, he seemed unwilling or unable to forge a consensus on national relations and republican rights. He announced early in 1988 that a Party Plenum was to be devoted to nationality relations.[10] In July he announced that it would not be held before 1989 at the earliest.[11] Later, the plenum was postponed until the summer of 1989.[12] It was with apparent reluctance, then, that Gorbachev came to address the issue.

When the administration did raise the issue, it was with uncharacteristic caution. This no doubt reflected Gorbachev's personal assessment of the causes and implications of nationalism. Gorbachev's criticism of nationalism was different from that of his predecessors. It was not the doctrinaire, ideological opposition of Lenin based on a "scientific" presumption that national identity was ephemeral. It was not the prejudiced ruthlessness of Stalin. Gorbachev did not share the plebeian sense of Slavic cultural superiority that appeared to move Khrushchev. Nor did Gorbachev have the basically conservative fear of anarchy that seemed to motivate Brezhnev. Gorbachev's opposition to nationalism was based on his sense that nationalism was a threat to the integrity and functioning of the Soviet state. Nationalism threatened to limit the prerogatives of central officials and, notably, of Gorbachev himself.

Gorbachev repeatedly asserted that granting concessions to nationalists and extending the rights of republics would hamper the operational abilities of central officials. In circumscribing the latitude of officials, nationalism would present a threat to Gorbachev's own program of economic and social renewal. Gorbachev announced to the Party Plenum early in January that there were no policy problems that did not have a national dimension.[13] In his remarks to the 19th Party Conference in July 1988, Gorbachev averred that nationalists "try to set people of different nationalities against each other" and that such actions "hinder the process of democratization and the cause of perestroika."[14] At the Party Plenum following the conference he called for stronger penalties against nationalism.[15] Later, in stating his objections to the "Estonian Clause," Gorbachev insisted that it would be disastrous and would jeopardize perestroika.[16] Early the following year, while addressing a favorite audience—representatives of the Soviet intelligentsia—Gorbachev argued that "the success of restructuring will depend to a decisive extent" on how the problems that have accumulated in the sphere of nationality relations are managed.[17] In a somber television address in the summer of 1989, Gorbachev spoke of national unrest as threatening a "nightmare" of violence and the destruction of the Soviet state.[18]

Gorbachev's opposition to nationalism raises an important question: When the nationalists argue that perestroika is their objective, when, like Sajudis, the Lithuanian reform movement, nationalists insist that their movements are in support of perestroika, how is it that Gorbachev can see the interests of the nationalists as inimical to the success of his programs? There are two principal reasons. First, political instability in the borderlands threatens Gorbachev's hold on the levers of central power. Widespread political unrest could tilt the balance of elite opinion away from the values of dynamic change toward the maintenance of political order at virtually any cost. The second factor is that the fusion of political and economic decision-making in the USSR makes it impossible to carry out economic reform in the absence of political reform. Certain aspects of the action programs of the nationalist movements are consistent with Gorbachev's perestroika. Other aspects, however, would limit the operational authority of the center and thereby diminish the center's ability to implement the specific policies and programs to carry out the rhetorical goals of perestroika in practice.

The Communist Party, the economic ministries, and the Soviet legislative bodies all have linkages between center and periphery which make it impossible to carry out perestroika without redrawing the basic sociopolitical contract of federal relations in the USSR. The economic malaise of the *zastoi* is customarily attributed to the favorite scapegoats of both Soviet and Western analysts, namely, central planning and the bureaucracy. But much of the immobilism is actually the product of various strategies of self-protection and self-assertion on the part of entrepreneurial officials in the regions. A pro-national if not "nationalist" agenda often plays an important role in framing the incentives of these officials in the borderlands. As the Soviet nationality theorist Eduard Bagramov rightly observed, "perestroika calls for deep changes in nationality affairs."[19]

In this situation of ambiguity as to the consequences of restructuring, the surprise announcement by Gorbachev at the 19th Party Conference that the time was propitious for political reform greatly increased the importance of assertiveness on the part of pro-national lobbies. Timing is ninety percent of politics. A redrawing of spheres of competence of the ministries or of the formal representation of the republican contingents in the central legislature would be an enduring change. Moreover, the time frame announced for the reform was specifically designed to be brief enough to not allow extensive political mobilization of opposition. Nevertheless, as we will see in Chapter 6, the constitutional amendments came surprisingly close to foundering over the issue of "republican financial sovereignty." Although the Estonians lost their bid for financial independence of the republic, they did manage to place on the political agenda with remarkable clarity and urgency the question of republican rights.

Prior to the 19th Party Conference, Gorbachev's uncharacteristic caution and diplomacy in the sphere of nationality relations can be attributed to two things. First, "solutions" to nationality disputes tend to be zero-sum, advancing the rights of one group at the expense of another. Second, Gorbachev's economic reforms exert pressures in two opposing directions at once. The reforms have both centralizing and decentralizing implications.[20]

The rhetoric of perestroika has encouraged us to concentrate on the decentralizing effects of the campaign. Restructuring is designed to put decision-making responsibility in the hands of those most likely to make rational economic decisions, that is, plant managers, farm officials, and regional leaders. This, it is presumed, will have the effect of countering the risk-avoidance of the managers as it builds the morale of the workers and farmers. A number of important institutional changes have taken place under the rubric of restructuring. The first was the introduction of the law on state enterprises that went into effect at the beginning of 1988.[21] The goal of the law was to depart from Stalinist economic practices by remaking Soviet enterprises into autonomous, democratic, and financially independent producers. A second major step was taken early in 1989 with the introduction of a new paradigm for the agricultural economy as a part of a new "agrarian policy."[22] The goal of the agricultural reform was to achieve a "radical transformation" of Soviet agriculture by "restoring the peasant as the lord and master" of the land. Programs such as these are quite properly seen as decentralizing.

A third and potentially more important step was the "General Principles for Restructuring the Leadership of the Economy and Social Sphere in the Union Republics."[23] This proposal for increasing the sphere of republican rights was a result of disagreements over the constitutional prerogatives extended to the republics in the constitutional amendments of 1988. When the draft amendments were publicized for an "all-union" discussion in October 1988, the immediate response from many republics was a strident complaint that the constitutional provisions fell far short of providing the economic autonomy the republics would need to implement perestroika. Consequently, in November TASS announced that a separate manifesto would be prepared which, in effect, would redefine center-periphery relations. The draft version of the "General Principles" officially embraced the concepts of expanded republican sovereignty, self-government, and self-financing. Nevertheless, when the public version of "The Principles" finally appeared, it was clear that this was a document of philosophical subtlety; the actual devolution of authority was difficult to ascertain.[24]

A great deal of attention has focused on "decentralizing" efforts. Less attention has been paid to the *centralizing* policies which are either a component of perestroika or have accompanied it. Indeed, much has been made of the "top down" quality of restructuring. It is often said that Gorbachev's populism is actually an attempt to "go under the heads" of those who stand to lose the most from restructuring, the middle-level bureaucrats. It is an effort to appeal to Ivan Ivanovich, the Soviet "everyman." But perestroika involves more than uprooting layers of complacent bureaucrats and restoring incentives for efficiency and productivity. It involves a frontal assault on the means by which privilege, benefits, and even status are distributed throughout the system. As we will see in Chapter 6, the administered economy is particularly fertile ground for "*na levo*" or unofficial uses of the information and resources of public officials for their personal benefit. The center is attempting to put an end to political corruption, establish greater political accountability, and promote ideological levelling. The wholesale purge of party and ministerial officials in the Central Asian republics is a case in point. Even as he seeks to turn decision-making responsibilities over to the localities, Gorbachev is desperately seeking to prevent the diversion of public office and power to personal gain. This aspect of restructuring is clearly centralizing.

The emotionalism of the political debates over republican rights is testimony to the importance of the symbolic meaning conveyed in the constitutional guarantees. Although these assurances were proffered to the national minorities as appeasement, they have acquired important symbolic importance. The goal of the national groups is to elevate those guarantees into the realm of practice. As Hélène Carrère d'Encausse expressed it, "Their aim is to 'freeze' the political framework of the Soviet system, federalism, and broaden their powers within this framework so that the national level [republican level] becomes the principal level of the whole system."[25] Perestroika, as most people in the Soviet Union are now aware, is a "creative process." As a defender of republican rights argued in *Pravda*, "One of the most important achievements and proofs of the rightness of the national policy followed by the party is the creation and stable existence of national statehood in the USSR."[26] It is this "stable existence," (in other words, the unexpected resourcefulness of national federalism) which makes it impossible for the center to dismiss the rights of republics. The quandary over the delineation of rights was no doubt best summed up in the artful ambiguity of the political slogan adopted by the 12th session of the Supreme Soviet in November 1988. It championed a redefinition of rights aimed at creating a strong union through simultaneously pursuing a strong center and strong republics.

Nationalism and Socialism

One might expect that federalism, of any brand, eventually legitimizes pluralism. Yet, in terms of its reigning ideology, Soviet socialism has been antagonistic to heterogeneity. This fact has puzzled and distressed many Marxist observers outside of the Soviet Union, especially those in Eastern Europe. Why, they ask in the perennial debate over the failure of a "pluralist, humanitarian socialism" to emerge, is the Soviet system so resistant to change and so resilient in the face of the pluralizing forces of modern technology, communication, and social change? The most frequent explanation for this phenomenon is an economic one. A centralized economy is rigid; rigidity stifles incentives; and stifled incentives lead to popular lassitude, indolence, and resignation. A citizenry resigned to this situation is not apt to challenge the political and ideational uniformity imposed by the prevailing political culture. If national federalism in the USSR is as resourceful as the analysis and data of this book would suggest, would this type of federalism not reveal important aspects of Soviet political dynamics? Would it not have implications for the direction of the further evolution of Soviet political society?

Once the exclusive province of Marxist scholars outside the USSR, the discussion of the previously heretical concept of "socialist pluralism" now has no less an important interlocutor than Gorbachev himself.[27] Indeed, the idea of socialist pluralism has become a favorite topic of *"politologi"* (politologists) in the USSR.[28] Some writers have gone further. One Soviet writer suggested that the contest between the central political authorities and the bureaucracy has resulted, for the first time since political consolidation by the Communist Party in the 1920s, in the emergence of "dual powers" in the USSR.[29] Would not these developments, assuming they are not checked by a sudden, ideologically driven re-Stalinization campaign, eventually lead to a national pluralism? While a socialist pluralism along syndicalist or corporatist lines might be theoretically appealing to some political constituencies in the USSR, there are strong reasons to conclude that a "multinational pluralism" is not likely to prove so in practice. These reasons fall into three categories: ethno-demographic, economic, and psychological.

If the national makeup of the USSR is the continuing rationale for the existence of the federal principle, there are many ethno-demographic asymmetries which will make any power-sharing arrangement less than satisfying to both regional and central interests. In 1987 the USSR was composed of 15 union republics, 20 autonomous republics, 8 autonomous oblasts, and 10 autonomous okrugs, each of which has some nominal political status and claim to representation. But there is a poor fit between the ethnographic and political-administrative boundaries in the USSR. For instance, the republics, oblasts, and okrugs of the Caucasus are principally populated by their indigenous namesake populations. Yet the namesake populations are by no means the exclusive inhabitants of these areas. In many respects the area could be described as a crazy quilt of small subnational groups. Similarly, the Turkophone and Persian-speaking populations of Central Asia can hardly be said to fit into four distinct national republics. Uzbeks live in Tadzhikistan and Tadzhiks live in Uzbekistan. The administrative delimitation of these republics does not make ethnographic sense now and made even less sense when it was first imposed upon them sixty years ago.

There was never a clear correspondence between the rights of national groups and their representation through the national republican party and ministerial apparatus. Even if there were, the national groups which occupy less than republic status would still be second class citizens. Some widely dispersed groups do not have any form of national representation. Germans, Koreans, and Jews, for instance, are groups which are not recognized with any formal republican structures. Some seven million people do not have any national politico-administrative structure at all. The largest republic, the Russian republic, dwarfs the others in terms of its size, its demand on resources, and its psychological predominance by virtue of history, tradition, and, most important, the privileged position of the Russian language in the Union. Without parity in some forum, republics are not likely to compete in a federal process in terms proportional to their size, contribution, or influence. Sub-republican groups would not participate at all. Nor, in fact, do all groups want to participate in a measure proportional to their place in the ethno-demographic composition of the society. There are claims from some national minorities for non-proportional representation. Some defenders of republican rights have expressed the hope that restructuring would result in the creation of "a federation in which national units would have equal rights," hardly a democratic notion.[30]

A second group of impediments to multinational pluralism is economic. Federalism in the USSR is not just an "administrative-political" concept since, in the USSR as in any federal state, many of the ultimate questions of federal authority concern finances and movement of resources. In the USSR the centrally directed economic ministries extend their authority over the internal jurisdiction (areas of "competence" in Soviet parlance) of the republics. Were sole responsibility for financial decision-making to be handed over to the republican governments, replacing "state capitalism" with "republican capitalism" (republican level *khozraschet*), the unavoidable consequences would be autarky in some republics and increasing inequality among republics. The "diktat of the branch principle" at the center would simply be replaced by the "diktat of the republican level."[31] A socialist, planned economy could not survive this type of reform. Moreover, the socioeconomic characteristics of the populations of the technologically advanced and more skilled Baltic republics would quickly improve while other republics would quickly deteriorate. Given the regime's long-standing commitment to equality, it is unlikely that a political agenda promoting inequality could be long sustained in the USSR.

A third impediment to harmonic national relations is the psychology of contemporary Soviet politics. In the hushed period before "openness" the discussion of many nationality problems took place behind a veil of abstract Marxist-Leninist formulas. The discussion of nationality problems was marked, as the Chairman of the Soviet Government Publishing Committee observed, by "ritual recitation, generalization, circumlocution, and conventional wisdoms."[32] Many critical questions were simply not raised. But does this mean that certain sentiments, feelings, and general speculation did not have an effect on the way people saw their own situations? An ironic consequence of this "hushed period" was that, even while minority groups felt that they had been victimized by the Russian majority, the Russians often saw themselves as being plundered by subsidies designed to overcome the "backwardness" of the peripheries. Among the Russians these sentiments fueled the Russian nationalism movement, championing the virtues of the Russian people as against—in some cases, as superior to—the other nationalities of the USSR.[33] The Gorbachev agenda has tended, if not to support Russian nationalism, at least to favor some of its favorite programs. For example, the Politburo decision in 1986 to abandon the "Trans-Siberian Canal" was a symbolic victory for the Russian nationalists who had long lobbied against this project.

Among the minority populations, there is distinct resentment over the privileged position occupied by the Russians in the union. The access to power that is bequeathed by the fact that the Russians are situated at the "core" in terms of culture, economics, and politics is a source of continuing conflict. Not only do the Russians dominate at the core, but as the pivotal nationality group, they often occupy the key positions at the periphery. As one commentator pointed out, the Russians "predominate among the heads of the main agencies of power, in the Academy of Sciences, in the Central Committee, in the All-Union Central Trade Union Council . . . and also hold special positions in the national republics."[34] Such observations underscore how easy it would be for a resourceful politician, operating under the liberalized protocols of glasnost and perestroika, to mobilize national resentments. Chapter 6 discusses the obvious cases of mobilization by representatives of national minority rights. The more dangerous use of this technique would come from one who undertook to "stir up the 'bourgeois-nationalist elements,' 'sow enmity and discord among the peoples of the USSR,' or to 'undermine the friendship of the peoples of the USSR with the Great Russian people.'"[35]

Ethnographic diversity, economic problems, and popular political psychology combine to diminish the prospects for political harmony in the USSR under an institutional arrangement of "multinational pluralism."

Unity and Diversity in the Soviet Multinational State

A multinational pluralism is unlikely to be sustained in the USSR by virtue of the logic of the ethno-demographic balance, economic arrangements, or popular attitudes. Yet it is obvious that, however long or short its existence, the USSR will not cease to be a multinational state. What, then, are the prospects for political stability and longevity? In the face of the centripetal forces we have described, is political stability likely at all? The obvious importance of the question for international order makes it one of the most frequently addressed speculations in the field of international affairs. One hears speculation referring to a range of alternatives: dissolution of the union; more centralization in the hands of Moscow; loose confederation, with Moscow playing a brokerage role; or muddling along in a situation not unlike that of the pre-perestroika days.[36] There may be some slight utility in characterizing all the conceivable outcomes of a situation, but this hardly provides us with insight into the internal dynamics of change. The substance of this study is that there are two important dimensions to these dynamics; one concerns the structure of the Soviet federal system, the "territorial" dimension. The second concerns the nature of bureaucratic nationalism.

Territorial federalism is a structural device which is best suited to dealing with a situation of contraries. It prescribes a forum and a system of values for dealing with a situation characterized by dynamic tension. It defines the "rules of the game" in a way which patterns interaction among the constituent units. The durability of territorial federalism as a form of government depends upon the ability of the society to balance the interests of disparate regional constituencies. Territorial federalism, in other words, is best summed up as a means of achieving unity under conditions of geographical diversity. Its appeal stems from the fact that the constituent federal units share long-term common interests in maintaining political unity even though there may be profound divisions over particular issues. Territorial federalism satisfies those groups who, paradoxically, seek, on the one hand, disengagement from the system and, on the other hand, feel a sense of deprivation at being excluded from participation. It is designed to address the psychological ambivalence that characterizes so many subnational groups, the simultaneous feelings, as Ivo Duchacek has expressed it, of "let us alone" and "let us in."[37]

But in offering both a sense of separateness and inclusion, territorial federalism can reinforce localist identities. Ironically, the very structures adopted to contain fissiparous national sentiment are those which tend to sustain, reinforce, and ultimately exert an independent force in favor of nationalism. As Herman Bakvis pointed out, "the political rules and structures governing the distribution of powers and resources . . . often have the reciprocal effect of reinforcing the identities and character of the subcultural blocs in question."[38] As the segmented patterns of communication become routinized, federalism can serve to reinforce those ethno-regional identities which, as in the Soviet case, it was designed to neutralize.

The second important dimension is the "national" component of national federalism. It is important here to avoid the anthropological fallacy. Nationalism in the USSR is not primarily a product of primordial national sentiments. Basic and deep psychological attachments to national identity are both obvious and profound. But the relationship between ethnic identity and political attitudes is a complex one; strong subnational identity and "Soviet patriotism" need not be exclusive sentiments. Exclusivist nationalism as an ideology, as a movement, and ultimately as a political force, does not follow solely from ethnic attachment. In general, nationalism may be defined as politicized ethnicity. On its own, ethnicity has no political implications whatsoever if it is not mobilized in the form of a nationalist movement. Competitive, open, nationalist movements do not exist in the USSR because the rules of the political game do not support them. Groundswells of cultural sentiment are not the same as organized political movements. A main theme of this book is that nationalist sympathies are channeled by means of the bureaucratic processes unique to the Soviet system. It is within these bureaucratic fora of competition that confrontation takes place over critical values.

The most salient feature of the Soviet policy process is that it is dominated by bureaucratic procedure. Political exchange takes place within the broad context of the Soviet bureaucracy—a context subject to many of the same pathologies of other large, complex organizations. In this arena of bureaucratic confrontation, the national identity of the institutional actors heavily influences the perceptions of institutional interests. In this forum of national confrontation, lobbyists rely upon abstract and flexible formulas of Marxism and Leninism to buttress their arguments for national rights. The winners and losers are not merely offices and agencies, but the "greater" and "lesser" homelands.[39] The arena of competition is not that of deliberative institutions, of parliaments and adversarial process, but of bureaucratic pulling and hauling. Because the stakes are so high, the contest is often concealed. It is precisely this zero-sum bureaucratic competition along national lines that has given rise to such hyperbolic expressions as "counterrevolutionary nations."[40]

Is there a formula for the solution of these disparate demands within the system of Soviet socialist multinational federalism? To answer this question we turn in Chapter 2 to an examination of the principles at the foundation of Soviet socialist federalism. We seek to discern the reason for the adoption by the Bolsheviks of federalism, a principle so foreign to Marxism. Chapter 3 offers an account of the evolution of Soviet constitutionalism. Chapter 4 details the criticism that Soviet scholars and political officials have addressed to the operation of the federal system. Chapter 5 describes bureaucratic nationalism focusing on the two interacting forces of the territorial bureaucracies and the national leadership in the republics. By implication, this chapter raises the question, Can policy be "national in form" and yet "socialist in content?" This chapter also develops the concept of the "national climate." The sixth chapter examines the national resurgence that culminated in 1988 in unprecedented challenges to the constitutional order. The final chapter summarizes the argument with an eye toward the future.

Notes

1. TASS (23 March 1988).

2. *Sovetskaia Estoniia* (17, 18, and 19 November 1988).

3. Merle Fainsod, *How Russia Is Ruled*, rev. ed. (Cambridge: Harvard University Press, 1965), p. 368.

4. Section III, Chapter 8, Article 70 of the Soviet Constitution. It should be noted that when discussing Western federal theories Soviet scholars refer to unitary [*unitarnyi*] systems. Thus the expression *edinyi* might also be translated "integral."

5. V.A. Nemtsev, "Raionnyi organ vlasti i ego territoriia," *Sovetskoe gosudarstvo i pravo* No. 8 (1969): pp. 69–73.

6. *Pravda* (13 January 1988).

7. Donna Bahry, *Outside Moscow: Power, Politics, and Budgetary Policy in the Soviet Republics* (New York: Columbia University Press, 1987), p. 163.

8. One observer of Soviet nationality policies has gone further to claim that "On coming to power, Gorbachev does not appear to have had a clearly formulated nationality policy or, for that matter, any desire to alter the overall approach he had inherited." Bohdan Nahaylo, "Gorbachev Disavows Merging of Nations," *Report on the USSR* Vol. 1, No. 5 (3 February 1989): p. 23. Darrell Hammer noted that "Gorbachev . . . has spent his entire career in the RSFSR

and initially seemed insensitive to the nationality issue." Darrell P. Hammer, "'Glasnost' and 'The Russian Idea'," in *Russian Nationalism Today, Radio Liberty Research Bulletin* (19 December 1988): p. 11.

9. Roundtable discussions on nationality questions appeared, for instance, in *Voprosy filosofii* (September 1988), *Druzhba narodov* (December 1988), and in *Vek XX i my* (December 1988). A debate organized by the "Znanie" society was aired on Soviet television starting on January 18, 1989. At the same time, scientific-practical conferences were sponsored by the military under the rubric "Leninist principles of nationality policy of the CPSU and the contemporary tasks of international education." See *Kommunist vooruzhennykh sil*, No. 5 (March 1989): pp. 3–11.

10. *Pravda* (19 February 1988).

11. The plenum was referred to several times. It was noted in Gorbachev's speech to the Party Plenum in July 1988, that the nationality plenum would be held as early as 1989. Later, it was announced that it would be held in summer 1989.

12. See Ann Sheehy, "The Forthcoming CPSU Central Committee Plenum on Interethnic Relations," *Radio Liberty Research* 439/88 (28 September 1988).

13. Reprinted in M.S. Gorbachev, *Izbrannye rechi i stati* Vol. 4 (Moscow: Politizdat, 1987), p. 329.

14. See his report to the 19th Party Conference, June 28, 1988 in *Pravda* (30 June 1988).

15. *Pravda* (31 July 1989).

16. *The New York Times* (28 November 1988). It is interesting to note that one of Gorbachev's closest pro-perestroika associates, Aleksandr Yakovlev, has reversed the formula, arguing that only perestroika could solve the problems of "increasing corruption, social injustice, local feudal structures, ecological crimes, and inadequate attention to national histories, languages, and ethnic cultures" that have been accumulating for decades. See his remarks quoted in *Report on the USSR* Vol. 1, No. 10 (1989): p. 47.

17. *Pravda* (8 January 1989).

18. *Pravda* (2 July 1989).

19. E. Bagramov, *Pravda* (14 August 1987).

20. Philip Hanson rejected the view that decentralization has produced heightened nationality tensions in the USSR. He argued that decentralization has in fact been slight. Furthermore, Hanson argued that this would be a gradual process; ethnic conflict arising out of regional economic differentials would take a long time. Philip Hanson, "Economic Decentralization and the Nationalities Issue," *Radio Liberty Research Bulletin* 127/88 (15 March 1988).

21. A text of the law appeared in *Pravda* (1 July 1987).

22. *Pravda* (17 March 1989).

23. A draft version of this document prepared by the USSR Supreme Soviet Presidium, was published in all the Soviet central newspapers on March 14, 1989. It was announced that a draft law on the subject would follow.

24. Some initial Western responses were tempered with reserve. See John Tedstrom, "USSR Draft Program on Republican Economic Self-Management: An

Analysis," *Report on the USSR* Vol. 1, No. 16 (21 April 1989): pp. 1–8. In assessing the implications of this change, Tedstrom cautions that "powerful ministries and other central organs will withold critical information or disregard the plans drafted at republican levels."

25. Hélène Carrère d'Encausse, *Decline of an Empire: The Soviet Socialist Republics in Revolt* (New York: Newsweek, 1979), p. 268.

26. A. Zharnikov, "Dialektika natsional'nykh protsessov" *Pravda* (27 September 1987): p. 2.

27. Mikhail Gorbachev, *Perestroika: New Thinking for our Country and the World* (New York: Harper and Row, 1987), p. 77.

28. See, for instance, A. Krukhmalev, "Sotsialisticheskii pliuralizm: sushchnost' i osnovnye cherty," *Kommunist vooruzhennykh sil* No. 5 (March 1989): pp. 20–26.

29. This expression is used by by Andrei Nuykin in *"Idealy ili interesy,"* *Novy mir* No. 1 (January 1988): p. 210. The reference is to p. 210. For a discussion see Archie Brown, "The Soviet Leadership and the Struggle for Political Reform," *The Harriman Institute Forum* Vol. 1, No. 4 (April 1988): p. 7.

30. See the remarks of R. Ovanesian, *Pravda* (8 January 1989).

31. See E. Ezhov, "Diktatura otrasli," *Ekonomicheskaia gazeta* No. 17 (1989): p. 5; V. Laptev, "Sil'nyi tsentr–sil'nye respubliki," *Ekonomicheskaia gazeta* No. 17 (1989): p. 17.

32. M. Nenashev, *Pravda* (24 November 1987).

33. For an overview of the thinking of leading Western scholars on Russian nationalism see the special edition of the *Radio Liberty Research Bulletin, Russian Nationalism Today* (19 December 1989).

34. See his remarks in the roundtable discussion in *Vek XX i mir* No. 12 (1988): p. 10.

35. Such, indeed, were exactly the charges that were leveled in 1953 against Lavrentii Beriia. See *Pravda* (17 December 1953).

36. See Zbigniew Brzezinski, "Will the Soviet Empire Self-Destruct?" *The New York Times Magazine* (26 February 1989): pp. 38–40.

37. Ivo Duchacek, *Comparative Federalism: The Territorial Dimensions of Politics* (New York: Holt, Rhinehart, and Winston, 1970), p. 356.

38. Herman Bakvis, "Federal and Consociational Arrangements," *Publius* Vol. 15 (1985): p. 62.

39. A discussion of "greater" and "lesser" homelands appeared in a Moscow public affairs television broadcast devoted to problems of nationalism. The expression was used by a leading commentator on nationality affairs, Eduard Bagramov. A transcription of the broadcast is available in *Daily Report: Soviet Union* Foreign Broadcast Information Service (11 June 1987): p. R2.

40. See the celebrated pro-perestroika manifesto, "Printsipy perestroiki," *Pravda* (5 April 1988).

2

A Federal Solution
to the National Problem

There is only one solution for the national problem.

—Lenin

Marxists have traditionally been hostile to the federal principle. According to Marxist theory, federalism could only be seen as a retrograde development. Basing federal divisions on a principle of ethnic or "national" identity was viewed as particularly misguided. According to the Marxist perspective, the nation itself was nothing more than an intermediate stage along a continuum leading from capitalism to an "internationalist" socialism. Capitalism provided an engine of economic change, bringing about the comingling of nations and leading, eventually, to the assimilation of small nations by larger nations. As socialism approached, nations gradually lost their rationale for existence. Nationalism as a political doctrine then too could be expected to lose political significance. Under these conditions, Marxists saw little wisdom in extending formal recognition to national groups in a federal structure of the socialist state. To do so could only prolong the demise of nationalist yearnings.

Such was the theory. Despite the theory, the first socialist state was also to become a federal state. How did this come about and what were its implications for the nature of federalism in the USSR? The first thing to be observed in answering these questions is that the federal structure in the USSR did not emerge as a means of accommodation among competing peripheral constituencies. Rather, it emerged as a temporary and, in intent at least, transitional compromise between a relatively strong central power headed by the Bolsheviks and weak and fissiparous peripheral groups. The Bolsheviks did not intend for the federal structure to be a permanent organizational feature of socialism. It was to be merely a stage on the path to a unified socialist society.

It is ironic that today the federal form is established in the Soviet Constitution and proclaimed by the Party Program. More important, this federal form is embodied in the ministerial organization, reflected in the branches of the party, regarded as justified by the vast majority of Soviet scholars, and defended enthusiastically by proponents of minority rights. The history of this transformation is closely linked to the adoption of a federal state as a means of dealing with what Lenin referred to as one of Russia's "burning questions" (*bol'nye voprosy*), the nationalities issue. In the pages to follow, we examine the multi-ethnic situation in Russia and the USSR. We review Marxist and Leninist perspectives on nationalism. We see how the national problem constrained the instincts of Marxist theoreticians and how political expediency inclined Lenin toward the "federal solution," a decision which would have enduring consequences for national relations in the USSR. We see how the principle of "national statehood" eventually became enshrined as a fundamental principle of Soviet socialist federalism. Finally, we consider how the theoretical premises of Leninism have been adapted to the demands of the present under the rubric of "Leninist nationality policy."

The National Problem in 1917

Among the many unresolved problems of the Tsarist empire as it raced toward internal collapse was the issue of animosities among the scattered ethnic minorities or "nations." The "burning nationalities question" prompted Lenin to refer to the Tsarist empire as the "Prison of Nations." The complex pattern of Russian colonial domination through a hierarchy of subordinate groups set empire against nation, nation against empire, and nation against nation. Nationalist animosities and resentment toward the St. Petersburg government fueled and crystallized nationalist self-identification. At the same time, the relatively favored groups found that the sharp edge of Russian domination was dulled by their ability to dominate the less favored.

The national composition of the Tsarist empire was the culmination of a long process of territorial expansion and colonization. From its origins in the European plains, the empire grew in a series of great, expansionist waves. The conquest of Kazan and Astrakhan by Ivan the Terrible added the Turks of the Volga region. Siberian expansion in the seventeenth century added Turks, Mongols, and other smaller groups. By the early eighteenth century the Dniepr populations of western Slavs and Cossacks had been added. Peter the Great expanded northward with the addition of Baltic territories. Under Catherine's reign Russia pushed southward toward Turkey, bringing Russia to the shores of the Black Sea. In the early nineteenth century Georgia, Finland, and Poland were added to the realm. By mid-century the remaining Transcaucasian territories were incorporated. Finally, under the reign of Alexander II, in the latter part of the nineteenth century, the Central Asian areas of Turkestan were joined to the empire.

In comparison with the other nineteenth century colonial empires, Russia was unusual. European empires extended colonial control across the sea. Russia, in contrast, extended its political and economic domination to geographically contiguous areas. Defenders of the Tsarist empire argued that it was different from the colonial empires of the West European nations by virtue of the territorial contiguity of its possessions. They insisted it was a "natural" political formation. They argued that national consolidation had taken place in all great nations through acquisition at the territorial periphery followed by cultural assimilation. According to this line of reasoning, the Russian empire was different from the European empires in size, not quality. Lenin joined those who denounced this line of thought as the "salt water fallacy." Lenin argued that the possessions of the Tsarist realm were "colonies of the clearest sort."[1]

The land empire that resulted from Tsarist expansionism was unprecedented in its multi-national composition. The census of 1897 included data on some 194 ethnic groups, comprising over fifty percent of the total population of the domain. The figures alone did not do justice to the ethnic diversity of the groups in the borderlands. While the populations of some large ethnic groups (notably the Russians and the Ukrainians) were fairly concentrated, others were either contained as ethnic and cultural "islands" within larger, dissimilar groups, or dispersed, as in the case of the Jews, throughout a variety of territories.

Many of the national groups of the Tsarist realm had not passed through a true process of national consolidation. In most colonized areas of the world, the metropolitan administration played a key role in grooming native elites and developing organizational infrastructures which later served as the basis for the development of nationalist movements and, eventually, for national consolidation itself. The Tsarist empire differed in this respect from other colonizing powers. The principle of autocracy continued to guide Tsarist administration. The regime adopted administrative formulas which impeded national development just as they inhibited economic and social development. Russian rule was organized through a system of ten general governorships in the borderland areas. Seats of these governorships were in regional capitals such as Kiev and Vilnius. Central Asia had two governorships as did Siberia. A slightly different arrangement in Transcaucasia provided for administration under a viceroy. Tsarist officials maintained an attitude of superiority and condescension over the subjugated peoples. Tsarist policies were segregationist, designed to protect presumed Great Russian cultural superiority from the influence of inferior cultures.

The varied pattern of ethnic distribution made a true confederation of ethnic minorities impractical. At the same time, the resilience of ethnic identification and the often fierce attachment to ethnic traditions made assimilationist government policies difficult to administer. Upon the collapse of the monarchy, the importance of nationalist discontent among the national minorities was quickly appreciated by the provisional government. The new government moved swiftly to abolish numerous legal restrictions on members of the national minorities.[2] Committees were established to administer the borderland areas, but with the wavering authority of the provisional government itself, never managed to gain legitimacy. In the borderlands the national conflicts were generally of two types. One consisted of long-standing internecine disputes among the groups in the borderlands vying for regional hegemony. A second more important type was conflict that arose out of native resentments in the borderlands against Russian rule, especially resentments aimed at the policy of the Tsarist administration to provide privileged access to land for Russian settlers.

The Marxist Premises

Marxist thought in the nineteenth century was both critical and programmatic, that is, it sought to analyze the political economy of the nineteenth century as well as offer an agenda for change. The most enduring legacy of this early period of Marxism, however, is the sustained critique of the political consequences of extremes in the distribution of wealth and power in mid-nineteenth century society. Three premises form the core of the Marxist critique. These are the concepts of: (1) economic determinism; (2) dialectical materialism; and (3) anthropocentrism.

The principle of economic determinism maintains that economic development is at the heart of the progress of civilization. Consciousness, cognition and emotions—including political loyalties—are determined by economic processes. Economic conditions change through a dialectical process of historical advance. The degree of interaction among people is determined by the economic conditions and by rules imposed by political authority, the "superstructure" of the economic forces.

According to the Marxist interpretation of history, primitive and feudal societies were characterized by relative isolation of peoples from one another. With the introduction of capitalist economic relations, ethnically based formations were fused into progressively larger "national" units. Eventually this led to the emergence of nation-states under the direction of powerful central political authorities. As nation-states grew in number and size they assimilated small, peripherally located ethnic communities into larger national groups. New forms of national identity were forged in this process of national consolidation. The maturation of capitalism introduced a new stage of still larger, transnational formations. Banks and industrial and commercial syndicates began to transform the conventional sovereignty of the nation-state. Eventually, and as a natural continuation of these processes, the interests of the small ethnic group as well as the larger national group were subsumed under the category of proletarian class interests. Since proletarian interests transcended the historical category of the state, the psychological loyalties of the worker would also transcend the state. Patriotism would be displaced by proletarian class solidarity.

Marx did not have a carefully defined concept of the nation, using the term frequently in the various senses of country, state, and society. But seen within the terms of the Marxist framework, the nation was generally viewed as a collective whose origin was economic processes and whose external features were expressed in terms of common customs, rituals, a common language, and similar political sympathies. As the economic forces changed, so, naturally, would the nation. This proposition was announced in one of the most famous passages of the Manifesto stating that "national differences are vanishing." Whether Marx himself ever anticipated this to mean that all discernible differences among peoples would ultimately attenuate is a matter of scholarly debate. But, as a practical matter, assimilation implies the disappearance of national characteristics and traditions—an issue charged with symbolic political significance.

Accompanying this articulation of the "logic" of Marxism, however, was practical Marxism. Practical Marxism was action-oriented, pragmatic, political, and intensely sensitive to the pursuit of power in an effort to aid changes that were expected to result from socialism. The differences between the theoretical and practical strains of Marxism suggest why the early Marxists were forced to function on two relatively separate tracks, dismissing nationalism in theory and yet acknowledging it as a real force in practice. The impossibility of completely separating the two forced both Marx and Engels, as Walker Connor has concluded, "to be influenced more substantively by national concepts than they were probably aware."[3] This influence had some surprising consequences. We must recall that the anti-nationalist doctrine of "proletarian internationalism" and the notion that the "worker has no country" were formulated amid the politically charged atmosphere of competing European nationalisms. It is ironic that 1848, the year of publication of the anti-nationalist tract *The Communist Manifesto*, was also a year of nationalist fervor throughout Europe. The slogan of the nationalist movement—the "self-determination of nations"—found its first public statement in the Proclamation on the Polish Question, which was drafted by Marx himself and endorsed by the London Conference of the First International in 1865. Walker Connor rightly points to the irony of the fact "that this most famous credo of nationalism should make its first appearance in a public document which was drafted by history's most famous internationalist."[4]

In practice Marx saw nationalism merely as a stratagem used by the bourgeoisie to project its class interests in an effort to capture the loyalties of the workers. National consciousness was thus part of an "illusory communal interest."[5] The fact that national consciousness was illusory, of course, did not mean that it could not have effects and that it could not be mobilized. Nationalist sentiment had proved very useful to the bourgeoisie. There was no reason why its attractions could not be harnessed in the service of socialism. Marxism accommodated the view that nationalism could be progressive or retrograde, depending on whose interests it supported. Communism, strictly speaking, was beyond nationalism. Under socialism nations would disappear. But, during the period of transition to communism, nationalism could be considered progressive to the extent that it facilitated progressive forces.

On matters of how nationalism was given voice and recognition, Marxists were less pragmatic. Marxism was in principle opposed to to federal structures. Marx attacked the liberal notions of Montesquieu and Rousseau, both of whom favored federated systems as more democratic than unitary states. Marx's early and radical followers viewed the broad distribution of decision-making authority—which federalism entailed— as slowing the maturation of contradictions in society. Since these contradictions were assumed to spell the eventual collapse of the pro-capitalist order, federalism was viewed as revisionist and regressive. A unitary government would hasten capitalism's assimilationist tendencies along. Engels insisted that the "proletariat can only use the form of the one and indivisible republic."[6] Marx did, as in the case of the proposed British federation, support federal solutions under limited circumstances. But this was a tactical rather than a principled concession on his part. In such cases a federal solution was appropriate specifically as a transitional stage.[7] In the latter half of the nineteenth century, Marxists continued to regard national sentiment as subordinate to class interests. The resilience of nationalism as a factor in the politics of Eastern Europe eventually made it a practical necessity for the Marxists to eventually adopt more detailed responses to the challenges of nationality politics.[8]

The workers' organizations founded in the 1870s in Russia paid little attention to the national question. The first direct treatment of nationalism as a policy issue of the Russian social democratic movement appeared in the First Congress of the Russian Socialist Democratic Labor Party (RSDLP) in Minsk in 1898. Echoing a resolution passed at the International Socialist Congress two years before, the Minsk Congress adopted a resolution which defended the "right of nations to self-determination." The deliberations of the Second RSDLP Congress, held in Brussels and in London in 1903, again took up the issue of nationality. The Congress adopted a program which included the self-determination principle (Article 9). This caused a serious division between left-wing "internationalist" ideological purists such as Rosa Luxemburg, on the one hand, and, on the other hand, a coalition of defenders of national minorities and more pragmatic party members.

The question of national rights had already been debated at the 1899 Brunn Congress of Austrian Social Democrats. The delegates to the Congress entertained a perspective deeply influenced by the Hapsburg empire's multi-national composition. Consisting of Austrians, Czechs, Poles, Hungarians, Ruthenians, and other, smaller ethnic groups, the multi-national Austro-Hungarian empire offered challenges to the socialist theory of the nation-state. How could a socialist state accommodate this kind of national heterogeneity? Two proposals were advanced. The first was anthropological, the second was territorial. The territorial proposal was essentially the federal model. The multi-national state would be segmented into smaller, national constituent states whose territorial identification provided the basis of their integrity. The anthropological proposal sought to identify the basis of the state with the national group itself, substituting national-cultural autonomy for the more traditional claim of the preeminence of property and territory.

The Congress did not resolve the issue. But the idea of extra-territorial group rights was taken up by two influential Austrian Social Democrats, Karl Renner and Otto Bauer. In their polemical writings elaborating the thesis of extra-territorial recognition and representation of national groups, Bauer and Renner sought to reconcile national movements with the socialist strivings for proletarian unity. They did so by rejecting what had long since become an unquestioned truism for Marxists—that the nation was an ephemeral category. Bauer advanced the iconoclastic thesis that nationalism was on the rise and that the triumph of socialism would therefore "result in an increasing differentiation of nations . . . a sharper expression of their peculiarities, a sharper separation of their natures."[9]

The idea of extra-territorial autonomy appealed particularly to the members of the Jewish Bund (Jewish Socialist Party) in Russia, due to their "extra-territorial" distribution. The Fourth Congress of the Bund (1901) advanced the idea that "Russia must be transformed into a federation of nationalities," with the notion of federation being used in an explicitly extra-territorial sense."[10] Bauer and Renner's works were subsequently translated into Russian, popularizing within Russian Marxist circles the debates over the issues of the relationship of the nation to the state, the interpretation of self-determination, and the principle of extra-territorial recognition.

Of the two leading Russian Marxist parties, the Social Revolutionary Party, with its philosophy of a free association of communes, was the first to expressly announce itself in favor of federalism and the principle of national-cultural autonomy. Mensheviks and Bolsheviks continued to reject both federalism and cultural autonomy. At the August Conference in Vienna the position was softened, though not entirely changed. The conference concluded with a resolution that national-cultural autonomy was not contrary to the party's program guaranteeing self-determination.[11] Thus, by the outbreak of the First World War, all of the major parties, long since committed to some form of self-determination for nations, had come to entertain if not accept some form of extra-territorial recognition for the minority populations.

Lenin's Theory of Nationality

Lenin's approach to the questions of multi-nationality has come to be known in the USSR as "Leninist nationality policy." Not everyone agrees as to the exact definition of this policy, nor, especially, is there universal agreement as to what the policy implies today given the changed circumstances of socialism. Despite the disagreement, the formulas of Leninist nationality policy continue to be invoked in the USSR as the rationale and intellectual basis for present-day policies regarding the nationalities. Much of this disagreement can be attributed to the fact that Lenin's thinking on the subject had both a theoretical and a practical component. The theoretical component drew heavily upon the historical debates of Marxism, while the practical component was deeply influenced by Lenin's own experience, his sense of political expediency, and, during the years in power, by the politics of the consolidation of Bolshevik power. The following discussion seeks to clarify the Marxist theoretical foundation of Lenin's policy and then proceeds to an analysis of the more practical aspects.

Lenin's thinking on national questions developed in four stages.[12] The first stage includes Lenin's early and fairly cursory treatment of the subject. This spans the period from 1897 until his exile from Russia. A second stage begins with Lenin's re-evaluation of the importance of nationalism during the period of political reaction following the 1905 revolution. Living in exile and watching the gathering forces of nationalism as the world moved toward war, Lenin began to theoretically elaborate the positions that he had previously taken on mainly polemical grounds. It was during this period that Lenin began reading widely on the subject of nationalism and even commissioned Stalin to begin writing on the subject. Lenin's new, more theoretically detailed understanding of nationalism found expression in an outpouring of writing on the subject in such works as his "Critical Remarks on the National Question" (1913). This small pamphlet contains the most complete statement of Lenin's theory of nationalism. Finally, there is a brief fourth stage in the evolution of his views at the end of his life, starting in late 1922.

Despite the fact that there are identifiable "stages" in Lenin's thought, one is struck by the continuity in his views on nationalism. After the publication of "Critical Remarks," the "principles" of Lenin's approach to nationalism changed hardly at all. The one important exception was his reversal on the federalism question.

The theoretical basis of Lenin's policy is found in two fundamental Marxist premises, to which Lenin added his own decidedly idiosyncratic interpretations. The first premise is the idea that economic relations are at the heart of social and political processes. In colloquial Marxist terminology this idea is referred to as economic determinism, although this phrase is somewhat stronger than what Lenin had in mind. The second major premise concerns the etiology of nations. It claims that nations (national groups, national collectivities, tribes, and so on) are the products of processes uniquely associated with a historical stage of economic development. A particular economic stage would establish conditions which permitted a certain kind of national formation. The following stage would antiquate that formation but, in so doing, would create the conditions for a successor stage. Collectivities rise and fall in accordance with economic stages. Implied in this view is the idea that nations and national identities are ephemeral. Political loyalties follow the same logic. "On any really serious and profound political issue," Lenin asserted, "sides are taken according to classes, not nations."[13]

To these two basic Marxist premises Lenin added a series of idiosyncratic definitions of key terms in the analysis of nationalism. In these interpretations he frequently disagreed, sometimes to an extent bordering on hysteria, with many of his contemporaries. His unusual interpretations of the day-to-day questions of how to manage, solve, or overcome the problems of multi-ethnicity have far-ranging significance today for state and party policies. The concepts include national identification (that is, loyalty to one's nation); the relationship between nation and class; relations between nation and the party; factionalism and nationalism; self-determination; national autonomy; national culture; political self-administration; and, finally, the scheme for determining nation-state relations, namely, the idea of socialist federalism.

Lenin saw capitalist private property as the historical force that brought nationalism into existence. Capitalism was, therefore, ultimately the principal cause of antagonism and enmity among nations. From his theoretical perspective, Lenin perceived two historical stages in the development of nations and national consciousness. In the first stage he perceived the awakening of national life, national movements, and the creation of nation-states. This was the dawn and flower of nations. But if capitalism brought nations into being, it would also eventually prove their undoing. Following this stage of national emergence, Lenin saw a conflict stage. In this conflict stage the nation grew less important than the interaction among nations. This stage was witness to the development of different arenas of international relations, the breakup of national frontiers, and the dissolution of national identities, affinities, and attachments. Finally, this stage brought about the creation of an international unity of capital, commerce, politics, science, and culture.[14]

Lenin considered himself an internationalist. He maintained that the "aim of socialism is not only to end the division of mankind into tiny states . . . but to integrate them."[15] The label "anti-nationalist" might have offered a more fitting description of the attitude of Lenin toward nationalism. "Marxism," he wrote, "is incompatible with nationalism, even the most 'just,' 'pure,' refined, and civilized nationalism."[16] He claimed that "aggressive bourgeois nationalism . . . drugs the mind of the workers, stultifies and disunites them in order that the bourgeoisie may lead them on the halter."[17] Although he thus disdained nationalism, he nevertheless recognized its utility. He saw it as an instrument by which the objectives of socialism could be advanced. Not expecting nationalism to be an enduring force, he never bothered to offer an explicit definition of the "nation" in his own work. Toward the end of his life he insisted that "an abstract formulation of the question of nationalism in general is completely pointless."[18] Meanwhile, others, including his plodding student on the subject, Stalin, struggled vainly to put legalistic boundaries and limits on this most amorphous of anthropological concepts.

According to the Leninist scheme, the nationalist enmity that suffused the Tsarist colonies was the product of past oppression. Lenin expected that as socialism removed the sources of that oppression, the psychological underpinning of national identification would be eliminated and national enmity would give way to proletarian psychological identification and, eventually, to political solidarity. With its motive forces dissipated, nationalism would naturally attenuate and lose its political force. Until that time, nationalism offered itself as an instrument by which power might be consolidated, put in the hands of the workers, or at least the party, and then used to advance the aims of socialism, hastening capitalism's demise.

In the practical operation of socialism the crux of the nationalist question centered on the concept first expressed by the nineteenth-century catch phrase of "national self-determination." Originally a paean to the nationalism of nineteenth-century political realists, the concept was appropriated as a fundamental tenet of democratic populism and, eventually, was used by such political idealists as Woodrow Wilson in defense of democratic self-expression. As we have seen, his slogan of the nationalist movement earlier found its way into the political agenda of socialism. The first public statement appeared in the socialist treatise the *Proclamation on the Polish Question*. Drafted by Marx himself and endorsed by the London Conference of the First International in 1865, the Proclamation included the idea of self-determination more as an empathetic recognition of the resentments born of colonial exploitation than as a principle of Marxist theoretics. Slogans often acquire a life of their own, however. Once the idea of self-determination had become a rallying cry in the political rhetoric of motives, it became a fixed, though intensely provocative, element in the agenda of socialism. The Program of the Second International, as endorsed by the London Conference of 1896, noted that "the Congress advocates the full right of self-deter-mination of all nations."[19] Later, the Program of the RSDLP upheld the "right of self-determination for all nations comprising the state." The Second Congress of the RSDLP in 1903 (the first Marxist Congress to take place in Russia) included in its program Lenin's own proposals for the national question which included three key points, one of which was the right of self-determination.[20]

In the charged political atmosphere of the time, with idealists, realists, nationalists, and "internationalists" defending the "right of national self-determination," it is little wonder that there was confusion as to what self-determination implied. For Lenin self-determination meant offering a temporary concession to nationalist sentiment in exchange for political support of socialism. It was a tactical alliance for a limited objective. Lenin's interpretation of self-determination did not make the intuitive sense to Lenin's contemporaries that it made to him. Lenin's view took exception, for instance, with the resolutely anti-nationalist position of Rosa Luxemburg, Trotsky and others. At the same time, Lenin's view circumvented the practical concessions that would follow from the nationality-oriented Renner-Bauer formula.

Lenin fashioned an interpretation of national self-determination which offered a "voluntary and free choice" to the national groups to enter the Bolshevik ranks. Once that offer was accepted, the "right" to direct and control their national destinies was quickly assumed by the party. Thus the "right" of self-determination came to be a one-time choice rather than a legal right to continuing self-government. Lenin's reasoning was that the right of self-determination hinged upon the "right" of secession. But if a nation were freely offered that right, it would not use it. If denied the right, on the other hand, a nation would fight for it. Hence, Lenin held it was necessary to offer this right "in principle" so that it would not be demanded in practice. Lenin's formula was appealing to many in that it appeared to offer the national leaders in minority areas real local control. In actuality, it guaranteed them only verbal assurances.

Many of Lenin's fellow socialists had been critical of the idea of granting national self-determination for fear it would encourage localism or even separatism. For practical considerations, Lenin thought separation and secession unlikely. He wrote in 1913 that "separation is by no means our plan. We do not predict separation at all."[21] He set out the substance of his position on the secession issue in "The Right of Nations to Self-Determination," published as a journal article in 1914. In the article he explained in detail how a right "in principle" need not imply the exercise of that right. Later, in 1916, he asserted that "The more closely the democratic system of a state approaches complete freedom of secession, the rarer and weaker will be the striving for secession in practice."[22] In the anxious days after the February Revolution he insisted that "the more resolutely our republic recognizes the right of non-Great Russians to secede, the more strongly will other nations be attracted toward an alliance with us."[23]

Lenin drew a crisp distinction between the ideas of "national autonomy," which he favored, and "national cultural autonomy," which he opposed.[24] He derided and ridiculed the idea of national culture, characterizing it as a "clerical or bourgeois deception."[25] He considered national culture to be little more than a window dressing of bourgeois ideological domination. At the same time, he argued in favor of the political concept of "national autonomy." Lenin argued that the principles by which national autonomy would be recognized under socialism included: the right of all nations to self-determination and free secession; the right to the formation of "independent" governments for the national groups; full legal, political, and economic equality of all nations in all spheres of social and political life of the country; the equality of languages; and a guarantee of protection against a compulsory government (that is, official) language.

These guarantees would not constrain socialism, Lenin thought, because they were accompanied by two additional planks to the platform. These planks sustained Lenin's confidence that localism could be avoided.

These two planks were, first, the existence of a single party and a single organization of the proletariat irrespective of national background and, second, the organizational principle of democratic centralism within the party. For all his acumen and political insight, Lenin was a poor student of bureaucracy.[26] He tended to equate hierarchy and control with responsiveness. He naively thought that democratic centralism would operate within a tightly structured organization. This, he thought, implied an easily controlled party organization which would exert its power and authority through a top-down expression of democratic centralism.[27]

The Federal Solution and Leninist Nationality Policy

Prior to the Revolution, Lenin simply rejected federalism. He did not think it offered a practical solution to the national question.[28] He was hardly alone in this view. Many people agreed on the impracticality of nationality based federalism. With a few notable exceptions, the national groups simply were not sufficiently localized in any specific territories or homelands. As a contemporary of Lenin's wrote, "The nations are so intertwined with each other that there is hardly anything that can be identified as 'national territory' within which one could easily establish federative or autonomous political institutions."[29]

In his writings, up to the very brink of the Bolshevik seizure of power, Lenin spoke only infrequently and summarily about federalism. When he did discuss federalism prior to the Revolution, it was invariably in pejorative terms. Although he was a staunch advocate of self-determination (at least as he understood this concept), he insisted that self-determination and federalism were not to be confused. One gets the impression that Lenin feared support for the former might brand him with advocacy for the latter.[30]

The issue of a nation-based federal structure had been raised repeatedly with respect to the party structure. The Minsk Congress of the RSDLP in 1898 discussed the issue, but the Congress passed a resolution favoring a single-party structure organized without reference to nationality. The issue was on the agenda again at the January Conference of the RSDLP in 1912. At the January Conference, Lenin adamantly resisted suggestions to incorporate the federal principle in the structure of the party. He labeled the proposals at the conference "federalism of the worst type" and objected to what he called attempts "to adapt socialism to nationalism."[31]

Lenin had written that Marxists are "opposed to federation and decentralization" and that "while, and insofar as, different nations constitute a single state, Marxists will never under any circumstances advocate either the federal principle or decentralization."[32] In April of

1917 Lenin urged the party "to create as large a state as possible."[33] A short time later he asserted "we do not favor the existence of small states."[34] In one of his most celebrated theoretical treatises, *The State and Revolution*, Lenin ridiculed the idea that federalism and democracy were somehow structurally linked. "A prejudice is very widespread," he noted, "among petty bourgeois democrats, that a federal republic necessarily means a greater amount of freedom than a centralized republic. This is wrong. . . . The greatest amount of local, regional, and other freedom known in history was accorded by a centralized and not by a federal republic."[35] In tones that border on hysteria, he lambasted his opponents for attempts to read pro-federalist perspectives into Marx. "Marx disagreed with Proudhon," Lenin argued, "precisely on the question of federalism. . . . Federalism as a principle follows logically from the petty-bourgeois views of anarchism. Marx was a centralist."[36] Thus, right up until the revolution Lenin, like his mentor, was a centralist.

It was only in the dramatic events after October 1917 that Lenin adopted the view that the yearning for voice and representation of the regions was a political resource to be exploited even at the cost of compromising his principled objections to federal arrangements.[37] Why did he change his position on federalism? In a sense he did not change. Lenin's support of the federal principle was essentially tactical. Lenin saw federalism as temporary; a federation, he maintained, constituted only a transitional step to a unitary government. He claimed that federalism was a "transitional form [of government] enroute to the unity of the laborers of all nations."[38]

Lenin referred, as Stalin would repeatedly, to the lesson of the Swiss and American federations, which evolved, in his view, from independent states, through confederation to federation and, ultimately, to centralized unity. Lenin saw federation as the "surest step to the most solid unification of the different nationalities of Russia into a single, democratic, centralized Soviet state."[39] He defended his position with references to Engels' assertion that a federal republic was a "step forward" toward centralized unity.[40]

Lenin was not overburdened by the contrast between his theoretical writings and his new "pragmatic" position on the federal question. What threatened was nothing less than dismemberment of the empire; potentially a devastating blow to the fortunes of world socialism. As Lenin observed, "If the Ukrainians see that we have a republic of Soviets, then they won't break away; if they see we have a republic of Miliukov, then they will go their separate way."[41] Lenin accepted the right to self-determination and the right of secession (which he thought it implied) as rights "in principle." He saw the minorities' fear of Russian dominance as the motivating factor in secessionist sentiment. If he could allay those fears, separation could be prevented, and unification was possible. For this reason it would be necessary to maintain the political allegiance of the colonial areas. Federalism could offer this. When the time came, the federal form could wither away. The pace at which transitional, socialist federalism would lead to a unitary form of government has been a subject of intense and bitter dispute within the USSR.[42]

Federalism, then, was Lenin's answer to the nationalities question. But what kind of federalism? The First All-Russian Congress, held in May 1917, adopted a federalist proposal for the form of government.[43] In April 1918, a constitutional commission was established to prepare a draft of a new document to describe the relations between the regions and the center. The original question was whether the basic principle of organization should be structural or spatial. Some argued in favor of a corporatist principle, the "economic principle," which gave socio-economic groups such as communes, trade unions, and cooperatives political status as the constituents of the system. But it was a hybrid compromise combining nationality and territory that won the day. The national-territorial principle gave formal status and political recognition to the leading groups and recognized their claim to a homeland. National statehood came into being. This national-territorial principle gave a sense of self-determination, a promise of autonomy, and a feeling of natural representation to the national minorities. At the same time it integrated them into the central institutional framework in such a way that their legal rights could not be institutionally defended.

Only at the end of his life, after he had been partially paralyzed by stroke and forced to retire from active political participation, did Lenin realize the extent to which his government and party were promoting forced assimilation rather than the natural, gradual integration he anticipated. This was the fourth and last period of Lenin's nationality theorizing. While he was not capable at this point of reversing the trend toward national repression, he did manage one last gesture by interdicting Stalin's attempt to concentrate economic commissariats in Moscow in the plans for the Treaty of the Soviet Union of 1922. As the Commissar of Nationalities, Stalin was the responsible official in a commission established in August 1922, to draft the Treaty of the Union which would outline inter-republic relations. Lenin's insistence on reviewing the draft reflected his distrust of Stalin's increasingly tactless approach to nationality problems. Lenin objected to the draft, Stalin revised it, and it was adopted as the Treaty of the Union in the waning days of 1922. But policy is made in the process of implementation. Lenin would not survive to see this nominal victory carried through in practice.[44]

Lenin's positions on the issues of national self-determination, national autonomy, and federalism constitute what has become known in the

USSR as Leninist nationality policy. What exactly is this policy? Walker Connor defines the original policy as the "formula for performing the task of harnessing the powerful forces of nationalism to the revolution and then vanquishing them thereafter."[45] Richard Pipes concurs with this view, calling the original Soviet federal structure "an instrument for welding together the scattered parts of a disintegrated empire."[46]

Since Lenin's day, interpretations of the Leninist nationality policy have changed. A typical contemporary definition is the one offered by Eduard Bagramov, a leading press commentator on nationality affairs in the Soviet Union today. He summarized Leninist nationality policy as "the continual strengthening of the free and voluntary union of peoples based on the fullest trust and a clear consciousness of fraternal unity."[47] Gorbachev identified the goal of Leninist nationality policy "as achieving a situation in which every person and every nation can develop freely, and every people can satisfy its requirements in all spheres of sociopolitical life, in its native language and culture, and in its customs and religious beliefs."[48]

Additional insight can be gained if we look at the problem not from the central perspective, but from that of the periphery. In the Soviet borderlands, proponents of the rights of the national minorities tend to emphasize the formal guarantees of Leninist nationality policy in an effort to mobilize the legitimacy of Lenin's name in their own defense. Leninist nationality policy is thus often brandished as a shield against overbearing policies of the center. As James Critchlow noted, it has long been a standard practice of defenders of minority rights to use Leninist quotations to "buttress every argument for national rights."[49]

These instrumental and political definitions provide us with insight into the motives of political actors, but do not reveal much of the substance of policy. They do not, therefore, afford useful analytical definitions. The definitions of Connors and Pipes capture the tactical quality of early Leninist nationality policy. Bagramov's and Gorbachev's definitions suggest the instrumental quality of contemporary policy. Critchlow's definition reveals the fact that Leninist nationality policy has many sides. The perspective of the periphery is different than that of the center. But how do we capture all of these aspects in a definition which provides insight into both the Leninist principles and the dynamics of Soviet nationality politics?

A more general definition of Leninist nationality policy, one which includes the elements listed above, must emphasize the main feature of Leninist nationality policy, namely, its purposive quality. Lenin's purpose in managing nationality relations was national integration. He expected and hoped for the integration of humanity into a "nationless" collective. Given his theoretical views, Lenin could feel confident that concessions granted in the form of national autonomy and federalism would not be permanent. As he saw it, capitalism was integrative, but socialism was even more so. Nationalism would disappear as the vestiges of capitalism atrophied.

> Socialism organizes production without class antagonism, and thus supports the well-being of all citizens. In so doing it gives full scope to the "sympathies" of the population. It therefore facilitates and greatly speeds the rapprochement (*sblizhenie*) and fusion (*sliianie*) of nations."[50]

Originally Lenin did not think that this form of integrationism risked charges of assimilationism—meaning in the Russian and early Soviet context, Great Russian Chauvinism—because, given the Marxist teleology, integration was inevitable. Thus the "fusion" referred to above was viewed by Lenin as leading to assimilation into a class (proletariat) rather than a nation (Russia or, for that matter, even the USSR).

What then is the substance of Leninist nationality theory as it has developed over the years? Today, Leninist nationality theory contains four components. Its first component concerns the Marxist comprehension of the etiology and evolution of nations. The second concerns the objectives of inter-ethnic relations as contributing to the accession of socialism. In other words, axiom one gives the *dynamics* of nationalism, axiom two gives the *goals*. As axioms, both of these are fixed; they are the givens of the situation. The two unknowns in the situation are, first, the *pace* at which the processes of socialism carry forward, and, second, the specific *instruments* by which those processes are advanced. Leninist nationality theory can then be described as a theory of "teleological integrationism." The policy is chiefly concerned with how, not whether, this integration takes place. In sum then, Leninist nationality policy— as opposed to Leninist theory—is concerned wholly with the pace and instruments of teleological integrationism.

The "dialectical" interpretation of history gives a flexible and dynamic turn to Lenin's thought and practice, allowing him to apparently reverse his views with no theoretical contradiction. His doctrine of "alliance for limited objectives" served as a rationale for his polemical and tactical style. He turned his tactical approach to his advantage. Against the abstract internationalists, Lenin appeared to be the defender of national rights. Against the Great Russian Chauvinists, he appeared to be the defender of democracy and national rights. Against "bourgeois nationalists," he appeared to be the defender of national autonomy but not the proponent of suicidal secessionism. His idiosyncratic view of national self-determination, with its facile distinction between recognizing a right and yet not supporting the exercise of that right, offered a solution to the problem of separatism. Against the promoters of forced integration, he favored "natural" integration. On the language issue, for instance, he proclaimed himself against a "state language," calling it superfluous since a large proportion of the population would adopt a common language "by virtue of the demands of economic turnover without any 'state' privileges for any one language."[51]

Lenin's thinking on nationality questions continues to be of paramount importance in the USSR because there is so much disagreement over the pace and instruments of policy. Like Marx before him, Lenin saw nations as historical categories destined to wither away. The exact interpretation of the "fusion" of nations has become a litmus test of the orientation in the debates regarding the moral and legal standing of minority group rights in the USSR. The critical question for Leninist nationality policy is essentially the same question for federal theory, although they are stated differently. Even as the key question on the federal agenda has been the speed at which a unitary form of government is approached, so has the nationality agenda hinged on the rate at which the peoples of the USSR merge into one undifferentiated, classless, proletarian mass. National differences, according to this view, would wither as nations passed from stages of national development (*rastsvet*), through a "growing together" (*sblizhenie*), to an ultimate state of merging or "fusion" (*sliianie*). As Soviet sources so often cite the famous "fusion" reference of Lenin's to the effect that the nations are approaching a monolithic whole, so federal theorists see the administrative divisions of the system as playing temporary roles as they strengthen the forces of cohesion and lead the society toward a unitary polity.[52] The source of controversy is the "speed" of the process and the proper means for directing it. Here, as elsewhere, disagreement on means can often fuel disputes more bitter than disagreements on final objectives.

Notes

1. The comment was made specifically with respect to Central Asia. V.I. Lenin, *Polnoe sobranie sochinenii* Vol. 30 (Moscow: Izdatelstvo Politicheskoi Literatury, 1960–65), p. 35.

2. See the *Sbornik ukazov i postanovlenii Vremennogo Pravitel'stva* Vol. 1 (Petrograd, 1917). Decree of March 20, 1917, as cited in Richard Pipes, *The Formation of the Soviet Union: Communism and Nationalism, 1917–1923* rev. ed. (Cambridge: Harvard University Press, 1964), p. 50.

3. Walker Connor, *The National Question in Marxist-Leninist Theory and Strategy* (Princeton: Princeton University Press, 1983), p. 19.

4. Connor, *The National Question*, p. 11.

5. Robert Tucker, *Stalin as Revolutionary, 1879–1929: A Study in History and Personality* (New York: W.W. Norton and Co., 1973), pp. 123–125.

6. This remark, made in Engels' *A Critique of the Draft Social-Democratic Programme of 1891* is favorably quoted in Lenin's *State and Revolution*. Lenin noted that "Engels, like Marx, upheld democratic centralism, the republic–one and indivisible. He regarded the federal republic either as an exception and a hindrance to development, or as a transition from a monarchy to a centralized republic, as a "step forward" under certain special conditions. Among these special conditions, he puts the national question first." Lenin, *Polnoe*, Vol. 33, pp. 73–74.

7. Engels opposed the "Zonderbund" in Switzerland as a federal solution to the problem of compartmentalized cantons. Marx took a more lenient position with respect to federalism regarding proposals in the 1860s for the creation of a "British Federation." Following Lenin, Soviet writers often cite this as evidence that he favored federation as a solution to minority rights within a multinational empire. See Lenin, *Polnoe*, Vol. 33, pp. 73–74, nt. 95.

8. Treatment of the issues involved in the political debates regarding nationalism before the Bolshevik revolution may be found in Jurij Borys, *The Sovietization of Ukraine, 1917–1923* (Edmonton: The Canadian Institute of Ukrainian Studies, 1980): pp. 12–51; Walker Connor, *The National Question in Marxist-Leninist Theory and Strategy* (Princeton: Princeton University Press, 1984); Horace B. Davis, *Nationalism and Socialism: Marxist and Labor Theories of Nationalism to 1917* (New York: Monthly Review Press, 1967); and Pipes, *The Formation*, pp. 21–49.

9. Pipes, *The Formation*, p. 26.

10. Pipes, *The Formation*, p. 28, ft. 40.

11. Pipes, *The Formation*, p. 34.

12. Interpretation and argumentation bearing on the national question occurs throughout Lenin's writings, but much of it is repetitive. The principal works which address questions of nationalism include: "The Tasks of the Russian Social Democrats" (1897); "The National Question in Our Program" (1903); "The First of May" (1905); "Critical Remarks on the National Question" (1913); "On the National Program of the RSDLP" (1913); "On the Right of Nations to Self-determination" (1914); "On the National Pride of the Great Russians" (1914); "The Socialist Revolution and the Right of Nations to Self-determination" (1916); "Theses on the National Question" (1917); and "The State and Revolution" (1917). For consistency of reference, all subsequent citations to Lenin's work are from the Russian language edition *Polnoe sobranie sochinenii* 55 Vols., 5th ed. (Moscow: Izdatelstvo Politicheskoi Literatury, 1960–65). Complete English translations may be found in Lenin, *Collected Works*, 45 Vols. (Moscow: Progress Publishers, 1964). There is a large secondary literature on Lenin's nationality theories. Readers should consult the select bibliography. Especially useful analysis may be found in Walker Connor, *The National Question in Marxist-Leninist Theory and Strategy* (Princeton: Princeton University Press, 1984); and Peter Zwick *National Communism* (Boulder: Westview Press, 1983).

13. Lenin, *Polnoe*, Vol. 24, p. 134.

14. Lenin, *Polnoe*, Vol. 24, p. 124.

15. Lenin, *Polnoe*, Vol. 27, p. 256.

16. Lenin, *Polnoe*, Vol. 24, p 131.

17. Lenin, *Polnoe*, Vol. 24, p. 121.

18. This passage appears in Lenin's long-suppressed notes on nationalism that were reprinted during de-Stalinization in the party theoretical journal *Kommunist* No. 9 (1956): pp. 22–25.

19. See Borys, *The Sovietization*, p. 21.

20. The two others were: full equality of all citizens regardless of gender, religion, race, and nationality; and local [oblastnoe] self-administration.

21. Pipes, *The Formation*, p. 45.

22. Lenin, *Polnoe*, Vol. 27, p. 255.

23. Lenin, *Polnoe*, Vol. 32, p. 7.

24. He wrote in April, 1917, that "the party of the proletariat emphatically rejects what is known as 'national cultural autonomy'." Lenin, *Polnoe*, Vol. 31, p. 440.

25. He wrote that "national culture is the culture of the landlords, the clergy, and the bourgeoisie." Lenin, *Polnoe*, Vol. 24, p. 121.

26. Lenin's lack of prescience regarding the effects of bureaucracy on socialism is examined in Moshe Lewin, *Lenin's Last Struggle* (New York: Random House, 1986).

27. Democratic centralism is defined in the CPSU Ustav adopted in February 1986, as: "a) election of all leading party bodies, from the lowest to the highest; b) periodic reports of party bodies to their party organizations and to higher bodies; c) strict party discipline and subordination of the minority to the majority; d) the decisions of higher bodies are obligatory for lower bodies." This definition is unchanged from the version adopted in the 1961 Party Ustav.

28. Lenin's opposition to federalism was by no means an extreme position for the time. Many contemporary thinkers opposed federal solutions. The Constitutional Democrats (Kadets) also opposed federalism, arguing that a functioning federalism presupposed rough equality between the constituent governments. Great Russians were not apt to assent to a formula which suggested equality between the Russians and their colonies. See Pipes, *The Formation*, pp. 30–34.

29. S.G. Shaumian, *O natsional'no-kul'turnoi avtonomii* (Moscow: 1959), p. 10.

30. Lenin, *Polnoe*, Vol. 27, p. 256.

31. Lenin, *Polnoe*, Vol. 22, p. 229. The fact that the RSFSR does not have a separate party organization today dates from this dispute.

32. Lenin, *Polnoe*, Vol. 24, p. 143.

33. Lenin, *Polnoe*, Vol. 31, pp. 167–168.

34. Lenin, *Polnoe*, Vol. 32, p. 342.

35. Lenin, *Polnoe*, Vol. 33, p. 74.

36. Lenin, *Polnoe*, Vol. 33, p. 53.

37. Most Soviet scholars date this change in position to the Third All-Russian Congress of Soviets in January 1918. See S.S. Galilov, *Razrabotka V.I. Leninym printsipov stroitel'stva Sovetskogo mnogonatsional'nogo gosudarstva, 1917–1922 gg* (Moscow: Izpolit, 1958), p. 56; D.A. Chugaev, *Lenin–osnovatel' Sovetskogo mnogonatsional'nogo gosudarstva* (Moscow: 1960), p. 17; S.I. Iakubovskaia, *Obrazovanie i razvitie Sovetskogo mnogonatsional'nogo gosudarstva* (Moscow: Izdatelstvo AN SSSR, 1966), p. 11.

38. Lenin, *Polnoe,* Vol. 41, p. 164.

39. Stalin, *Sochineniia,* Vol. 4, p. 66.

40. Lenin, *Polnoe,* Vol. 33, p. 72.

41. *Polnoe,* Vol. 31, p. 436. These remarks were made by Lenin in April 1917. Note also Stalin's observation at the VII (April) All-Russian Conference of Bolsheviks in 1917 that "9/10 of the nationalities after the destruction of Tsarism will not want to break away." As quoted in I.P. Trainin, *"Sovetskoe mnogonatsional'noe gosudarstvo,"* *Sovetskoe gosudarstvo i pravo* No. 10 (1947): p. 22.

42. The extent to which Lenin viewed federalism as justified by conditions prevailing in the USSR is a matter of dispute among Soviet scholars. Some have attributed to him a view that suggests more permanence to federalism than the view attributed to Stalin. After the publication in *Kommunist* of a previously suppressed letter on the subject, many Soviet scholars argued that the "transitional" view of federalism was actually a Stalinist distortion, not a view of Lenin's. On this issue see Grey Hodnett, "The Debate over Soviet Federalism," *Soviet Studies,* Vol. 18, No. 4 (1967), pp. 458–481, especially p. 460.

43. Pipes, *The Formation,* p. 77.

44. The story of the relationship between the two men regarding this question is recounted in Hélène Carrère d'Encausse, *Decline of an Empire: The Soviet Socialist Republics in Revolt* (New York: Newsweek, 1979), pp. 17–24.

45. Connor, *The National Question,* pp. 36–37.

46. Pipes, *The Formation,* p. 111.

47. Eduard Bagramov, "Zhivoi vopros zhivoi zhizni," *Agitator* No. 23 (December 1987): p. 9.

48. See Gorbachev's address to the people of Azerbaidzhan and Armenia which appeared in *Bakinskii Rabochii* (27 February 1988) as reprinted in *Current Digest of the Soviet Press* XL, No. 8 (1988): p. 6.

49. James Critchlow, "Signs of Emerging Nationalism in Central Asia," in Norton T. Dodge, ed., *The Soviets in Asia* (Mechanicsville, MA: Cremona Foundation, 1972), p. 26.

50. Lenin, *Polnoe,* Vol. 30, p. 21.

51. Lenin, *Polnoe,* Vol. 23, p. 317.

52. In addition to the "fusion" passage cited above, compare the passage on *"sliianie"* in Lenin, *Polnoe,* Vol. 27, p. 256.

3

The Evolution of
the Soviet Federal System

Soviet autonomy is not a rigid thing fixed once and for all time; it permits of the most varied forms and degrees of development.

—Stalin

The first document adopted by the first official organ of Soviet power, the Second All-Russian Congress of Soviets, meeting on November 7, 1917, promised to guarantee "all nations inhabiting Russia" the "complete right of self-determination."[1] A week later Lenin's "Declaration of Rights of the Peoples of Russia" was announced by the Soviet government. The Declaration offered an array of promises. It declared: (1) equality and sovereignty of the peoples of Russia; (2) the right of self-determination extending to secession and the formation of an independent government; (3) the rejection of all national and national-religious privileges; and (4) the free development of all national minorities and ethnographic groups inhabiting the territory of Russia.[2] This document was quickly followed by the "Appeal to All Laboring Muslims of Russia and the East," promising to defend the rights of Muslims and urging their support for the Soviet regime.[3] So began the process that Soviet sources refer to somewhat ambiguously as *"natsional'noe stroitel'stvo"* (national construction). It was a process complicated by territorial concessions resulting from the separate peace of Brest-Litovsk, the travail of the ongoing civil war, the lack of administrative experience on the part of the new rulers, and by the extreme variations in political styles among regions with differing languages, cultures, and political traditions.

In the struggle for ascendancy after the seizure of power, the Bolsheviks, with promises of peace, land, food, and power to the Soviets, won popular support in the Russian heartland. But even as they gained the support of the Russian core, the Bolsheviks' initial bids for popular support in the borderlands of the Empire were not successful. In the

Baltics, in the Western provinces and Ukraine, in the Caucasus, and in Central Asia popular support initially swung behind the national intelligentsia. Internally divided, poorly organized, and not driven by the millennial zeal of a revolutionary ideology, however, the members of the local political elite lacked the political resources, organizational capability, and the political appeal necessary to counter the communists' promises. The Bolsheviks possessed an ardor inspired by a vision of a revolutionary future and a shrewd pragmatism inspired by years of experience as political underdogs. The Bolsheviks held forth the offer of a "new society" beyond the divisiveness and national enmity of Tsarist colonialism. At the same time, the Bolsheviks were ready to exploit local political cleavages by making alliances with even the most reactionary groups when it served their purposes.

Out of pride and a lingering Great Russian Chauvinism, the White armies of Denikin and Kolchak were unwilling to forge alliances with local political figures. Discredited by the humiliating military defeat of World War I, the forces of the status quo and monarchist restoration could excite few political imaginations among those who had been subject to Tsarist colonialism. The prospect of change offered by the Bolsheviks eventually proved magnetic. In this atmosphere, the nascent political organizations in the borderlands proved unable to rival the Bolsheviks. Even as the principles of local autonomy were elevated in Bolshevik theory, the economic and political subordination of the borderlands to the center proceeded in practice.

The Extension of Soviet Power to the Borderlands

If one conceives of the situation in terms of the military metaphors so prevalent at the time, there were four geographical "fronts" on which the Bolsheviks sought to resist the unravelling of the former Empire. To the north there was Finland. Shortly after the Revolution, Finland and parts of Poland broke away from the young Soviet state. Powerless to prevent this, the Bolshevik leaders accepted it philosophically. The western front, still engulfed in the War effort, included the Baltic countries, Belorussia, most of Poland, and Ukraine. To the south was the mosaic of cultures of the Caucasus. Further to the south and to the east were the even more remote territories of Turkestan that had fallen under Tsarist control in the nineteenth century, chiefly as a result of the Anglo-Russian rivalry.

On these various geographical "fronts" the imposition of Soviet control took place in three distinct phases. The first phase immediately followed the Bolshevik Revolution. The second phase extended over the period of political consolidation. This phase varied from region to region with some areas in Central Asia not coming under direct Soviet control until the early 1930s. The last period started with the 1939 occupation of the Baltic countries and concluded with the annexation of territories at the close of World War II.

The revolutionary doctrine of Marxism-Leninism was global in its sweeping vision of a future society freed from exploitation and not ruled by the laws of capitalism. Bolsheviks naturally sought to spread the effects of the revolution and the establishment of the first socialist order as widely as possible. To the Bolsheviks this entailed preventing the imperial borderlands from reverting to pre-socialist forms of political control. One of the first goals of the Soviet government that came into being in January 1918 in the form of the Russian Soviet Federated Socialist Republic (RSFSR) was socialist expansionism. The young government's expansive designs, however, were cut short by the exigencies of the withdrawal from the First World War. The Treaty of Brest-Litovsk signed with Germany in March 1918 forfeited nearly a fourth of Russia's territory, nearly a third of its population, and the important agricultural resources of Ukraine. The treaty was unpopular with many of the party's leaders, but Lenin saw it as a necessary if humiliating concession in order to strengthen the chances for success of the first Soviet state. The direct consequences of the accord did not last long. The treaty was abrogated within a year following the capitulation of the Axis powers in November. The indirect consequences were more enduring. The lessons of Lenin's pragmatic compromise were clear. In a hostile international environment, with the capitalist nations eager to take advantage of vulnerabilities, world communism would need to rely on resources other than an expectation of the automatic spread of socialism.

During the Brest period, the Bolsheviks continued to exert influence in Ukraine. In November 1918, a temporary Worker-Peasant Government of Ukraine was established. In that same month, an Estonian Soviet Republic was declared. That December, Latvian and Lithuanian Soviet Socialist Republics were formed. In January 1919 a Belorussian Soviet Socialist Republic was formed. In February 1919 the Belorussian and Lithuanian republics were combined. By June of 1919 the All-Russian Central Executive Committee passed a decree providing for the unification of Russia, Ukraine, Latvia, Lithuania, Belorussia, and the Crimea. Yet, while these political formations existed on paper and these dates are still given by official Soviet sources as the dates of inception of these respective republics, none of these political formations proved enduring. Each was relinquished owing to insufficient political support.

The struggle for the consolidation of Soviet power varied widely throughout the borderland regions. In the Caucasus local figures remained in power for three years following the October Revolution. Not until the April 1920 insurrection in Baku was the Azerbaidzhan SSR established. In November 1920 the Armenian SSR was created. In February of the following year the Georgian Soviet Socialist Republic was formed. In December 1922 these formations were again transformed into a Transcaucasian Socialist Federated Soviet Republic.

In Central Asia an April 1918 decree of the Bolshevik government recognized the Turkestan Autonomous Soviet Socialist Republic. In August 1920 the Kirgiz Autonomous Soviet Socialist Republic was recognized. In April 1920 the Khivan Khan fell and the Khorezm People's Soviet Republic was formed. In October of that same year the Bukharan Emir fell and the Bukharan People's Soviet Republic was formed. At the close of 1922 the First All-union Congress of Soviets passed the treaty on the formation of the USSR. The formation of the union was followed by reorganization of the southern tier republics. In October 1923 the Khorezm Republic joined the USSR, and in September of the following year the Bukharan Republic followed suit. After a period of redistricting, Central Asia was divided in October 1924 into the Uzbek Soviet Socialist Republic and the Turkmen Soviet Socialist Republic. Initially, parts of Kazakhstan and Kirgizia were incorporated into the Russian Soviet Federated Socialist Republic as Autonomous Soviet Socialist Republics. Not until June 1929 was the Tadzhik Soviet Socialist Republic created in its present form. In 1936 the Kazakh and Kirgiz Soviet Socialist Republics were formed. At the same time the Transcaucasian Federated Republic was again divided into Armenia, Georgia, and Azerbaidzhan. By the time of the adoption of the 1936 (Stalin) Constitution, there were 11 republics (RSFSR, Ukrainian, Belorussian, Georgian, Armenian, Azerbaidzhan, Kazakh, Uzbek, Turkmen, Tadzhik, and Kirgiz).

The Baltic countries represent a special case of Soviet designs because they were seen not only as areas of expansion for socialism, but also as having a geopolitical and commercial importance to the regime. As we have seen, Lenin and the other Bolsheviks maintained an eccentric interpretation of autonomy and independence, and could thus later claim that they had never meant or promised independence in the "bourgeois" sense of the concept. Nevertheless, events forced the young Russian government into recognizing the independence of the Baltic countries in a most unambiguous manner. For instance, a treaty signed in August 1920 noted that "Russia unreservedly recognizes the independence, self-subsistency and sovereignty of the Latvian State and voluntarily and forever renounces all sovereign rights over the Latvian people. . . ."[4]

The formal guarantees of independence won by these countries was relinquished, however, by the Molotov-Ribbentrop non-aggression treaty of August 23, 1939. Hitler had earlier compelled the Baltic countries to sign non-aggression treaties with Germany in June of 1939. Stalin followed suit by forcing upon the Baltic countries "non-aggression" treaties in the end of September 1939. The Latvian government, for instance, was required to sign an agreement giving the Soviets control of Latvia's islands in the Baltic Sea for the use of Soviet military and naval bases. The charade of friendly relations came to an end in June 1940 when Soviet troops occupied the countries. By early August of 1940 all three countries were incorporated into the USSR as Soviet republics.[5]

The Soviet Constitutions and Federalism

In January 1918, the Third Congress of Soviets undertook to embody the changes that were taking place in the USSR in constitutional form. The congress passed a resolution declaring the existence of "a federation of Soviet republics founded on the principle of a free union of the peoples of Russia." The following July, the first socialist constitution came into force, a federal constitution.[6] This "1918 Constitution" was followed by a Treaty of Union in 1922. The treaty later served as the basis for the second Soviet Constitution, adopted in 1924. Twelve years later a new constitution, the 1936 "Stalin" Constitution, was adopted. In the 1960s Khrushchev made reference to the need for yet a new constitution, and appointed himself chairman of a committee charged with drafting it. Fifteen years later, in 1977, the committee's product, the "Brezhnev Constitution," was unveiled. The recent constitutional amendments of November 1988 stand out as more important than any of the preceding constitutional revisions. The following pages survey the evolution of Soviet Constitutions. No description of Soviet constitutionalism would be complete without reference to the party. The Party Program and the Party Statute are arguably more "fundamental" than the fundamental law. Practice indicates that they are indeed more difficult to revise than the constitution.

The first Soviet Constitution was adopted in July 1918. It announced the legal creation of the Russian Soviet Federated Socialist Republic (RSFSR).[7] The first "fundamental law" of socialism was distinguished from more traditional constitutions by both its tone and content. It was both programmatic and ideological in its complexion.[8] The organization of state-party-society relations described in the document set the stage for the historical evolution of Soviet political institutions. It recognized the institutional "triad" which continues to exist in the USSR, dividing power among the: (1) party; (2) government (commissariats and, later, ministries) and (3) soviets (legislative bodies). The first Soviet Constitution does not explicitly mention the party as an instrument of Soviet government. It does, nevertheless, implicitly grant a role to the party by acknowledging the ideological and teleological goals of Soviet society.

In this way it provides an implicit rationale for the party acting as a shadow government.

The constitution vested control of the means of production in the government. The land, natural resources, and banking system were nationalized and the factories, mines, and other means of production and transport were placed under the direction of the Supreme Soviet of the Public Economy (VSNKh). The constitution provided for a legislature by creating an All-Russian Congress of Soviets. For reasons of both ideology and politics, suffrage was intentionally restricted by this constitution. Tradesmen, clergy, tsarist police officials, and those living on unearned income were excluded from voting. The procedures and principles of representation were designed to exclude the "exploiters" of the early period.

The RSFSR was called "federated" because it contained within it smaller politico-administrative units, eight so-called "autonomous republics" and thirteen "autonomous regions." But the real departure from the concept of a unitary form of government came with the discussions preceding the adoption of the Treaty on the Formation of the USSR late in 1922. A commission had been set up in August 1922 for the purpose of drafting a new constitution. The commission, in which Stalin played a central role, produced a draft which extended the centralized government machinery into the borderland peripheries under the rubric of "autonomization." Lenin joined the advocates of minority rights in opposing the draft plan. The Commission relented and produced a revised, less centralized version of a political compact. Even as the discussions of the constitution continued, practical steps were being taken to adopt a "Treaty of Union" which would draw the border republics into closer association with Moscow. An October CPSU Central Committee resolution called for the creation of a union; plenary meetings of the party central committees in the republics followed. Congresses of the soviets of the republics "unanimously" voted in favor of the plan. Despite criticism from Georgia and Ukraine, a new Declaration on the Formation of the USSR was adopted. Finally, a Treaty of Union, incorporating the RSFSR, the Ukrainian SSR, the Belorussian SSR, and the Federal Republic of Transcaucasia into a Union of Soviet Socialist Republics was concluded on December 30, 1922, by the First Congress of Soviets.

In the Treaty, the principle of federation was expressed in a separation of functions between all-union and republican organs of government. All-union organs were in charge of foreign relations, military affairs, transport, and communications. Such functions as financial affairs, food production, labor, and transport were to be dually administered by center and republic. Justice, education, health, social welfare, and internal affairs, however, were to be left in the hands of the republican commissariats.

The materials of the Twelfth Party Congress of the Russian Communist Party (Bolsheviks) held in April 1923 made clear the continuing tension between the center and the peripheries. A resolution of the congress referred in critical terms to "a significant proportion of Soviet functionaries" who regarded the USSR not as a union of equal republics, but as a step toward the liquidation of the republics, as "the beginning of a so-called indivisible whole."[9] Lenin, who did not attend the congress for reasons of health, sent a letter, dated December 22, 1922, to be read to the delegates. (On the Question of Nationalization and Autonomization). The letter expressed his changing notion of a voluntary union.[10] As control was being re-extended over the colonized areas, the varied multinational composition of the state was held out as a rationale for a new formulation of federal relations. It was this formula which resulted, on January 31, 1924, in the adoption of the second Soviet Constitution.

Like its predecessor, the 1924 Constitution distinguished between government, state, and party functions. Its legislative provisions described an all-union Congress of Soviets which was to meet annually until 1927 and, afterwards, every two years. The membership of the congress ranged from 1540 to more than 2000. Elections were held for each congress. When the congress was not in session, power was exercised through the all-union Central Executive Committee (TsIK). A Presidium exercised power for the TsIK when it was not in session. The Presidium's members were elected by the convened TsIK from among its number. Moreover, the TsIK elected the Council of People's Commissars. The TsIK was bicameral, including a Soviet of the Union and a Soviet of Nationalities. The Soviet of the Union was elected by the congress delegates from among their numbers on the basis of the population of each republic. The Soviet of the Nationalities was elected by the Congress of Soviets of the union republics, autonomous republics, and autonomous oblasts on the basis of a fixed formula. The TsIK was to hold at least three sessions during each of its convocations between the all-union congresses of Soviets. On paper this arrangement gave a good deal of representation to the republics.

The third Soviet Constitution, or as it is often called, the "Stalin" Constitution, identified the USSR as a "federal state formed on the basis of a voluntary association of equal Soviet socialist republics." (Article 13) The Stalin Constitution, adopted by the extraordinary Eighth Congress of Soviets on December 5, 1936, was said to introduce the victory of socialism. Its legislative provisions championed the principle of general, direct, and equal suffrage. The previously disenfranchised groups discussed above (i.e., the clergy, etc.) were reintegrated. The electoral system provided for secret ballot, but with only single-slate candidacies.

In many respects the rights of the republics appeared to be enhanced in the Stalin Constitution. Each republic had a right to its own constitution (Article 16), was guaranteed the "right to freely secede from the USSR" (Article 17), and was offered the right to exercise residual powers (Article 15). The new constitution nominally expanded the representation of the republics by boosting their deputies in the Soviet of Nationalities from five to twenty-five. The autonomous republics, under the old arrangement, enjoyed equal representation with the republics. The new arrangement altered this equivalence by leaving the autonomous republics with eleven deputies. Moreover, Stalin took the opportunity to define three conditions under which a national group was entitled to republican status. He pointed out that the republic "must be a border republic . . . because, since the union republics have a right to secede from the USSR, a republic . . . must be in a position logically and actually to raise the question of secession from the USSR."[11] Second, the national group must constitute a compact majority within the republic. Third, the group should have a substantial population, which Stalin, apparently arbitrarily, fixed at one million. A group of this size, it was reasoned, would be capable of standing alone and thus would have, "in principle," a chance of succeeding as a separate state.

The 1936 Constitution did away with the Congress of Soviets in favor of an enlarged Supreme Soviet. Deputies were elected to the bicameral Supreme Soviet for four-year terms. Each new election ushered in a new consecutively numbered convocation (*sozyv*). Within each convocation, sessions (*sessiia*) were numbered consecutively. The Supreme Soviet ordinarily met twice a year, although prior to Stalin's death in 1953 this rule was not strictly followed. The Stalin Constitution also introduced a new nomenclature, identifying the territorial units of *krai* and *oblast*.

The prerogatives of the republics were nominally extended by two amendments in the 1940s. On February 1, 1944 the Law on the Creation of Military Forces of Republics was passed. At the same time a law permitting the republics to conduct foreign affairs was also passed.[12] On March 15, 1946, an amendment provided for the Chairman of the Presidium of the Supreme Soviets of each of the republics to become a vice-chairman of the USSR Supreme Soviet. Meanwhile, the number of republics had increased. The original treaty forming the USSR had united four republics. The number later increased to six and, with the promulgation of the Stalin Constitution, to eleven. At the close of the post-war territorial consolidations, the number stood at sixteen. The

Karelian republic was reduced to autonomous republic status in 1956, bringing the number of republics to its present fifteen.

A mood of decentralization set in during de-Stalinization. Khrushchev announced publicly that changed conditions called for a revision of the 1936 Constitution. In April 1962 a constitutional commission was established to produce a new draft. No doubt in part because of the resentment amid the mid-elite provoked by Khrushchev through his administrative changes, Khrushchev was removed from power before the commission could make public its product. A political consensus for a new constitutional draft did not emerge for another fifteen years. But by this time, under Brezhnev's leadership, the mood was decidedly centralist. This was reflected in the draft constitution unveiled on May 27, 1977 which proclaimed itself the constitution of "developed, mature socialism." The final form of the Brezhnev Constitution enacted into law on October 7, 1977, adopted a slightly new nomenclature, championed some new political slogans, and changed the formulas of representation somewhat. But the overall delineation of powers between the central government and the constituent republics was unchanged.

The Stalin Revolution and Party Supremacy

The shape of the federal structure of the USSR today cannot be understood without reference to three factors: the Marxist-Leninist ideology; the crucible of the revolutionary situation; and the centralizing pressures exerted upon the Soviet Union as it passed through the revolution of Stalinism. The ideology was discussed in the previous chapter. The foregoing sections of this chapter have addressed the territorial aspects of political consolidation. The remaining issue, the impact of Stalinism, is, both within and outside of the USSR, the most provocative and often disputed factor.

Since glasnost has expanded the domain of political discourse in the USSR, the prevailing tendency is to attribute the rapid centralization of the Soviet polity to the forced modernization under Stalin. As a recent commentary noted:

> the years of the "great change" . . . saw the beginning of forced collectivization. Economic accountability in industry was done away with. The scientifically-based and balanced plan of the first 5-year period was replaced by a race to attain arbitrarily set targets. Thus the bureaucratism of the center vanquished federalism in the organization of national life.[13]

To what extent is the "abandonment" of federalism attributable to Stalin alone?

The gradualism of the period of the New Economic Period (NEP) brought the USSR to what Stalin and his entourage saw plainly as a historical turning point. Stalin saw that a transformation was taking place as members of the peasantry, unschooled in the ways of the world, unmoved by Marxist philosophizing, and unsteeled by participation in pre-revolutionary clandestine politics, were increasingly joining the ranks of the party. Many peasants had reached an accommodation with the provisions of New Economic Policy. They were beginning to respond not to the development of socialism but, rather, to marketplace incentives the NEP created. Industry was increasingly in the hands of technical specialists, "experts" who were often politically neutral. The sharp class cleavage between workers and exploiters that was anticipated by Marxist doctrine was diffused by the heterogeneity of social, cultural, and national conflicts. The oligarchy that ruled over a coalition of peasants, workers, intelligentsia and specialists—Kirov, Ordzhonikidze, Kaganovich, Voroshilov, Molotov, Kuibyshev, with Stalin at their head—could prevision the eventual demise of the regime unless a new direction was launched. Yet the country was not prepared for the new direction and, as some presciently observed, would not be able to support it.

These two factors, the necessity for change and the incapacity of the government to support it in any organized fashion, drove the leadership to embark upon a forced modernization and industrialization campaign which first burdened, then distorted, and ultimately corrupted the economic, social, and political systems. The industrialization was foisted upon the backs of the peasants, who responded with predictable peasant conservatism, provoking yet more frenetic measures from the leadership. The result was a war-like mobilization that took place in a crisis atmosphere.[14] The conflict between city and village replaced that between worker and exploiter. The village became the battleground in the "class war." Mass "defections" from the village went over to the side of the city, enlisting in the ranks of the armies of industrialization. Forced modernization exacerbated social cleavages, encouraging many people to indulge the deep resentments borne of the turmoil of the revolution. Resentments over the human cost and the sacrifice of socialist construction were directed outward, buttressed by the historic xenophobia of the peasants, fueled by the severity of the international market of the 1920s and 1930s, and given credence by the political hostility of inter-war Europe and Japan. Stalin did not create these situations, but he discovered how to channel the resentments.

Just as these aspects of social upheaval were taking place, the overly ambitious goals were provoking the administrative apparatus to new levels of state interference. Ultimately, this resulted in the takeover and monopolization of virtually all sources of initiative and control throughout the economy. Once fully captured by the state administrative organizations, the economy of "material balances" of commodities, goods, services, and labor became the exclusive province of petty officials responding to cues from bureaucratic rather than production criteria. Unavoidably, the economic system developed along channels of producer sovereignty, generating an elaborate system of quotas, targets, bonuses, and "material incentives." These in turn led to the creation of an equally elaborate set of stratagems for avoidance, evasion, hedging, and self-protection, and, eventually, to the creation of a stratum of beneficiaries of the system. Through the mechanisms of social learning, the system began to replicate itself, propagating a value system in the new recruits of the practical if unwritten rules of achievement and advancement.

Against the backdrop of the social changes unleashed by the war, the Revolution, modernization, and greater access to the West made possible through NEP, Stalin sought to use the new political currents for mobilizing political support against his opponents. For Stalin, federalism was useful because it was associated with his mentor's name. Lenin's influence loomed ever larger as his memory was eulogized during the socialist hagiography of the 1930s. Stalin deliberately encouraged this mythification of Lenin; it allowed him to bask in Lenin's reflected glow.

The federal structure was rationalized by Stalin as a basis for maintaining the Leninist line on nationality policy. The Lenin-Stalin formula operated at first to guide nationality relations. Later, it also served to guide interrepublican and federal relations. It was based partially on Stalin's idiosyncratic interpretation of Marx and partially on calculations of political expediency. From Marxism, Stalin appropriated the ideas that: (1) No nation can be free which suppresses another nation; (2) The nationality question should be considered in terms of the historical stage and the class conflicts prevailing at the time; and (3) Working class solidarity requires the unification of all workers regardless of national origin. From Lenin and political expediency, Stalin acquired the principles that: (a) The national question and the colonial question were closely connected; (b) The national question played a role in the proletarian revolution; (c) Nations required a right to "self-determination," the right of secession, and the right to "independent national statehood"; and (d) The solution to national conflicts required not only legal but factual equality. This in turn implied the fraternal help of the proletariat to all "backward" peoples.[15]

Stalin, like Lenin, regarded federalism as transitional. He explained that:

in all existing federative organizations—the most characteristic of the bourgeois-democratic type are the American and Swiss federations. Historically they have been formed from independent governments, from a confederation to a federation, but in fact they have transformed to a unitary government, maintaining only the form of federalism.[16]

Moreover, Stalin turned the use of the purported federal structure of the state to his benefit by using it as a political weapon against his foes. His discussion of nationality policy during the late 1920s and the 1930s was invariably tied to the assertions of "deviations" in nationality policy by his opponents or by nationalist apologists in the localities. Stalin sought to identify assimilationism with Great Russian Chauvinism, thereby branding his opponents with the onus of association with Tsarist policies. Ironically, his own policies were indistinguishable from those that he ridiculed. The "essence of the deviation towards Great Russian chauvinism," he explained,

> is an effort to ignore national differences of language, culture and mode of life; an effort to prepare the way for the liquidation of the national republics and regions; an effort to undermine the principle of national equality and bring into disrepute the party policy of nativizing the administrative apparatus, and of nativizing the press, schools and other state and public organizations.[17]

He claimed that deviation towards nationalism was an attempt to identify the interests of the party with those of the bourgeois exploiters.[18]

Stalin's accusations of deviation found a certain resonance among the minority borderland populations, of course, because Stalin, by way of contrast with his straw men "deviationist" opponents, appeared to champion a color-blind policy of national equality. At the same time, Stalin's accusations appeared to be consistent with Marxist and Leninist thought. He thus could claim to be a defender of the "autonomy" of the national populations. He argued against "those who sought to do away with the boundaries" of the national republics as following a "most subtle and therefore the most dangerous form of Great-Russian nationalism."[19] But his definition of autonomy was, to use his own term, "elastic." "Soviet autonomy," he noted, "is not a rigid thing fixed once and for all time; it permits of the most varied forms and degrees of development. It ranges from narrow administrative autonomy . . . to the supreme form of autonomy—contractual relations."[20] He went on to add that the "elasticity of Soviet autonomy constitutes one of its prime merits."[21]

In his early, theoretical writings Stalin had argued against cultural autonomy in favor of regional autonomy. He made the familiar Leninist argument that cultural autonomy must be rejected because it was "artificial and impractical." Claiming that it attempted to draw people into a single nation who are being dispersed by the "march of events," he argued that cultural autonomy stimulates nationalism by cultivating "national peculiarities."[22] He argued in favor of regional autonomy because it specified a relationship with "a definite population inhabiting a definite territory" and did not "serve to strengthen partitions, but unites the population."[23]

Even while cloaking his arguments in the language of the protection of minorities, Stalin developed the most "Sovietizing," centralizing policies. At the forefront was the centralizing impetus of the equalization policy. As Stalin told the Tenth Party Congress,

> the essence of the national question in the Soviet [Union] is to liquidate the backwardness (economic, political, and cultural) of the nationalities. We inherited this backwardness from the past. This is in order to give the possibility to the backward peoples to catch up with central Russia in government, cultural, and economic relations.[24]

Stalin's approach to educational policy in the borderlands, for instance, superficially supported the minorities by defending the right to native languages. The thrust of this policy was to give concessions to the minorities in order that they would understand the importance of building the central government. He claimed that the "development of national cultures is bound to proceed with a new impetus when universal compulsory elementary education in the respective native languages has been introduced and has taken root."[25] His detractors, labeled nationalists or Great Russian chauvinists, failed "to realize that only if the national cultures develop will it be possible to secure the real participation of the backward nationalities in the work of socialist construction." He explained that his detractors did not realize that this is the "very basis of the Leninist policy of assisting and supporting the development of the national cultures of the peoples of the USSR."[26]

A suggestion of the importance that Stalin attributed, probably only subconsciously, to nationalism can be gathered from his remarks concerning the irredentist threat posed by the division of ethnic Ukrainians between east and west. Stalin explained that:

> There is a Ukraine in the USSR. But there is another Ukraine in other states. [sic] There is a White Russia in the USSR. But there is a White Russia in other states. [sic] Do you imagine that the question of the

Ukrainian and White-Russian languages can be settled without taking these peculiar conditions into account?[27]

The opportunity to alter this situation arose with the Molotov-Ribbentrop Agreement. The pact provided for the westward extension of Soviet borders to those more closely approximating the borders of the Tsarist period, thus initiating the third wave of border changes. During this period the Karelian ASSR was transformed into a Karelo-Finnish Soviet Socialist Republic. In October 1939, the Ukrainian and Belorussian Republics added parts of Poland. In June 1940 Northern Bukhovina was taken from Romania and added to the Ukrainian Republic. This area was incorporated into the Moldavian ASSR and then transformed, in 1940, into the Moldavian Soviet Socialist Republic. In this same year the three Baltic Republics, Estonia, Latvia, and Lithuania, were reincorporated into the USSR.

Stalin took the opportunity offered by the war to bring boundaries into ethnographic balance to the advantage of the USSR. This was celebrated in a eulogy to the Ukrainian nation in *Pravda* which noted that the power of the USSR made it possible to "realize the yearning for national reunion which the Ukrainian people have carried through the centuries."[28] Stalin's policies limited the appeal of irredentist claims. They also suggest the weight that national consciousness continued to have on Soviet practice during the Stalin period.

The Federal Structure and the Central Economic Ministries

How great then was Stalinism's contribution to determining the actual functioning of the federal structures of the socialist state? One point to note is that during Lenin's time the federal structure was *potentially* more important than it later became. Lenin's power was first exercised not through the party, but through the government. To be sure, government authority was quickly centered in the executive rather than legislative bodies of the government. In November 1917, the Central Executive Committee (TsIK) of the All-Russian Congress of Soviets granted the Council of People's Commissars (SNK) the "right to issue decrees of immediate necessity." The legislative wing of the Soviet system never regained full operation oversight, veto power, or directive control over the administrative wing.[29] The exigencies of War Communism established the paradigm for a centralized socialist economy. When the situation returned to normal, there was no ongoing bureaucratic structure to which to revert; the standard operation procedures of an earlier period were thoroughly discredited as remnants of the Tsarist administration.

Specific administrators and methods were rehabilitated, but the paradigm of administration had undergone a revolutionary change. The results of centralization were an absence of: (1) constitutional guarantees, (2) institutional countervailing forces, and (3) an effective political opposition. Policy opposition that did arise exhausted itself in disputes between local secessionist nationalists and pro-communist opposition.

The first five-year plan introduced the major shift of spending power toward Moscow away from the localities. Between 1928 and 1932 total expenditures increased at the center by a factor of four while central government expenditures increased by almost six times.[30] During the mid–1930s the localities would regain about half of the control they had lost over expenditures. Republican control over spending would fall again during the war to its lowest extent and only in the period following the war would it be restored to its mid–1930s level.

Despite administrative centralization, the authorities in Moscow were forced to rely upon the compliance of local officials. Therefore, the critical contest for political control in the borderlands came not with centralization as such—much of this was essentially "on paper"—but with the issue of the staffing of the local apparatus. In this respect the Bolsheviks again proved to be very pragmatic. By adopting a policy of "nativization" (*korenizatsiia*) of the indigenous administrative and party and managerial apparatus—that is, advancing individuals from a local ethnic minority within the apparatus of the region—the Bolshevik officials assured themselves of having friendly forces in positions of authority and power and, at the same time, satisfying local yearnings for local control. The Bolsheviks were no doubt assisted in this matter by the fact that the central government neither had the capacity nor, at the early stages, the intention of determining the *nomenklatura* of the borderlands. Nevertheless, during the process of nativization, the central authorities practiced a studied refusal to adopt a principle of proportional representation, reserving to the party the right to use judgment in appointments. As power flowed to the center after political consolidation, and as central government and party capacity increased, the *nomenklatura* formula gradually changed to the benefit of the center.

By the late 1920s the major battles over the "principles" of the organization of the socialist political and economic system had been fought and won. As we have seen, principles of "autonomy," "national statehood," and "rights to independence extending to secession" had triumphed in the political rhetoric. Political reality was quite different. Given the limited capacity of the central government, the national republics wielded certain *de facto* powers by virtue of the fact that policy was implemented through the various branches of the administrative apparatus in the localities. Whether these branches of the apparatus were more responsive to local or central interests often depended on the political acumen of local leaders as much as the formal designation of authority.

In the earliest days of Soviet power the administration was defined in terms of functional branches or groupings of enterprises and management offices divided in terms of their function or product line specialization. To the economic philosophers whose chief shibboleth was "production for use," the organization of the economy seemed naturally to flow from the nature of the production process itself. In this idealized, socialist economy the functional lines of demarcation were quite straightforward. Each sector of the economy required a functionally differentiated structure. Each sector, then, had associated with it a commissariat, or as it later came to be known, a ministry. In such a framework, agriculture was one sector, "public enlightenment" was yet another, and so on until all the goods and services were represented in the hierarchical organization.

The original administrative structure identified three tiers of commissariats: one level at the center; one shared central-republican level; and one level under the complete control of the republic. The Commissariats of Foreign Trade, War and Navy, Foreign Affairs, and Communication were positioned at the center. The Commissariats of Finance, National Economy, Food, Labor, and Inspection were to be jointly operated according to shared direction. Internal Affairs, Justice, Education, and commissariats relating to the "mode of life" were to be reserved to the republics. One additional commissariat, the Peoples Commissariat for Nationalities, was explicitly charged with protection of nationality rights, although, under Stalin's guidance as Commissar, it acted to promote central interests. The Narkomnats, as it was called, passed out of existence in July 1923. By 1929 the Commissariat of Agriculture was transformed into a joint commissariat in preparation for the intense period of agricultural collectivization. Shortly thereafter Internal Affairs was centralized, becoming an all-union commissariat in 1930. With the introduction of the Stalin Constitution, Health and Justice became joint commissariats. At the same time, a number of transitions from local identity to central identity were introduced. A number of autonomous regions became autonomous republics, autonomous republics in some case became union republics, and republican commissariats became union republic commissariats.

In Soviet parlance this functional division was known as the "*otraslevoi*," or "branch" principle of organization. The "branch" principle was first adopted when the organizational structure of the commissariats was established in November 1923, with the formation of the Narkomnats of the USSR.[31] The branch principle guided the organization of the commissariats throughout the 1920s and 1930s and, after March 15, 1946, their successors, the ministries.[32] According to the principle of branch organization, decisions radiate from the center to all parts of the economy of the USSR.

The question arises, then, of the day-to-day control over economic and material affairs that is in the hands of the territorially-defined (republican) federal structures. To the extent that the republican-level structures have authority over economic decision making, they are practicing, again, in Soviet parlance, the "territorial" (*territorial'nyi*) principle of organization.

In addition to the question of the competition between these two principles of management, there is also the competition between the vertical levels of the administrative process. This is the question of jurisdiction or, to use the Soviet expression, the issue of "competence" in a given area. The standard historical explanation for the division of authority among the three principal rungs of the ministries, (all-union, union republic, and republic) is that the all-union and union republic ministries administer functions requiring higher levels of centralization.[33] But the historical record does not bear out this explanation as an actual rationale. Until 1936 there were only a few commissariats of strictly economic purpose; most were concerned with utilities, services, or public works. For instance, Heavy Industry was an all-union commissariat while Light Industry was a union republic commissariat. Defense and Foreign Affairs were all-union commissariats until 1944, when, stangely, they were grouped with the Justice, Finance, and Health as union republic commissariats. The Ministry of Defense was returned to an all-union ministry only in 1978.

The tension between the centrally-oriented branch principle of organization and the republican-oriented territorial principle could only result in a continuing source of conflict. The political extremes of Stalinism could keep this conflict in check, but modernization and technocratic adaptation of the economy would eventually require a resolution of this tension either in favor of the republics or in favor of the center.

Notes

1. V.I. Lenin, *Polnoe sobranie sochinenii* Vol. 35, p. 11. The offices and structures of the Soviet state and Communist Party have changed names frequently over the years. A good source for identifying the various iterations of these structures is Edward L. Crowley, *et al.*, eds. *Party and Government Officials of the Soviet Union, 1917–1967* (Metuchen, NJ: Scarecrow Press, 1969).

2. *Dekrety Sovetskoi vlasti* Vol. 1 (Moscow: Politizdat, 1957), p. 40.

3. *Dekrety*, p. 114.

4. "Treaty of Peace between Latvia and Soviet Russia." Signed at Riga August 11, 1920. *League of Nations, Treaty Series,* Vol. 2, No. 3 (London: Harrison and Sons, 1920–1921), p. 213. (Reproduced in microform by Research Publications, Inc., New Haven, CT.)

5. The United States government extended formal diplomatic recognition to the three Baltic countries in 1922. Since that time the United States has never recognized the incorporation of these countries into the Soviet Union. The United States government continued to extend diplomatic status to representatives of the governments in exile and demonstrated its continued commitment to recognizing the independence of the Baltic countries through a variety of means. The U.S. Ambassador in Moscow and cabinet-level officers of the U.S. government, for example, did not, in the period before 1988, visit the Baltic republics.

6. One of the first and still most lucid discussions of the relationship between nationality and the federal structure may be found in Julian Towster, *Political Power in the USSR* (New York: Oxford University Press, 1948), pp. 50–92.

7. The committee designated to draft the constitution had Sverdlov at its head, but Stalin played a major role. The outcome of the committee's disputes was to grant recognition along national-territorial lines rather than to corporatist organizations, and to situate the urban proletariat as the principal pillar of regime rather than to constitutionally recognize a workers-peasants alliance.

8. It is interesting to note that Soviet "politologs" have long regarded the Soviet Constitutions as more important for their educational than for their legal qualities. An authoritative Soviet history source, for instance, describes the 1918 Constitution briefly, but points out as one of its more important facets the fact that it was translated into many languages and had a "wide foreign response." B.N. Ponomarev, ed., *Istoriia Kommunisticheskoi partii Sovetskogo soiuza* (Moscow: Izpollit, 1973), p. 258.

9. See V.V. Koroteeva, *et al.* "Ot biurokraticheskogo tsentralizma k ekonomicheskoi integratsii suverennykh respublik," *Kommunist* 15 (1988): p. 23.

10. See *Dvenadtsatyi s"ezd RKP(b): Stenograficheskii otchet* (Moscow: Politizdat, 1968).

11. Joseph V. Stalin, "Report on the Constitution," in *Leninism* (New York: International Publishers, 1942), pp. 399–400. Some authorities on Soviet constitutionalism have asserted that Stalin's formula is no longer taken seriously by Soviet constitutional scholars. See Donald Barry and Carol Barner-Barry, *Contemporary Soviet Politics*, 2d ed. (Englewood Cliffs, NJ: Prentice Hall, 1982), p. 108, ft. 23.

12. While some observers initially interpreted this as a decentralizing move, most have seen it in terms of the objectives of Soviet foreign policy. A discussion of the rationale for these laws may be found in Vernon V. Aspaturian, "The Union Republics and Soviet Nationalities as Instruments of Soviet Territorial Expansion," reprinted in Vernon V. Aspaturian, ed., *Process and Power in Soviet Foreign Policy* (Boston: Little, Brown and Company, 1971), pp. 452–490.

13. Korotaeva, p. 24.

14. As Soviet society moves farther from these events it becomes more apparent to many Soviet citizens how heavily the political idioms of the

revolutionary period were infected by the crisis atmosphere, and how these continue to influence the political culture. One writer to a *Pravda* editor recently opined, "why is it that we do not harvest wheat but instead 'carry out a struggle for the harvest?' Why is it that the milkmaids do not milk cows but 'carry out a battle for milk?' Why is it that construction workers do not construct but 'we stand on the construction front'? Why is it that we do not 'stop drinking but carry on a struggle with the 'green snake'? Why is it that tasks are not solved but are 'placed at attention'?" *Pravda* (7 April 1987): p. 3.

15. The discussion of the principles of Soviet nationality policy are a regular and familiar feature of political discourse in the USSR. For a recent scholarly treatment see, for instance, M.I. Kulichenko, ed., *Rastsvet i sblizhenie natsii* (Moscow: Politizdat, 1981).

16. I. Stalin, *Sochineniia* Vol. 4, p. 66.17. I. Stalin, "Extract from a Report Delivered at the Sixteenth Congress of the CPSU, June 27, 1930," reprinted in *Marxism and the National and Colonial Question* (London: Lawrence and Wishart, 1936), p. 256.

18. Stalin, "Extract," p. 267.

19. Stalin, "Extract," p. 257.

20. Stalin, "Extract," p. 81.

21. Stalin, "Extract," p. 81. 22. Stalin, "Extract," p. 57. 23. Stalin, "Extract," p. 57. 24. Stalin, "Extract," p. 103. 25. Stalin, "Extract," p. 261. 26. Stalin, "Extract," p. 261. 27. Stalin, "Extract," p. 266. 28. *Pravda* (12 January 1954). 29. Peter Vanneman, *The Supreme Soviet* (Durham: Duke University Press, 1977), pp. 30–32.

30. Donna Bahry, *Outside Moscow: Power, Politics, and Budgetary Policy in the Soviet Republics* (New York: Columbia University Press, 1987), p. 43.

31. See *Vestnik rabochego i krest'ianskogo Pravitel'stva Soiuza SSR* No. 10 (1923): Article 299.

32. For the observation that the branch principle has always guided the organization of the ministries see V.M. Manokhin, ". . . S uchetom otraslevogo i territorial'nogo printsipov . . . ," *Sovetskoe gosudarstvo i pravo* No. 10 (1978): p. 22. "It is correct, obviously, to recognize that the strengthening in the 1936 Constitution of the first Narkomat [Narodnyi komissariat] was the affirmation of the branch principle of government administration, although that principle was not actually articulated there." Manokhin contrasts this with the 1977 Constitution which does explicitly proclaim the branch principle.

33. N.A. Volkov, *Vysshie i tsentral'nye organy gosudarstvennogo upravleniia SSR i soiuznykh respublik v sovremennyi period* (Kazan: Izdatelstvo Kazanskogo Universiteta, 1971), p. 111.

4

Administering Soviet Federalism: Criticism and Reform

The relatively independent "national factor" has historical roots which will make it necessary to deal with the inertia of outlived traditions for a long time to come.

—Eduard Bagramov

Shortly after Stalin's death, the role of "national statehood" (*natsional'naia gosudarstvennost'*) as a principle of socialist governmental organization re-emerged as a controversial topic in Soviet politics. The attitudes of leading policy makers in the USSR vacillated on the subject. This ambivalence was reflected in central policy in the early post-Stalin period. Khrushchev's motives in carrying out various reforms were not clear to officials in the peripheral areas and were often understood, rightly or wrongly, as attacks upon national statehood. Yet at the same time Khrushchev undertook policies which central bureaucrats saw as benefiting the peripheries at the cost of the central apparatus. It is quite possible that Khrushchev did not have clear and sustained motives, but rather sought to achieve a variety of shifting policy goals, changing policies as he went.

The tension between the republics and the center was underscored by the competing organizational principles of branch and territory. In seeking a structural solution to these tensions of centralization, some people began to speak of abandoning the federal structure altogether. What emerged was a debate on the advisability of defederalization. The importance of the debate was underscored by a passage contained in the 1961 version of the Party Program of the CPSU, which darkly observed that the boundaries of the national republics were "losing their former significance." The observation merely acknowledged publicly what was evident: that the centralization brought about by the administration of the economy through Moscow-based and Moscow-oriented ministries was reducing the importance of the politico-administrative divisions. One political implication of abandoning the federal structure would be that of revoking, or at least substantially de-emphasizing, the political legitimacy of national statehood.

There are several factors which may account for the fact that the issue of federal arrangements came to be the focus for this debate in the 1950s and 1960s. First, within the USSR, the debate on Soviet federalism was precipitated by the efforts of Khrushchev and his entourage to lift the veil on the past, exposing the excesses and brutalities of Stalinism. In the process, Khrushchev raised a host of questions related to Soviet political functioning. In the Soviet provinces, increased sentiment in defense of federalism was no doubt propelled by the example of the resurgence of national aspirations in Eastern Europe unleashed by de-Stalinization. In addition, the Soviet provinces were witnessing a gradual accumulation of technical and political sophistication. Perhaps most important was the fact that the relationship between Soviet center and periphery grew increasingly complicated and unsatisfactory for all parties. A great deal of bureaucratic distress focused on an institution called "dual subordination."

Dual Subordination

The ministerial structure is divided into three tiers, the union ministries, the union republic ministries, and the republic ministries. The sphere of activity of a given tier is generally determined by whether its activity is of all-union importance. Typically, defense, heavy industry, and other branches with all-union significance were classified as all-union ministries. Most production industries and goods and services were concentrated at the intermediate union republic level. Republican ministries usually only have authority over activities which are peculiar to the republic or only have "local significance." The branches of the republic ministries are usually health, social services, communal economy, daily services, and the like.[1]

The ministries are organized along branch lines. Branch management pertains to the administration of a sector of economic or sociocultural activity. It is defined as management "along vertical lines from high to low in the domain of the entire USSR just as in the domain of each union republic, and each autonomous republic."[2] By way of contrast, territorial management is the management of all spheres of social and government life in the domain of each administrative-territorial unit (*respublik, krai, oblast, raion, gorod,* and *selo*). "The essence of such management," a Soviet source explained, is "the coordination of the territorial organs with the branch organs." Territorial management is "carried out by the territorial organs designated as organs of general competence (oblispolkom, gorispolkom, the Council of Ministers of the union republic or autonomous republic)."[3] A simple way of comprehending the difference is to note that branch management is basically positioned in the center and radiates downward and outward in a hierarchical fashion while territorial management is based in the republics and unites them and the center in a more or less lateral fashion.

Both forms of management have certain advantages and certain disadvantages associated with them. Branch management is often accused of a variety of ills including the tendency for compartmentalization, enclosure, and bureaucratic insularity. As one writer noted, the tendencies for enclosure have their "own sources of energy, system of support and maintenance, and so on." These include the "tendency of many offices to satisfy the demands of their own enterprises first and foremost." In such cases a "ministry directs its subordinate enterprises only to the solution of production questions," leaving aside questions of the social costs of production.[4] The branch principle has the advantage of bringing the technological and financial resources of the entire country to bear on the solution of a particular policy problem. It is thus well suited to mobilizational goals. The chief advantage of the territorial principle is said to be its ability to take into account local conditions. Its chief drawback is its encouragement of localism. Since the territorial form of organization concentrates authority in the republics, it also allows for the accumulation of political resources in outlying areas.

A good deal of the practical control at the republican level of management is bound up with the definition of what Soviet sources refer to as "competence." Competence refers to administrative jurisdiction or authority in a certain area. The 1977 Constitution assigns jurisdiction in the following manner. Article 73 assigns to the all-union level a domain of competence which includes, among other things, the "establishment of the general principles for the organization and functioning of republican and local bodies of state authority and administration," and "the pursuance of a uniform social and economic policy." Subject to these broad restrictions, Article 76 observes that "a union republic exercises independent authority on its territory." In matters within its jurisdiction, a union republic "shall coordinate and control the activity of enterprises, institutions, and organizations subordinate to the Union."

The intermediate level, union republic ministerial structure is integrated into the republican level structure. In theory, the republican bureaucracies are directed in day-to-day operations by the centrally based offices. The union republic ministerial offices are called upon

> to carry out unified economic, technological, and social policy on the territory of the republic; to work out and bring to realization measures

for the improvement of the activity of the organs, organizations, enterprises, and institutions of their system; to increase the effectiveness of production; and to improve the services of the population taking into account concrete conditions.[5]

Thus union republic ministries have one foot in Moscow and one foot in the republic. This overlapping authority frequently has resulted in an awkward pattern in the distribution of responsibilities. Enterprises which are directly subordinate to a union republic ministry take directions from the central institutions which, in turn, take directions from the USSR Council of Ministers. These enterprises, according to the constitutions of the various republics, are also simultaneously under the direction of the respective republic's Council of Ministers. This arrangement is referred to as "dual subordination" (*dvoinoe podchinenie*). As an administrative principle, dual subordination, in the words of one Soviet scholar, "can be viewed as the organizational form of the combination of branch and territorial administration."[6]

Dual subordination is a constitutional principle. Article 142 holds that "The Council of Ministers of a union republic shall coordinate and direct the work of the union republican and republican ministries and of state committees of the union republic, and other bodies under its jurisdiction." The same article holds that the union republic ministries and state committees of a union republic are to direct the branches of administration delegated to them, to exercise inter-branch control, and are to be subordinate to both the Council of Ministers of the union republic and the corresponding union republican ministry or state committee of the USSR. Accordingly, there are two competing lines of authority reaching down to these enterprises.

Such is the theory. In practice there is considerable disagreement as to the degree that the union republic ministries should be considered extensions of the central apparatus or as manifestations of the national statehood of the republic in question. As one writer critical of the arrangement expressed it during the first stages of the new definition of authority in the late 1960s, "The union republic ministries are specifically organs of the union republics. The experience of Soviet government construction shows that the legal position of these organs is defined by the Council of Ministers of the union republics."[7] Of course, in any given dispute over competence, the real issue is who has the last say. For this reason, the dual subordination arrangement itself *produces* disagreement. It divides local from central officials in terms of their perspectives. Officials of the central apparatus lay claim to a superior position with respect to knowledge of the "interests" of the all-union economy. Officials of the local branches respond by pointing to their superior understanding of the "potentials" of the local economy.

In practice, pride of place has allowed the USSR central officials the upper hand. Constitutional guarantees notwithstanding, the central officials have been in large measure responsible for defining the rights and privileges of their constitutional partners, the union republican ministries. The ancient principle of fairness—if I cut, you choose—is violated by the privileged position of the center. The center both defines the sphere of authority and exercises it.[8] This fact has not been lost on locals who have at times been intensely and openly critical of this central prerogative, asserting, for example, that "one can hardly agree with such a manner of practice."[9]

The only recourse that republican officials have to the privileged access to information and resources of their counterparts at the center is to refer to the declaratory and instrumental assurances written into the USSR Constitution and the Basic Laws which regulate the ministries. According to these documents, in certain spheres the center does not have directive authority, but only veto power. Moreover, these documents suggest that the Council of Ministers of the USSR does not have the right to change but only to suspend the implementation of the resolutions and directives of the Councils of Ministers of the union republics, and even then not in all questions, but only in those relating to the USSR as a whole.[10] Repeated calls have been made by spokesmen of the republics to "stabilize" the relationship between the central and republican bodies.[11] Yet the experience of all federalisms suggests that this type of devolution is not likely to be made in a display of benevolence by central leaders.

Defederalization and Sovnarkhoz

Scholars in the USSR have traditionally treated Soviet federalism as an organizational instrument for "solving the national question."[12] However, this has raised a dilemma for many Soviet scholars ever since central politicians in the USSR, starting with Khrushchev, began to speak of the national question as being "solved." If the national question were no longer relevant, many scholars observed, then what was the rationale for continuing to recognize, even in a purely formalistic sense, the "independence" of the fifteen constituent national republics of the USSR? If the class antagonisms of capitalism, thinly disguised in the rhetoric and motives of ethnicity, had disappeared leaving only "vestiges" of their pre-revolutionary forms, then could there be any reason for continuing to honor the concession of "national statehood"? If the national question was solved, had the time for a permanent transition to a unitary government not arrived?

In the 1930s and 1940s the relatively rare commentary on Soviet republican federalism stressed the "unified interests" of the Soviet state. The commentary at least suggested that the transitional view of federalism was still entertained not only by Stalin, but by leading academicians of Stalin's day:

> Our government is gradually moving to a federation on the basis of autonomy and contractual relations between Soviet republics and from contractual relations between republics to a union government.[13]

In the 1950s and 1960s a relatively small group of scholars began to raise the question of Soviet federalism. They gained notoriety for suggesting that the time of "unification" was at hand, that, in effect, the federal structure had served its purpose. Among influential political figures as well, the idea of "defederalization" gained wide currency; a fact reflected in the 1961 version of the CPSU Party Program adopted by the 22nd CPSU Congress in October 1961. The Program included the passage cited earlier to the effect that:

> The borders between the union republics within the USSR are increasingly losing their former significance, since all the nations are equal, their life is organized on a single socialist foundation, the material and spiritual needs of each people are satisfied to the same extent, and they are all united into one family by common vital interests and are advancing together toward a single goal—communism.[14]

The Party Program reflected the party leadership's official position in the bitter dispute regarding whether the time had come or was approaching when the republican structures of "national statehood," that is, the union republics themselves, could be dispensed with. The first major statement of the suggestion that the federal borders in the USSR had outlived their usefulness provoked an immediate and rancorous response.[15]

P. G. Semenov initiated the debate among academics and specialists in 1961 in a series of articles in which he bluntly advocated the dismantling of the republican structure.[16] "The mutual assimilation of nations," he argued, "in essence":

> denationalizes national-territorial autonomous units and even union republics. This brings Soviet society closer to the point at which the full state-legal merging of nations will be resolved in the foreseeable future.[17]

Along these same lines, I. Kislitsin also argued that the republican divisions would disappear in the "foreseeable future."[18] The school of thinkers that identified itself with proposals for defederalization argued that: (1) Lenin was opposed to permanent federal arrangements as a matter of principle; (2) the early federal arrangements were only intended to be temporary; (3) that current federal arrangements were less than "rational" (in the sense that this is used by Soviet economists); and (4) that the republican boundaries should be de-emphasized or abolished.

A rival school of writers quickly took up the gauntlet, challenging this view.[19] Conventional wisdom among Soviet academics soon branded the defederalists as "extreme" and "seriously mistaken." Yet those who criticized the defederalization proposal were themselves of differing persuasions. Some sought merely to defend the principle of national statehood from gratuitous assault, while others agreed in principle that the federal structure would eventually be replaced by a unitary structure, but that the time for transition had not yet arrived.

Opponents of the federal structure continued to write articles critical of the federal structure until about 1969. But now that the idea of the withering of the federal boundaries had been legitimized in the language of the CPSU Program, scholars simply referred to "Lenin's position" on the subject.

> The theoretically correct thesis, the one that agrees with Lenin's views, is presented in the CPSU Party Program. It affirms that the boundaries between union republics in the USSR are losing their former significance. Insofar as nations are equal in rights, their life is constructed on a single socialist basis and the material and spiritual needs of each people is satisfied in equal measure. All of them are united in common vital interests in one family and all move toward one idea—communism.[20]

Even as the defederalization debate was taking place in the academic journals and conferences, a more significant series of policy changes was being instituted. The policy changes no doubt lent vital importance to the ivory tower debates. There is little question that the critics of the policy changes were afraid to directly attack the manner in which decision making authority in the economy was redefined in the 1950s. Russian political style is such that debates carried on at a philosophical level were acceptable. Debates over specific policies related to "defederalization" were suspect, even dangerous.

While the defederalization debate was taking its course in academic forums, Khrushchev was conducting a parallel experiment in the realm of policy. Shortly after Stalin's death, Khrushchev came to see that in order to gain greater control of the cumbersome ministerial apparatus, he would need to break with the extreme hierarchical centralization which characterized the management system. While centralization seemed to promise central control, in actuality it lent itself to a system of bureaucratic cues which Khrushchev, who had been a middle level agricultural manager himself, knew from personal experience to be counterproductive. Khrushchev sought to decentralize by moving away from the branch principle of organization, turning over decision making authority to local bodies. This strategy, he hoped, would encourage initiative and boost worker morale in the outlying regions.

At a Central Committee Plenum in February 1957 Khrushchev announced plans for a major restructuring of the ministerial system of management.[21] The Plenum created 105 economic regions throughout the USSR and established Councils of Regional Economy (*Sovety Narodnogo Khoziaistva—Sovnarkhozy*) to oversee these.[22] The plan was a direct attack on the branch principle of administration. The Sovnarkhozy, by way of contrast, were said to be based upon a "production" principle, although their activity quickly became identified with a "territorial" principle since their charge was to manage production within a territorially defined area. In the process of the reform, twenty-five central ministries were abolished and their enterprises were shifted to the Sovnarkhozy. The Sovnarkhoz reform proved not to be a panacea for the problems that it was designed to solve. An April 1961 joint resolution restructured the Sovnarkhozy into 17 major economic regions.[23] Later, on September 19, 1963, a Supreme Sovnarkhoz of the USSR was created, further reversing the decentralizing trend.[24] Khrushchev's decentralizing efforts were unsuccessful, but the "collective education" which his cohort derived from the Sovnarkhoz period was extremely important. Henceforth, there would be no discussion of federalism by Soviet specialists which did not include questions of ministerial decision making.

The definitive decision on the issue of national statehood appears to have been made in anticipation of the approaching 50th anniversary of the USSR. In the period leading up to this, a great deal of academic attention was concentrated on proselytizing and propaganda. A resolution was adopted on the preparations for the 50th anniversary of the Soviet state affirming the official "interpretation" of the federal question.[25] A major decision was reached sometime in the fall of 1971 regarding the nationalities issue.[26] Semenov's last article in *Sovetskoe gosudarstvo i pravo* in 1972 made no reference to the issue of future boundaries, concentrating instead on the historical importance of federalism.[27]

The "Combined Branch-Territorial" Principle

Administrative change has frequently appealed to Soviet leaders as an instrument of policy because it promised relatively low-cost solutions to pressing economic problems. However, Khrushchev so repeatedly resorted to organizational change that mid-level managers in the ministries and party apparatus came to anticipate Khrushchev's "campaigning" style of problem solving. Problems would arise and grow severe, committees would be convened, decrees would be promulgated, agencies would be delegated responsibilities for carrying out a solution, resources would be allocated, and, then before much could be done to actually carry out the policies, new problems would arise, siphoning off the resources and diverting the attention of decision makers. Each organizational change invariably closed down some offices and shifted their responsibilities to others. Mid-level managers, expecting that the high level decisions would ultimately be reversed or simply forgotten, naturally grew more concerned about protecting their own positions and perquisities than about the success of the policy. Under such circumstances, mid-level managers grew philosophic about implementing policy even as they grew concerned with the security of their own positions within the hierarchy.

The problems of the psychology of the mid-level managers was well-known to the members of the political elite. Khrushchev had attempted to out-maneuver the mid-level managers through reorganizations and replacements. Khrushchev's successors opted for a more conservative solution to the problem. Stability and continuity became the order of the day. Immediately after assuming power the Brezhnev leadership carried out a recentralization in the party structure. In November 1964 the party apparatus, previously divided by Khrushchev into rural and urban components, was restored to its former structure.[28] Most remnants of Khrushchev's experiment with territorial economic management were officially eliminated by the September 1965 Central Committee Plenum. The Plenum formally reinstated the position of the ministries and the branch concept of administration.[29] Interestingly, however, the restoration of the branch concept was not lauded openly as an end to territorial control. Moving cautiously, Kremlin leaders referred to a "combination of branch and territorial principles." The Chairman of the Council of Ministers announced that the branch principle of administration

> should be combined with the territorial principle. This should solve the inter-branch tasks of the complex development of the national economy as a whole. Moreover, it should help the economies of the republics and the raions by enlarging the rights of the republics.[30]

The restoration of central prerogatives which took place after 1965 was undertaken in this spirit of compromise. The record of Khrushchev's policies left the Kremlin leadership with two conflicting lessons. The failure of Khrushchev's policies gave eloquent testimony to the perils of over-centralization, namely bureaucratic ossification and compartmentalism. But the organizational changes introduced to counter these, that is the panoply of decentralizing policies, offered even more immediate perils, namely localism and the erosion of political control. The new leadership, accordingly, devised a compromise formula of "combined branch and territorial principles," seeking to steer between the Scylla of localism and Charybdis of centralism.

An important step in the restoration, and indeed, in the evolution of the Soviet political system, was toward legal-administrative norms and away from the personalistic exercise of power. The restoration was carried out initially through the instrument of Soviet administrative law. In 1967 a law was adopted regulating the interaction of the various rungs of the ministries.[31] This was the first attempt in forty years "to set forth a clear delimitation of the norms and procedures" regulating the ministries.[32] The all-union ministries were given the responsibility of leading the corresponding (namesake) union republic ministries.[33] The orders, decrees, and instructions of the all-union ministries were held to be obligatory for the ministries subordinated to them. On July 28, 1979 a CPSU resolution on further improving the economic mechanism and the tasks of party and state organs was promulgated. It was accompanied by a joint Central Committee and Council of Ministers resolution on improving planning and strengthening the economic mechanism for efficiency and quality. The joint resolution spoke of an improvement in the work of the branches in a "territorial context." Branch offices were to inform the Councils of Ministers of the republics—their putative partners—of the control figures and basic indicators of the draft plans of the enterprises and associations on their territory.[34]

While these administrative steps were being taken, the new Brezhnev administration, in good Leninist style, also began to develop a philosophical rationale for its approach to national and federal relations. At first Brezhnev was reluctant to speak out on nationalities issues. As he consolidated his authority, Brezhnev began to frame an ideological formula to parallel his administrative "compromise solution." He sought to appeal to the yearnings of the localities and at the same time find a solution appropriate to the logic of the vast bureaucratic machine. The formula which emerged from this bears all the features of an unhappy compromise. It was referred to as the "two tendencies" analysis. The formula includes both concessions to the localities and concessions to the center. Logical inconsistency was dismissed as irrelevant; this was a "dialectical" solution to the problem.

By means of his artful new synthesis Brezhnev sought to satisfy both local and central constituencies and wound up satisfying neither.[35] The entire period is characterized by endlessly repeated slogans uniting the general interest with the particular. The line of reasoning goes as follows. A new historical community, "the Soviet people," had come into being during the period of mature socialism. The Soviet people was an amalgam of all the constituent nations, nationalities, and national groups of the USSR. Each of these nations was gradually coming into line with the others in this new historical community. As each of the constituent nations and nationalities acquired the positive qualities of the Soviet people, so each also came to realize its true nature and discover its own possibilities. Thus each nation was experiencing *"rastsvet"* (development) and becoming itself even as it was undergoing *"sblizhenie"* (rapprochement). The nations were growing into one overarching "Soviet community."

In describing the dialectics of nationality, Brezhnev carefully deemphasized the idea impetuously and provocatively brought up by Khrushchev, namely that the "Soviet nations" were "fusing." "Fusion"— the idea that the nationalities were melding into one undifferentiated unity in the near future—became a key catchword in the Soviet political lexicon. True, in speaking of the Soviet economic system as the "language of Leninist nationality policy," Brezhnev did refer to the "fusion" [*sliianie*] of the economic possibilities and resources of each republic.[36] But Brezhnev did not intend this to mean that all differences among groups would be eliminated. Brezhnev's formula essentially boiled down to the proposition that prosperity for all meant prosperity for each.

Brezhnev did not invent the "two tendencies" line of reasoning. He appropriated it from the academy. Academician Zlatopol'skii, who had earlier played a leading role in the federalism debate, propounded this theme in a major collection of essays published in 1968 entitled *National Statehood of the Union Republics* (*Natsional'naia gosudarstvennost' soiuznykh respublik*). The basic idea of the book, as it was summed up by one reviewer, was the concept of the "two tendencies," in the sphere of government-legal relations. Here, the two tendencies referred to the simultaneous "strengthening of the unity of federation (Union of SSRs) and of the development of the national government of the union republics."[37] The development of the Soviet federation was characterized

by two important tendencies which have found expression in the new Soviet Constitutions. First, the strengthening of the union basis in organization of the entire Soviet multinational government as dictated by the progressive growing together of nations and peoples of the USSR. Second, by the development of the Soviet federation characterized by the strengthening and widening of the guarantees of sovereign rights of the union republics.[38]

Brezhnev sought to shape the compromise by pursuing two goals. He told the 25th Congress in his general report in 1976:

> We have to strengthen both bases of democratic centralism. On one hand, we have to develop centralism, placing at the same time a limit on bureaucratic and localist tendencies. On the other hand, we have to develop democratic bases, the initiative of the locality, and unburden the high echelons of leadership from minor issues, to enhance the operationality and flexibility in the implementation of decisions.[39]

Even as the open advocacy of "defederalization" was chilled during the Brezhnev period, the proponents of the unitary principle were not completely silenced. They were permitted to continue to write and publish in a political climate in which otherwise dissident and unapproved literature was dealt with harshly and summarily.

One of the most visible and influential writers on federalism, a professor at Moscow State Institute of International Affairs of the Ministry of Foreign Affairs, was Aleksei Ilych Lepeshkin. In the mid–1970s, in a series of articles and books, Lepeshkin subjected the defederalization suggestion to withering criticism. He raised the rhetorical question:

> But what in fact is this "denationalization" if it really has any meaning now? It means the dismantling of national statehood, the elimination from the government apparatus of its structural divisions reflecting both general interests and national interests of individual nations. Denationalization means the gradual withering of Soviet federalism, in all of its forms and aspects, and the change to a unitary form of a socialist republic. Supporters of the concept of denationalization think this is already taking place now in the period of mature socialism and this will conclude in the near "foreseeable" future.[40]

A supporter of national statehood, yet a "moderate" on the question of the transitional character of Soviet federalism, Lepeshkin continued to argue that federalism, though justified, should only be seen as a transitional stage.[41] Lepeshkin cited Lenin to the effect that federation is a "transitional form to the complete unity of the laborers of different nations."[42] Lepeshkin bolstered his arguments by citing the Party Program adopted at the 8th congress of the RKP(b) in 1919. He noted that, "as one of the transitional forms on the course to complete unity, the party puts forward a federative association of governments organized according to the Soviet type."[43]

Lepeshkin was careful to reject the proposition that the federal principle was adopted only as a solution to the nationalities problem.[44] This, he argued, leads to the conclusion that it has outlived its usefulness.

The creation of a Soviet federation was aimed at the goal of the historical epoch of the transition from capitalism to communism as one of the forms on the way to complete unity. Consequently the goals and tasks of Soviet federalism are considerably deeper and wider in content and volume than the elimination of national egoism and the establishment of full equality of nations in our country.[45]

He argued that there can be no doubt that the solution to the national question does not mean the end of the historical goal of Soviet federalism.[46] Lepeshkin argued that government structures

of certain national groups, no doubt, will change in the process of communist construction as they are directed toward the new tasks of national statehood construction. But the statehood of the Soviet peoples themselves, as well as their highest form—the federation—will remain until the achievement of the full unity of nations, that is, as long as a socialist government exists.[47]

Lepeshkin referred to the "socioeconomic, political and cultural factors" which provide the rationale for maintaining the current federal arrangement.

Among the reasons for maintaining the federal structure, Lepeshkin pointed out the following: (1) the importance of maintaining a material-technical base of communism; (2) the fact that, although the national question has been solved, problems of "national relations" remain, due to the ideological immaturity of some people and the efforts of imperialism to sow the seeds of nationalist discord; and (3) the importance of the elaboration of "Soviet culture" in an internationalist spirit.[48] Summarizing his position on the debate of the previous 15 years, Lepeshkin suggested improvements to "optimize" the federal structure. These included: (1) improvement in the economy entailing management on the basis of a close combination of economic interests of the union government with the economic interests of the national republics; (2) rethinking of the basis for national representation in the government and party as a result of population shifts brought about by interrepublican migration; (3) the improvement of Soviet federalism through better delimitation of competence (jurisdiction) between the union ministries and the republic ministries; and (4) "further democratization." Three of these issues would reemerge fifteen years later as central issues in perestroika. The other issue, that of the competence (jurisdiction) of ministries, would not wait that long.

Brezhnev and *Zastoi*

The direct successor of the "federalism debate" was a dispute carried on in the economic and management literatures—and presumably in innumerable offices—over the issue of the competence of the republican organs of policy management and control. The issue of competence is very subtle. The reason that Soviet discussions, especially during the 1960s and the 1970s did not use the term 'jurisdiction' to refer to the operational scope of the government organs in question is that 'competence' is an administrative concept rather than a legal one. The very use of the administrative (rather than legal) notion of competence in this regard spoke to a fundamental truth: in a socialist system where politics and economics are so closely wedded, federalism cannot be divorced from top-down control over the political and administrative apparatus. As a dean of the faculty of administrative law at Kazakh State University expressed it, "at the basis of the division and reapportionment of the competence of the organs of the USSR and the union republics . . . lies two principles, Soviet federalism and democratic centralism."[49]

The competence issue was important for several reasons. First, there were insistent problems that arose in the handling of the "dual subordination" arrangement. Second, the republican apparatus was used to implement policy and, therefore, the central apparatus took measures to ensure that local leaders had a strong material incentive in carrying out central goals.[50] Third, there was a dispute as to whether the republican-union division of authority was zero-sum or benefited both parties. Finally, the republican apparatus was viewed as a major mechanism of public participation.

The question of the "competence" of various branches of the ministries concerns the operational authority to implement policy. This was especially important in the republics because the branches were staffed and directed in most cases by the nationals of the republic. Defenders of the republican "link" of the policy process expressed their views of the importance of strengthening the republican apparatus in the heavily cloaked language of Soviet political discourse. The solution to the problem of

distribution of competence between organs of the USSR and the union republics in the current time is the development and strengthening, along with the organs of all-union subordination, of the organs of union republican subordination. These [union republican organs] reflect the interests of the USSR at large and the interests of the republic in particular.[51]

Since this distribution of competence was so sensitive, one could expect disagreement. A particularly bitter dispute arose in the mid–1970s as to whether the division and "redivision" of authority and competence between the all-union and republican rungs was advantageous to one or to both parties. Some interlocutors saw the issue in terms of the zero-sum advantage of the center over the republics. Others saw the opposite. The "widening of the rights of the federal organs," one writer explained

> certainly does not entail the corresponding decrease in equal measure of the rights of the members of the federation. On the contrary, the widening of the rights of the union republics certainly does not take place solely at the expense of the competence of the USSR, as some writers suggest.[52]

Those in favor of advancing the interests of the central apparatus with respect to the republican branches argued that certain branches of the republican administrations should be transferred to the union branches.[53]

Enthusiasts of central authority also defended the republican branches on the grounds that the branch system affords a form of political participation in the Soviet system. Since the republican administrations typically includes native personnel, especially in the visible posts, participation in the economic apparatus is, according to these writers, a form of representation of the interests of the nations, a "voice" of national statehood. Soviet sources frequently cited the formal and informal arrangements for the participation of republican representatives in central decision making. Representatives of the republics, they asserted, were included in the collegium of the Council of Ministers, in the government committees of the Council of Ministers, and other less important bodies. They often noted that the number of representatives in the Council of Nationalities of the USSR Supreme Soviet was increased from 25 to 32 deputies. Representatives of the Supreme Courts of the union republics were in the Plenum of the Supreme Court of the USSR. Since 1966 all the union republics were at least said to have representation by virtue of the fact that the Chairman of the State Planning Committee (*Gosplan*) of each of the republics sat on the central *Gosplan*.

On some occasions the republican apparatus was credited with specifically defending symbolic issues of national-cultural importance. For instance, one group of writers attributed a change in the Constitution of the Georgian SSR to the efforts of the republican apparatus.[54] The original published draft of the Brezhnev version of the Georgian SSR Constitution failed to identify Georgian as the language of the republic. The absence of this key symbolic passage was immediately conspicuous and resulted in spontaneous and widespread public disturbances. The status of the national language was restored in the final document. There is a lesson to be drawn from the treatment of such subjects. It is instructive that the writers cited above neglected to mention the fact that the constitutional changes could hardly be attributed to the efforts of the republican apparatus alone. Readers familiar with the sequence of events could easily read between the lines.

When the long-awaited draft of the new Soviet Constitution was unveiled by Brezhnev in 1977, a major "discussion" campaign was initiated. The issue of the federal structure was repeatedly, though rather obliquely, raised in central and local newspapers. When the draft version of the 1977 (Brezhnev) Constitution was adopted, the federal structure was described in language which vindicated the federal principle and, along with it, the idea of national statehood. In his report presented with the draft version of the 1977 Constitution, Brezhnev noted "the basic lines of the federal structure of the USSR have fully justified themselves. Therefore there is no need to undertake any fundamental changes in the form of the Soviet socialist federation."[55] However, Brezhnev did in a sense dignify the proponents of defederalization by openly rejecting their argument. "Some comrades," he said, are "seriously mistaken" in that they would propose

> introducing into the Constitution the idea of a unitary 'Soviet people,' eliminating the union and autonomous republics or drastically curtailing the sovereignty of the union republics, depriving them of the right to secede from the USSR and the right to maintain external relations.[56]

But implied in the mild rebuke is the idea that the comrades who held that position were in error, but not necessarily politically irresponsible.

Notes

1. The distribution of enterprises and, in general, assets among the three major tiers of the ministries had changed with successive waves of administrative reform. After Sovnarkhoz and before July 1970, the all-union group contained only machine building ministries. All the other ministries were union republican or republican. In June 1969 the all-union ministries, and *glavki* accounted for 41 percent of the enterprises; the union republic ministries comprised about 35 percent. The remaining 25 percent were controlled by the republic level ministries. A.S. Petrov, "Ekonomicheskaia reforma: tendentsii organizatsii otraslevogo upravleniia promyshlennost'iu," *Sovetskoe gosudarstvo i pravo* No. 3 (1971), p. 20.

2. M.Kh. Khakimov, *Novaia konstitutsiia SSSR i upravlenie narodnym khoziaistvom: uchet otraslevogo i territorial'nogo printsipov* (Tashkent: Fan, 1979), pp. 23–24.

3. Khakimov, *Novaia konstitutsiia*, pp. 22–24.

4. V.M. Manokhin, ". . . S uchetom otraslevogo i territorial'nogo printsipov . . . ," *Sovetskoe gosudarstvo i pravo* No. 10 (1979): pp. 22–23.

5. V.I. Shaibalov, "Soiuzno-respublikanskie ministerstva soiuznykh respublik (nazrevshie problemy)," *Sovetskoe gosudarstvo i pravo* No. 10 (1984): p. 25.

6. Khakimov, *Novaia konstitutsiia*, p. 18.

7. V.I. Shaibalov, "K sovershenstvovaniiu pravovogo polozheniia ministerstv soiuznykh respublik," *Sovetskoe gosudarstvo i pravo* No. 2 (1968): p. 68.

8. Nor is the authority of the union republic officials only challenged by the central ministerial officials. The local officials must also contend with the institution of *"podmena."* This term refers to a tendency of party organs to usurp functions of the state institutions. Thus, the lives of local officials are further complicated by the fact that they must not only contend with officials placed in a superordinate position within the ministerial hierarchy, but also with officials in the party who periodically intervene to reach solutions from yet a different institutional perspective. On *podmena* see Ronald J. Hill, "Party-State Relations and Soviet Political Development," *British Journal of Political Science* Vol. 10 (1980): pp. 149–165.

9. V.I. Shaibalov, "K sovershenstvovaniiu," p. 68.

10. See, for instance, V.A. Kirin, "Kompetentsiia soiuza SSR i soiuznykh respublik v oblasti zakonodatel'stva," *Sovetskoe gosudarstvo i pravo* No. 5 (1970): pp. 5–6.

11. See the appeal by the head of the legal section of the Latvian Council of Ministers for "stability." I.O. Bisher, "Ministerstva soiuznykh respublik: nazrevshie problemy," *Sovetskoe gosudarstvo i pravo* No. 5 (1973): p. 29.

12. See I.D. Levin, *Suverenitet* (Leningrad: Iurizdat, 1948), p. 311; O.I. Chistiakov, *Stanovlenie Rossiiskoi Federatsii (1917–1922)* (Moscow: Izdatelstvo MGU, 1966), p. 23.; and D.L. Zlatopol'skii, *Federativnoe gosudarstvo* (Moscow: Izdatelstvo MGU, 1967), p. 3.

13. S.Ia. Golembo, "Mikhail Ivanovich Kalinin o Voprosakh teorii i praktiki sovetskogo gosudarstva," *Sovetskoe gosudarstvo i pravo* No. 6 (1947): p. 6.

14. *"Programma Kommunisticheskoi Partii Sovetskogo Soiuza,"* *Kommunist* No. 16 (1961): p. 84.

15. The best introduction to the debate may be found in Grey Hodnett, "The Soviet Federalism Debate," *Soviet Studies* Vol. 18, No. 4 (1967): pp. 458–481; and "What's in a Nation," *Problems of Communism* (1967): pp. 2–15.

16. The principal works which champion defederalization are: I.M. Kislitsin, *Voprosy teorii i praktiki federativnogo stroitel'stva Soiuza SSR* (Perm, 1969); P.G. Semenov, "Programma KPSS o razvitii sovetskikh natsional'no-gosudarstvennykh otnoshenii," *Sovetskoe gosudarstvo i pravo* No. 12 (1961): pp. 25; V.I. Kozlov, *Soiuz svobodnykh i ravnykh* (Moscow: 1964) pp. 56–57.

17. P. G. Semenov, "Programma KPSS o razvitii sovetskikh natsional'no-gosudarstvennykh otnoshenii," *Sovetskoe gosudarstvo i pravo* Vol. 12 (1961): p. 25. Also see P.G. Semenov, "Natsiia i natsional'naia gosudarstvennost' v SSSR," *Voprosy istorii* No. 7 (1966): pp. 72–81; I.M. Kislitsin *Voprosy teorii i praktiki federal'nogo stroitel'stva Soiuza SSR* (Perm': 1969) p. 92.

18. Kislitsin, "Voprosy," pp. 92–93.

19. For instance, E.V. Tadevosian, *V.I. Lenin o gosudarstvennykh formakh resheniia national'nogo voprosa v SSSR* (Moscow: Izdatelstvo MGU, 1970), pp. 164–171; and *Sovetskaia national'naia gosudarstvennost'* (Moscow: 1972), p. 192; M.I. Kulichenko, *Natsional'nye otnosheniia v SSSR i tendentsiia ikh razvitiia* (Moscow: 1972), p. 540; Lepeshkin, *Sovetskii federalizm* (Moscow: Iuridicheskaia literatura, 1977).

20. M.G. Kirichenko, "Razvitie Kommunisticheskoi partii leninskikh idei o sovetskoi natsional'noi gosudarstvennosti," *Sovetskoe gosudarstvo i pravo* No. 2 (1969): p. 19.

21. The goal of the reorganization was to bring the "center of operational management of industry and construction closer to the enterprises." R.Kh. Aminova, ed., *Istoriia rabochego klassa Uzbekistana* Vol. 3 (Tashkent: 1966), p. 47.

22. An earlier form of "Sovnarkhozy" existed until the early 1930s, but these institutions were industrial conglomerates. They were later merged into the ministries.

23. *Bol'shaia sovetskaia entsiklopediia* Vol. 24, Book 1 (Moscow: Sovetskaia Entsiklopediia, 1976), p. 50.

24. *Bol'shaia*, p. 50.

25. The resolution was not a joint resolution but only a TsK KPSS resolution entitled *"O podgotovke k 50–letiiu obrazovaniia Soiuza Sovetskikh Sotsialisticheskikh Respublik"* (21 February 1972).

26. See George Breslauer, *Khrushchev and Brezhnev as Leaders* (Allen and Unwin, 1982).

27. P.G. Semenov, "Istoki sovetskogo federalizma," *Sovetskoe gosudarstvo i pravo* No. 10 (1972): pp. 3–8.

28. For a detailed analysis of the party bifurcation see Barbara Ann Chotiner, *Khrushchev's Party Reform: Coalition Building and Institutional Innovation (Westport: Greenwood Press, 1984)*.

29. It should be noted that this restructuring followed the party reunification and the March 1965 agricultural Plenum. The order of events reflected the new leaders' priorities. See Chotiner, *Khrushchev's Party Reform*, pp. 273–290.

30. A.N. Kosygin, *Izbrannye rechi i stati* (Moscow: 1974), p. 269.

31. See the "Obshchee polozhenie o ministerstvakh SSSR" adopted by the Council of Ministers of the USSR on 10 July 1967, reprinted in *Sobranie postanovlenii SSSR* No. 17 (1967): Article 116.

32. K. E. Kolibab, "O pravovom polozhenii ministerstv SSSR," *Sovetskoe gosudarstvo i pravo* No. 1 (1968): p. 19.

33. Kolibab, p. 19.

34. For a discussion see Manokhin, ". . . S uchetom."

35. For a discussion of Brezhnev as "artful synthesizer" see George W. Breslauer, *Khrushchev and Brezhnev as Leaders* (London: Allen and Unwin, 1982), pp. 179–199.

36. L.I. Brezhnev, *Leninskim kursom* Vol. 4 (Moscow, 1974), p. 57.

37. Iu. Sudnitsyn, "Interesnyi trud o sovetskoi natsional'noi gosudarstvennosti," *Sovetskoe gosudarstvo i pravo* No. 6 (1970): p. 146.

38. M.I. Piskotin and K.R. Sheremet, "Sootnoshenie Konstitutsii Soiuza SSR i Konstitutsii soiuznykh respublik," *Sovetskoe gosudarstvo i pravo* No. 10 (1978):p. 19.

39. As quoted in K.D. Korkmasova, "Sovetskaia natsional'naia gosudarstvennost'—vazhnyi faktor internatsional'nogo edinstva narodov SSSR," *Sovetskoe gosudarstvo i pravo* No. 8 (1976): p. 15.

40. Korkmasova, p. 3.

41. A.I. Lepeshkin, "Sovetskii federalizm v period razvitogo sotsializma," *Sovetskoe gosudarstvo i pravo* No. 8 (1975): pp. 3–12.42. Lepeshkin, "Sovetskii federalizm," p. 3.

43. *KPSS v resoliutsiiakh i resheniiakh s"ezdov, konferentsii i plenumov TsK* Vol. 28 (Moscow: 1970), p. 45.

44. Lepeshkin, "Sovetskii federalizm," p. 4.

45. Lepeshkin, "Sovetskii federalizm," p. 5. For those who see the federal principle as singularly associated with the solution to the nationalities problem, see D.L. Zlatopol'skii *SSSR–Federativnoe gosudarstvo* (Moscow: 1967), p. 3; O.I Chistiakov, *Stanovlenie Rossiiskoi Federatsii (1917–1922)* (Moscow: 1966), p. 22.

46. Lepeshkin, "Sovetskii federalizm," p. 7.

47. Lepeshkin, "Sovetskii federalizm," p. 8.

48. Lepeshkin, "Sovetskii federalizm," p. 7.

49. See S.I. Dosymbekov, "Sovershenstvovanie kompetentsii promyshlennykh ministerstv soiuznoi respubliki," *Sovetskoe gosudarstvo i pravo* No. 10 (1974): pp. 47–51.

50. One academic writer noted that the legal provisions regulating the relations between all-union and republican ministries give the republican structures an interest in seeing that local production meets central goals. "In agreement with article 9 of the Law of the USSR on the government budget of the USSR in 1970, one hundred percent of the profit from the turnover of all enterprises in the republic including enterprises of all-union subordination, goes into the budget of the union republic." As the writer observes, "Naturally, in these conditions the organs of the union republic have an interest in the swift fulfillment by the enterprises of the all-union subordination of the economic plans." S.N. Dosymbekov, "Uchastie soiuznoi respubliki v upravlenii promyshlennost'iu soiuznogo podchineniia," *Sovetskoe gosudarstvo i pravo* No. 2 (1971): p. 67.

51. Dosymbekov, "Sovershenstvovanie kompetentsii," p. 47.

52. See M.A. Shafir, "Kompetentsiia Soiuza SSR i soiuznykh respublik v Sovetskom gosudarstve," *Sovetskoe gosudarstvo i pravo* No. 10 (1972): pp. 13–14. The critical reference to "some writers" is specifically to the views put forward by I.M. Kislitsin in *Voprosy teorii i praktiki federativnogo stroitel'stva Soiuza SSSR* (Perm, 1969). For additional critical commentary on the "zero-sum" thesis see A.I. Lepeshkin, "Sovetskii federalizm," p. 12.

53. See for instance, A.S. Petrov, who called for the "liquidation" of the republican link of administration in branches of the national economy. Petrov supported the transfer of the functions of all these ministries, offices, and enterprises directly to the all-union ministries. A.S. Petrov, *Organizatsiia raboty ministerstv v usloviiakh ekonomicheskoi reformy* (Moscow: 1972), pp. 92–93.

54. M.I. Piskotin and K.F. Sheremet, "Sootnoshenie Konstitutsii Soiuza SSR i Konstitutsii soiuznykh respublik," *Sovetskoe gosudarstvo i pravo* No. 10 (1978): pp. 11–20.

55. L.I. Brezhnev, *Leninskim kursom* Vol. 4 (Moscow: Politizdat, 1978), pp. 382–383.

56. Leonid I. Brezhnev, "On the Draft Constitution (Fundamental Law) of the Union of Soviet Socialist Republics and the Results of the Nationwide Discussion of the Draft," (Report and Closing Speech at the Seventh Session of the Supreme Soviet of the USSR, Ninth Convocation, October 4–7, 1977) (Moscow: Novosti Press Agency, 1977)

5

Bureaucratic Nationalism

If you do not belong to your fatherland, you do not belong to mankind.
—Belinskii

Bureaucratic nationalism is the tendency for the "national factor" to be expressed within the various branches and subdivisions of the formal organizations of the Soviet system. Politicized ethnicity in the Soviet Union has, until quite recently, rarely resulted in the forms of anti-regime response that occur in open, competitive systems. Protests, demonstrations, marches, and other organized vehicles for the articulation of demands have not traditionally been considered legitimate expressions of dissent in the Soviet political system. From the Kronstadt revolt of 1921 to the Georgian separatist demonstrations of 1989, the exercise of such practices has historically been identified by the central leaders with anti-Sovietism and treason. But the underlying resentments and discontents which have given rise to these manifestations could hardly be extirpated by central fiat. Under these circumstances, national discontent has historically found expression through a form of diversion.

As we have seen, ethnic identification in the USSR is by no means unique to only those groups who have been accorded republican status. Nevertheless, the identities of those groups have been amplified by the formal recognition supplied by a legitimized government structure and, to a lesser extent, by the accumulation of intra-republican resources made possible through the branch government and party structure. Ethnic identification alone, one should hasten to add, does not constitute nationalism. Nationalism only exists under circumstances in which ethnicity is politicized and mobilized. Otherwise national discontent only produces anomie, withdrawal, resignation, and *zastoi*. Politicized ethnicity requires leadership. The basic assertion of this book is that two interacting factors have sustained nationalistic sentiment in the USSR: territorial bureaucracies and national leadership.

This chapter describes the constitutional and doctrinal bases of republican rights in the USSR. In light of these doctrinal foundations, we explore the contribution of the two factors of national bureaucracies and national leadership to the creation of what Soviets refer to as a "national climate" in the republics.

The Status of Republican Rights

The Soviet Constitution of 1977 consisted of an ideological preamble and nine basic divisions including some twenty-one chapters broken down into 174 separate articles. The nine basic divisions respectively addressed: the principles of the social and political system; relations between state and individual; the national-territorial (federal) arrangements; the legislative bodies; the administrative bodies at the all-union level; administrative bodies below the all-union level; the judicial system; state symbols; and procedures for emendation. The constitutional bases for republican rights are set forth primarily in chapters 8 through 19 (Articles 70–150).

The rights formally extended to the republics in this constitution essentially followed the delegation of powers set forward by the 1936 "Stalin" Constitution. There were a few exceptions. One is Article 75, a provision not contained in the earlier version of the Constitution, which somewhat abridged the right to secession. The article noted "The territory of the Union of Soviet Socialist Republics is a single entity and comprises the territories of the Union Republics." In addition, the original version of the Stalin Constitution included the right of union republics to their own military formations. This right was never exercised and it was not reaffirmed in the 1977 Constitution. The unifying influence of the Communist Party was only obliquely referred to twice in the 1936 Constitution. In contrast, the party's role in politics and society figured prominently in the more recent version.

According to the 1977 Constitution, the constitutional prerogatives extended to the union republics included the following: Each union republic was granted the right to "freely secede" from the USSR (Article 72). The union republics were described as "sovereign" states (Article 76). Subject to restrictions imposed by Article 73, a union republic was said to retain residuary powers (Article 76). A union republic's territory was described as inviolable. It could not be altered without the republic's consent (Article 78). A union republic was granted the right to enter into relations with other states (Article 80). The authority to "coordinate" and "control" the activities of production and administrative organizations located on its territory was granted to the union republic (Article 77).

In each of these areas of republican rights, however, the 1977 Constitution included restrictions upon the exercise of the powers delegated to the republics. The guarantee of Article 78 that "the territory of a union republic may not be altered without its consent" was subject to the restriction of Article 73, which held that "the determination of state boundaries of the USSR and the approval of changes in the boundaries between union republics" was under the jurisdiction of the USSR Supreme Soviet. Article 73 also could be interpreted in such a way as to prevent the exercise of the right of secession provided by Article 72. The right of a union republic to enter into relations with foreign countries, protected by Article 80, was restricted in practice by Article 73, which gave the USSR Supreme Soviet the authority to "establish the general procedures" and "coordinate" the activities of the union republics with respect to other states. The guarantee of Article 77 that a union republic had the authority to control the enterprises on its territory was subject to the restriction of Article 134 which authorized the USSR Council of Ministers to "suspend the execution of decisions and decrees of the Councils of Ministers of union republics." The provision of Article 76 of the retention of residuary powers by the union republics was restricted by Article 73, which granted the USSR Supreme Soviet the authority to determine the "conformity of the Constitutions of the union republics to the Constitution of the USSR." Most important, the Soviet Constitution did not spell out procedures by which disputes between the higher and lower bodies could be adjudicated by an independent institution.

Speculation about the long-term implications of national statehood was awakened by Gorbachev's announcement of a reform of the political system at the 19th Party Conference in the summer of 1988. Some five months later a law implementing the political reform was passed by the Supreme Soviet.[1] Yet the amendments had little direct impact upon the constitutional definition of republican rights. The amendments concerned primarily chapters 12 (the system of Soviets of Peoples Deputies), 13 (the electoral system), and 15 (the Congress of Peoples Deputies and the Supreme Soviet). The amendments introduced only cosmetic changes in the language of the rights specified in chapters 8, 9, and 10—the chapters which specifically address the definition of republican powers. A few additional amendments concerned the latter Articles of the constitution. For instance, Article 133 was amended to account for the new congress of Deputies as the basic organ of constitutional authority, but also added statements not in the earlier version, to the effect that the decisions and decrees of the USSR Council of Ministers were binding throughout the USSR. Moreover, a passage was mysteriously excluded by the amendments which, in Article 135 of the earlier version, had provided that the Presidium of the USSR Supreme Soviet determined the procedure for transferring enterprises from local to union subordination [No new source for this authority was specified.]

Western constitutional scholars are in agreement with many Soviets in concluding that the rights of the republics under Soviet constitutional doctrine extended primarily to: (1) verbal assurances of "sovereignty"; (2) formal recognition of "national statehood"; and (3) symbolic recognition of the republics as separate administrative units.

A few things were notably excluded from the Soviet Constitution. The constitution did not officially sanction the "rapprochement" or "fusion" of nations into an assimilated "Soviet people." On the other hand, there were no provisions in the constitution to guarantee the vitality of such institutional defenses of republican rights as national cultures, national mores, the education of young people in national traditions, and so on. There were no explicit promises offered regarding officially designated "national" languages of the republics. Some republics managed to maintain codicils to this effect in their republican constitutions. Even this was fraught with difficulty. For instance, the draft version of the 1978 Georgian constitution omitted any reference to Georgian as the national language of the republic. A spontaneous and widespread public outcry resulted in the restoration of formal recognition of the Georgian language as the official language of the republic.

The second source of doctrinal legitimacy in the Soviet Union is the *Ustav* (Rules or Program) of the Communist Party. Three versions of this document have been adopted, the first in 1919, the second in 1961, and the most recent in 1986.[2] For the reasons surveyed in chapters 3 and 4, the party has historically resisted the national principle in its internal organization. The party, as the slogans frequently repeat, "is the party of the whole people." Nevertheless, for reasons of expediency and efficiency, the party is internally structured according to the "territorial-production" (*territorial'nyi-proizvodstvennyi*) principle. In practice this means that all of the union republics, with the exception of the RSFSR, have nominal party organizations. The identification of a party member with the republican-level party organization, presumably supported by "intraparty democracy," is less important in practice than the influence of "democratic centralism" and the principle that the party is a "monolithic whole." The *Ustav* provides no specific defenses for the party organizations of the republics. Unlike the 1961 version, which referred to the diminishing significance of republican boundaries, the 1986 version discusses national federalism in less ideological terms, referring merely to the "resolution of the national question in its historic form."

The announcement that the 19th Party Conference in 1988 was preparing a resolution on the nationalities question fueled speculation that the final document would refer to the specific rights of the republics. In terms of rhetoric, the resolution was much more direct in its description of the plight of the republics than most observers expected. Nonetheless, few durable guarantees were proffered. The resolution said that the Party Conference maintained the view that perestroika would bring about the further development of the Soviet federation on the basis of democratic principles. This was to be carried out through "decentralization" in the areas of administrative functions, in the economy, in social and cultural spheres, and in the preservation of the environment. The term "decentralization" was specifically used with respect to the republics. "The socialist ideal," asserted the resolution, "was not a withering unification, but a full-blooded and dynamic unity in a multinational complex."[3] The vaunted "dialectical" formulas of the Brezhnev period were abandoned in favor of a much more realistic tone toward a center-periphery compromise.

The resolution identified a number of problems in the sphere of national relations. The problems were attributed to sources ranging from excessive bureaucratism at the center to "national egoism" in the localities. The resolution drew a sharp distinction between "national" and "nationalist," asserting that the party firmly supported the former and staunchly opposed the latter. Yet, despite the accurate descriptions of the problems and, to a lesser extent, the causes of national unrest, the resolution contributed little in terms of specific proposals for the enhancement of republican rights. Indeed, the resolution concluded on a note which for many defenders of republican rights must have been distinctly plaintive. The resolution proposed the age-old bureaucratic solution for temporizing, namely, the creation of another scientific research institute to study the problems.

A major party reform was announced in September 1988. It signaled a shift away from party interference in managerial decision making to a reliance upon legislative organizations. The announcement of party reform was followed by announcements at the local level of reductions of about thirty percent in the staff of party organizations scattered widely throughout the USSR. At the same time the creation of six Central Committee commissions was announced. These commissions were charged with direction and oversight of agrarian policy, ideology, international affairs, legal policy, party personnel policy, and socioeconomic affairs. Although each of these areas concern nationality affairs to some extent, it is significant that a separate commission was not created and charged with oversight of nationality affairs, federalism, and interrepublican relations.

In sum, the two doctrinal bases of republican rights in the USSR grant little in the way of durable guarantees to the republics. The Soviet

Constitution is a centralist document. Although the republics enjoy putative "autonomy," in practice the Soviet Constitution provides only symbolic protections for the rights of the republics. Moreover, the constitution neither provides legal defenses for republican rights nor protects the broader sociopolitical institutions and practices which, in traditional western "liberal" systems, tend to provide a ballast for legal rights. The constitutional amendments of 1988 themselves do little to alter this situation. The *Ustav* of the Communist Party recognizes the existence of subordinate republican-based party organizations, but these are not considered independent. The party reform of 1988 does signal an important shift of power away from the local party organizations to the legislative bodies. Whether this will be followed in practice by a coalescence of these prerogatives at the level of the republic remains to be seen.

Even if the legal arrangements do not serve to buttress republican rights, however, developments within the republics themselves have had this effect.

National Institutions

It is a truism of bureaucratic systems that much policy is made in the process of implementation. For this reason, policy made in Moscow frequently does not produce the outcomes that Moscow politicians and planners anticipate. Policy made in Moscow is implemented in the regions by staffs whose sympathies and loyalties are often strongly if not primarily attached to their respective regions. The situation closely approximates what Sidney Tarrow has called a "territorial bureaucracy."[4] First, as in all complex organizations, the bureaucratic structure tends to become highly stratified internally. Second, the gap between the horizontal strata is augmented by the distance between the place where rules are formulated (Moscow) and the place where they are implemented (republican capital). Communication failures between strata develop. Communication problems are made worse by the independence that territorial agents enjoy, because their actions are often hidden from their central superiors. Sensing problems, central managers adopt abstract "standard operation procedures" to provide conformity between goals and outcomes. But in the real world, a lack of fit between the rules and the tasks is unavoidable. Local officials, in many cases dutifully striving to satisfy central goals, naturally resort to informal "understandings" which circumvent the rules. When the informal understandings fail, a "crisis" results. At this point, the decision makers at the center intervene, only to discover evidence of diversion and administrative autarky.

In each of the national republics the managerial apparatus from top level officials down to the management of the factories, farms, and service industries, is to a large extent nativized. In some areas, notably the Baltic republics, the Russian central presence is strongly felt. But in the southern tier and western republics, the line level management is almost uniformly native. The research and academic communities in these republics, though bilingual, are nearly fully nativized. The cultural communities and the arts, of course, are native. The result is that the bureaucracies of these republics have a palpable native cast to the way they function, the way they implement central directives, and the way they see the future of the republic.

These circumstances have produced a "national" climate in each of the republics. This does not mean that, for instance, the Ukrainian scientific community is on the verge of revolt. This conclusion is not supported by the facts. The conclusion that the facts do support is that the way this community responds to central directives is heavily influenced by the bureaucratic perception of the "Ukrainian national interest." This is bureaucratic nationalism in practice.

Bureaucratic nationalism is not uniformly felt through all branches and offices of the far-flung Soviet administrative systems. An accurate assessment of the vitality of bureaucratic nationalism must take into account the internal dynamics of the institutions themselves in terms of central control and local prerogatives. Exact data regarding the size and disposition of the organizations is simply not available. Moreover, the situation varies markedly from republic to republic and even from bureaucracy to bureaucracy depending on the extent of local control and, often, the institutional perspectives of the subunit in question. Nevertheless, some general observations may be made. There are three primary divisions in the Soviet administrative system: party, government (ministries), and legislative. With respect to each of these divisions, we may identify three primary areas according to which the "national orientation" of the republican organizations may be measured: (1) structural linkages with the center; (2) nativization of cadres; and (3) proportional representation of the titular nationality group of the republic with respect to other national minorities.

The Party

The structural linkages between republican parties and the center are provided through the "territorial-production" organization of the party. In practice this means that the party has subdivisions which are associated with the lower-level administrative divisions including the republic, oblast, krai, and so on. Moreover, the party divisions are also associated with the "production" principle in the sense that they are oriented toward place of work—shop, office, committee, and so on. Thus, the Communist parties of the republics are embedded at an intermediate level within the structure of the Communist Party of the Soviet Union. The republican-level party organizations are not independent. They are not autonomous organizations, nor do they constitute "interest groups" in any meaningful sense of that term. They are branches of the central party and, along with other smaller party subdivisions, are referred to as existing in a "net of party organizations." Yet, the delegation of authority inevitably entails to some extent the limitation of top-down central controls.

Structural linkages between the center and republican party organizations are reinforced by both formal and informal contacts which arise out of republican party leaders' positions within the central party. At the 26th Party Congress held in Moscow in February and March 1981, all the republican party First Secretaries were elected to full membership in the Central Committee of the CPSU. All the republican Second Secretaries were either members or candidate members of the CPSU Central Committee. Major Obkom First Secretaries are frequently CPSU Central Committee members or candidates. This same pattern held true for the 27th Party Congress.

In these central party forums, republican party leaders are formally called upon to articulate the problems and the tasks of their party organizations. In addition, the regular participation of republican leaders in these forums provides for informal contacts and creates channels for the exchange of information. These serve as a basis for the creation of personal linkages and networks between the center and periphery. It is not clear to what extent local representatives use these informal contacts for articulation of local interests, although common sense would suggest that it is unlikely that the flow of information is exclusively in one direction.

The chief instrument by which central control is exercised over the republican party organizations is through cadres, that is, appointment and discipline policies. The direct control of Moscow over the republics is most directly illustrated by the turnover in the position of republican party first secretary. As a glance at Table 4 will show, if one leaves out the anomalous case of the Ukraine, office holders at the highest level of republican leadership had in November, 1988 an average job tenure of 1.7 years in office. As Hodnett has stated, "At the republic level, recruitment is basically a process that is managed from above, within the framework of the whole *nomenklatura* system of job appointment."[5] The top-down control of the appointment process takes place within the context of the national minority community. "Recruitment at the republic level," Hodnett argued further, "occurs in an environment in which ethnicity and local particularism are constantly operating factors to which the Soviet authorities and republic leaders must always address themselves."[6] Historically, the center has used the top-down lever of cadres policy to control implementation in the localities. However, this "lever" is somewhat constrained by a countervailing policy objective, namely, preemptive control of nationalism.

Preemptive control of nationalism has historically been exercised through a policy associated with the advancement of local leaders. This policy is known as "*korenizatsiia*" or "*nativization.*" The goal of the policy was to advance pliant local leaders and managers who provided an aura of local representation, who could motivate the local citizenry, and who could be relied upon to prevent anti-socialist diversion. Nativization, then, was supposed to produce in the republics an administration which was both "native" and efficient. But, although ethnic composition varies among republics, there is no republic which is exclusively populated by its namesake national group. What, then, constitutes "native" in a multinational republic? Empirical evidence suggests that there is a great deal of regularity in the predominant position of the titular nationality of the republic. Nevertheless, there is also a good deal of ethnic diversity within the various republican parties. Indeed, the lack of clear patterns has suggested to some researchers that there is no overarching nationality cadres policy. Mary McAuley, in a cross-republican analysis of party organizations, concluded that "the republics do not devise detailed policies on national recruitment."[7]

It is clear that there are pressures for ethnic levelling to which the party must be sensitive. For instance, the Kirgiz Communist Party (CPKi) apparatus was apparently under pressure to reflect the internal ethnic composition of the republic. Absamat Masaliev, CPKi first secretary in 1987, in a speech to a scientific conference, gave figures for the nationality composition of the republic as of January 1, 1987: Kirgiz—2,175,000 (53 percent); Russians—954,000 (23 percent); Uzbeks—454,000 (11 percent); Ukrainians—119,000 (3 percent); Germans—109,300 (3 percent); Tatars—77,000 (2 percent); and other (5 percent).[8] He provided the figures to defend the current ethnic composition of the Kirgiz Party apparat. The change in the proportion of ethnic composition is particularly revealing. In 1970 the Kirgiz component was 37.7 percent, while the Russian was 37.6. In 1973 the figures changed slightly, the Kirgiz proportion being 38.7 and the Russian 37.1. By 1981 the respective figures were 44.2 and 32.9. The gap widened even further in 1984: the figures were 47 percent Kirgiz as opposed to 30.8 percent Russian. The Kirgiz component was almost 50 percent by 1987. The figures suggest that the proportion of Kirgiz in the republican party organization grew from 38 percent in

1970 to 48 in 1987, mainly at the expense of the Slavic component of the party. Masaliev's comments amount to a defense of the current ethnic composition of the Kirgiz Party organization. They also suggest that the party has felt some pressure for adopting a formula for proportional representation. The issue of ethnic composition was explicitly addressed in the Kirgiz Party resolution "On Instances of Nationalistic Phenomena in Kirgizia and the Incorrect Attitude of the Republic's Party Central Committee Toward Them," issued in 1986.[9]

Some Western scholars have discerned formulas for the promotion of pliant party elites in the republics. Vernon Aspaturian, for instance, has argued that there has been a tendency to establish "proportional national representation in all political and social institutions" in the republics.[10] Whatever "tendencies" one may divine in Soviet behavior, there has in fact never been a statement of what top party officials derisively label an "arithmetic" formula for proportional representation of the national minorities. No such firm quota system has ever been publicly adopted. No "control figures" of nationality participation targets for the republican party organizations have ever been announced. To the contrary, Soviet sources repeatedly refer to the "international" composition of the party apparat, including the republican branches of the party. Indeed, it is precisely the unwillingness of party leaders to specify "arithmetic" formulas which leads to charges, by those who feel they have been excluded from proportional representation, of favoritism, nepotism, and the spreading of networks of political cliques based in "family circles." One suspects that the party's reticence on this issue is based on a fear of public disclosure of the actual process of personnel appointments.

A significant central initiative to reduce the size of the party apparat at all levels was launched by the 19th Party Conference in the summer of 1988. This was followed by a central committee plenum on party reorganization in September. Although it is still too early to assess the outcome of this policy initiative, it is nevertheless clear that local branches of the party organization were under pressure to quickly respond to the directives through overall staff reductions of about one-third. For instance, on October 28, 1988, the Moscow city party announced a thirty-percent personnel cut and reduced the number of its departments from seventeen to seven. In similar fashion, announcements were made by local party organizations throughout the USSR of proportional staff reductions. A few weeks earlier, on October 10, 1988, a plenum of the Ukrainian party central committee announced that its eighteen departments would be cut in half and that there would be a thirty percent reduction of "senior personnel." Whether the reductions are permanent and amount to a political purge of local "dead souls," or whether they are simply a "musical chairs" game, remains to be seen.

The Government Structure

The principal institutions for carrying out the directives of the Soviet government are the three tiers of the ministries and the associated agencies, committees, and associations. In June, 1986, the fifty-eight existing ministries were divided such that thirty-three were all-union ministries and twenty-five were at the union republican level, both levels being subordinate to the USSR Council of Ministers. The Council of Ministers is headed by a Chairman of the Presidium of the Council of Ministers, the Prime Minister, who was assisted by a first deputy chairman and a number of other deputy chairmen. In June 1986, the Presidium included some twelve members and the Council of Ministers included an additional 109 ministers, directors, and heads of agencies. Representation at the highest level is, according to the constitution (Article 129), provided by the inclusion of the fifteen chairmen of the Councils of Ministers of the union republics in the USSR Council of Ministers. Moreover, the republics were said to have an additional influence on the Council of Ministers by virtue of the fact that joint sessions of the USSR Supreme Soviet appoint the USSR Council of Ministers.

The managerial model represented by the central administrative structure is mirrored on a smaller scale in all of the republican level ministerial organizations. The republican Council of Ministers includes the ministers of union republic ministries in addition to the ministers who oversee republican level ministries within the respective republic. In symmetry with the Moscow model, the position of the chairman of the Presidium of the Council of Ministers of each republic has nested below it a number of ministerial and ancillary institutions which form the administrative branch of government.

The organizational structure was officially reaffirmed after the passage of the new constitutions by the Supreme Soviets in each of the union republics in 1978. This was followed by new statutes of the Councils of Ministers for the republics, which generally became effective in January 1979. It was this structure which Gobachev would later criticize at the 19th Party Conference as proliferating to "almost 100 union ministries and departments and 800 republican ones."[11] The Council of Ministers of a republic thereafter was constitutionally subordinated in practice to the Supreme Soviet of the republic. The chairman of the Presidium of the Supreme Soviet of the Uzbek republic in 1978, Narkhomadi Khudaiberdyev, remarked that, with respect to the organs of state administration, the new Council of Ministers statute was "exceptionally important [for the proposal] for regular review of the Council of Ministers of the republic before the Supreme Soviet of the UzSSR."[12] However, this legal right of review was limited in practice. There is little evidence to suggest that any substantial change in authority followed the adoption of the new statute.

The guiding principles of central ministerial direction came under direct attack during 1988. The reevaluation of the principles of center-republican administrative relations culminated, in March 1989, in the new draft document "General Principles of the Managerial Restructuring of the Economy and Social Spheres of the Union Republics."[13] The document averred to the fact that "to a considerable degree the democratic basis of the management of economic and social spheres in the union republics was substantially deformed." Nevertheless, the document sought to square the circle by devolving authority to local enterprises while maintaining the overall importance of the "single, all-union economic production complex." The improvement of the quality of life in the republics was to be attained, according to the document, by the achievement of the comprehensive renewal of Soviet society, *not* by the delegation of authority to the republican level ministerial offices. A Soviet economist bluntly stated the rationale for restraint: "The *diktat* of the central agencies should not simply be replaced by the *diktat* of republican organs."[14]

The degree of nativization within the ministerial staffs of the republics is difficult to measure. Republics vary; moreover, the Soviet statistical bureau, Goskomstat, has been unwilling to provide illustrative let alone statistically comparable figures on the staffs of various bureaucracies. The *"shtab"* (staff) of the ministries and other agencies has, indeed, often been treated as a state secret. Figures that have been provided (see Table 7) suggest a relatively low level of administrative and managerial infrastructure. However, these figures can hardly be taken as an accurate representation of the numbers of people involved in "administration." The figure that continually arises in discussions of the "top heavy" pyramid of administrative managers is eighteen million. Of this figure, some twelve and one half million were said in 1985 to be personnel in the enterprises and organizations working as directors of plants, factories, and combines or working as engineers or other technical specialists. Some 661 thousand were officials of the Supreme Soviet, peoples deputies, or members of the executive committees of the lower Soviets. Almost three million were in law enforcement, communication, or other technical services. Only 1,623 thousand people were directly occupied as administrative managers.[15] Nevertheless, there is a great deal of popular resentment against this stratum of officials. "It is absolutely obvious," noted one economist, "that 18 million administrative managers, even in a country as large as ours, is completely unjustified."[16] Soviet sources have provided no guidelines as to what "administration" includes or excludes.

Since 1985 there has been a concerted campaign to reduce the number of individuals involved in management. One source reported that, in the previous three years, the number of individuals in the Moscow offices of ministries and agencies was reduced by 23 percent and the "coordinating" staff was reduced by 33 percent. At the same time, the source noted, the total absolute number of individuals in managerial positions increased by 122,000. Why had this happened? The answer is a familiar one: Decisions to reduce the staff "meet with silent but unwavering opposition."[17]

Under present circumstances, it is impossible to measure the exact extent of the nativization of the various bureaucracies of the republics. Thus the evidence for nativization in the ministerial organization remains basically anecdotal and suggestive. While the careful observer can sense a definite pro-republic orientation among many of the republic level ministerial officials, we do not yet have a good standard of measurement to determine the exact intensities of intra-organizational identification. Nor do we have good measures of the extent to which one republic's officials differ from those of another on a scale of institutional loyalty. One indicator of the degree of nativization which might be suggestive is the ethnic density of the republic in conjunction with some measure of the psychological distance of the ethnic group from the Moscow-oriented centralist bureaucratic culture. Such a composite measure would suggest considerable bureaucratic nativization in Tadzhikistan and Moldavia, for instance, compared to relatively low rates in Ukraine. However, these measures remain speculative and suggestive until Goskomstat provides reliable figures.

The Legislative Organs

To what extent have the legislative organs served as vehicles for republican-based interest articulation? Under the arrangement existing prior to the political reform of 1988, representation took place on three levels. The first level concerned the representation within the Presidium. The second level included representation at the level of the individual deputies. The third level included the operational prerogatives of the republican-level Supreme Soviets. At the first level, the USSR Supreme Soviet Presidium included a chairman, a first vice chairman, and fifteen other vice chairmen, among other members. The fifteen vice chairmen were chairmen of the presidia of their respective union republics, thus offering each of the republics representation at the level of the presidium. At the level of the individual deputy, representation was accorded by the formula apportioning to each republic and autonomous oblast a certain number of seats. Each republic was entitled to thirty-two delegates in the Soviet of Nationalities. Finally, at the operational level, the Supreme Soviets of the union republics had the authority, according to Article 113, to initiate legislation in the USSR Supreme Soviet.

To what extent did these provisions guarantee the republics' representation within the Supreme Soviet? In practice it guaranteed very little. The chairmanship of the union republic presidium was a mainly honorific post, the occupants of which were nevertheless always carefully selected for their willingness to accommodate to central designs. While the individual deputies from the union republics and autonomous republics may have been more representative of the citizenry at large, their function was primarily to convey information from the center to the regions, not to carry demands in the opposite direction. And finally, even though the Supreme Soviets of the union republics had the right to "initiate" legislation, this rarely had little effect in practice. The USSR Supreme Soviet rarely functioned as an autonomous institution; legislation was not passed which had not first been prepared and approved by the party apparatus. Judging from the foregoing observations, we can conclude that the voice accorded the republics at the center via the legislative institutions was severely circumscribed.

Compounding these failures of the union republic institutions to provide vehicles for local interest articulation was the fact that the legal rights of the republics were limited by a variety of administrative and quasi-legal obstacles. In assessing the legal prerogatives open to the republics, Peter Vanneman concluded that "the equality of nationalities, much circumvented by non-legal means, may also be contravened in a multiplicity of legal juridical ways within the Supreme Soviet system itself despite appearances to the contrary."[18] The tactical approach of central authorities in dealing with republican-level institutions, it would seem, was, first of all, to oppose, neutralize, and if that did not work, circumvent the prerogatives of the localities. But the center could scarcely ignore all of the demands of the localities. Over the years, localist complaints encouraged the center to develop channels of interest articulation geared to defusing local anxieties.

Complaints regarding the lack of information and sensitivity in the center to republican concerns led to the creation in 1957 of a body charged with coordinating the interests of the republics. After Khrushchev's comments at the 20th Party Congress about the uneven development of the republics, an Economic Commission of the Council of Nationalities was created in February 1957.[19] The Economic Commission was composed of thirty-one members (two from each union republic) and a chairman, Olga Ivashchenko.[20] The commission had three objectives: (1) to recommend improvements in economic and cultural policy in the republics; (2) to review requests from the republics for deliberation by the Supreme Soviet; and (3) to prepare proposals for the coordination of republican and all-union economic plans. Although redrawing organizational lines in this fashion engendered criticism from ministerial officials for supposedly encouraging localism, the interrepublican experimentation continued. For instance, a joint decree of the party and Council of Ministers established a "Coordinating Council" for the Central Asian Economic Region in April, 1961.[21] The Council included the party first secretaries and chairmen of the Council of Ministers of each of the four Central Asian republics. The Council apparently never had much effect; it was assigned no permanent staff and had no jurisdiction over the union-republic and republican ministries. It was abolished in November 1962 by the same CPSU Central Committee plenum which split the party organs.[22] Similarly, the Economic Commission was phased out by a law adopted in October 1967 which created the Standing Commissions of the USSR Supreme Soviet. The fact that the center eventually responded to the ministerial officials' complaints suggests the perceived importance of the demands; the fact that the center abolished the bodies confirms it.

In the perestroika period Gorbachev has made an effort to transfer policy-making responsibility from the ministries to the legislative bodies. Gorbachev announced at the 19th Party Conference that many ministries had recently been dismantled and that the successor organizations had reduced their personnel by fourty percent. In the republics the apparat was being reduced by fifty percent. The weight of decision making responsibility was accordingly being shifted to the legislative bodies. In the past, especially at the lower levels, these organizations were often dominated by their executive committees, the *ispolkomy*. In order to short circuit "departmentalist" tendencies within the executive committees, Gorbachev suggested that the oblast and raion party first secretaries be routinely elected as chairmen of the *ispolkomy*.[23]

The National Elite and the Logic of Subordination

The dialectics of the center-periphery balance place the members of the political elite in the union republics in a position of considerable irony. Achievement of the center's goals depends to a large extent upon mass participation in the socialist economy. The republics' agriculture, extractive industries, and industrial bases, cannot develop without the commitment of the local populations. The degree of mass participation required, however, cannot be generated unless local political figures can inspire, enthuse, and mobilize the local populations in the service of Moscow's goals. For these reasons the central leadership has identified, cultivated, and promoted to positions of nominal influence within the republics a stratum of local political and economic leaders drawn from the local populations which may be referred to as the "national elite."[24] The national elite combines elements of both the "dignified" and the "efficient" traditions. In other words, members of the national elite not only serve as symbolic representatives for the minority populations in their regions but also imbue the administrative organs with the measure of legitimacy which they need to function.

The irony of the situation is that, for local leaders to succeed in their charges, they must develop and steward the resources necessary to inspire, enthuse, mobilize, and promote within their republics. That is, they must develop political resources. To the extent that they succeed at this, they concentrate in their hands the ability to conduct politics in the traditional sense of the word, namely, to help friends and hurt enemies. For obvious reasons, a local leader armed with these capabilities can pose a potential threat to leaders in Moscow.

The politics of the relationship between the national leadership in the republics and the leadership at the center do not necessary translate into privileges for one republic as opposed to another. As Bahry found, "there is little evidence that the political status of any republic's leader affected its success in the investment arena."[25] However, within the republic, the local leaders' successes in gaining favors from the center can profoundly affect the elaboration of a political network. Moreover, there is strong anecdotal evidence to suggest that Goskomstat intentionally has "balanced" investment figures in an effort to vindicate the inter-republican equalization policy on the books if not in practice. The explosion of journalistic exposés on political corruption that took place during the *zastoi* period suggests the extent of resources outside the officially monitored economy.[26] If we assume that there are resources outside the formal investment arena to which entrepreneurial local leaders have access, we can appreciate the importance of investigating the mechanisms by which local officials develop political resources. A number of important observations may be gathered merely from scrutiny of the role of local officials.

The members of the national minorities who are advanced by the center in virtue of their ability to enthuse and mobilize the citizenry must be able to deliver such benefits as the socialist economic system provides. A national leader's success is in turn dependent upon his ability to establish a network of sympathetic patrons. At the same time, he must build the resources to help friends and hurt enemies and strengthen his hand for bureaucratic struggles with the center and other regions in the continuing contest over central allocations. The republican politician in the USSR, therefore, must conform to fit the peculiar attributes of his role.

The main attributes of the role are largely determined by the logic of the centrally dominated decision-making process and the peripherally dominated implementation process. The national leader is first of all subject to *divided loyalties*. Split between power (Moscow) and principle (the homeland), the leader must resolve the cognitive dissonance of his contrary loyalties. Generally the division of loyalty prevents the surrogate from being completely coopted into the programs, goals, and interests of the center. On occasion, the center can use this situation of dual allegiances to its own advantage. For instance, Moscow leaders used this aspect of the surrogate's position against Dinmukhamed Kunaev when they made the allegation that he failed to protect the interests of his ethnic homeland. Thus, as a commentator on Kunaev's "complicity" in the outbreak of riots in Alma-Ata in December 1986 noted, it was "the inability (or unwillingness) to consider in the proper measure the national interests of the different groups of the population . . . that led to the recidivism of nationalism."[27] Usually, however, the charges go in the other direction; namely, that the political leader fueled nationalism by defending the republic with excessive zeal. It was on such charges that Ukrainian party leader and Politburo member Petro Shelest was dismissed in May 1972. Although Shelest was not publicly charged with nationalism at the time of his ouster, many informed Western observers saw this as the cause; and, more recently, with the relaxation of glasnost, Shelest confirmed their speculations.[28]

Second, the national leader functions in a context of partial cooptation, his position defined by a tacit contract between center and periphery. This contract involves *political exchange*. The terms of the exchange are fairly simple. If the national leader provides orderly satisfaction of central economic goals and prohibits ideologically threatening political diversions, then the locality is left to pursue its own interests in the cultural sphere. The pursuit of cultural autonomy has been an important goal of national leaders throughout the Soviet republics. For instance, despite increased ardor among central officials for building Russian language proficiency in Central Asia, the use of the language continues to diminish. Central Asian leaders privately take pride in the fact that their languages are being gradually restored to a first position in the republics.[29]

Third, the *patron-client relationships* which generally characterize the network of mutually-reinforcing political interdependencies among Soviet bureaucrats and party personnel are substantially stronger in the republics due to ethnically-based cronyism and nepotism. Without the external discipline of the market, economic relations fall prey to manipulations. Without the probing interference of an independent press, personalistic cadres policies rely on ascriptive criteria of kinship and ethnic group as a determinant of advancement. The single most recurring criticism from the center in times of purge is that of nepotism.

Fourth, the national leader constantly faces the requirements imposed by the system of *lobbying for central allocations*. The system constitutes essentially a zero-sum context of inter-regional competition. Each locality is pitted against the others in the struggle for central favor and attention. To succeed in this context, the successful national leader must develop his political resources while he routinely understates them to the center.

While the center exerts pressure for the observance of the ideological norms of the regime and the terms of the economic production contract, there is considerable *central acquiescence* in the face of minor violations of socialist norms of propriety and the general indifference to many of the standard operating procedures of the administration. This can be interpreted as a form of collusion of the center with the local surrogates. Central leaders often turn a blind eye to minor corruption until a succession crisis or external event makes a confrontation inescapable. Then central leaders find that public charges of corruption provide the best method for disestablishing a local leader. First they embarrass him politically, replace him with a more compliant leader, and then continue to exposé the scandal until his personal entourage is also displaced. Such charges, though they are often no doubt true and damning in their own right, serve as a useful pretext for periodic renewal of cadres in the outlying areas.

Sixth, *conflict avoidance* is a hallmark of the successful national leader. Arrangements which compromise local opposition are preferred to overt confrontation. Arrangements which discredit local whistle-blowers are preferred to open discussion. In cases where a national leader seeks to exert pressure on the center, he may threaten to make revelations embarrassing or damaging to the central officials. This is a hazardous tactic. It was reportedly attempted by Kunaev's supporters in Kazakhstan after word had been leaked that Kunaev, the Kazakh Communist Party's first secretary, was to be replaced. As Gennadii Kolbin, Kunaev's successor, told the Kazakh Party Central Committee, the participants in the Alma-Ata riots had been urged on by assertions that the center had appointed a non-Kazakh to head the party organization. Since these assertions were made prior to the official announcement of Kunaev's ouster, Kolbin charged that Kunaev had attempted to stir national sentiment in an effort to embarrass the center into rescinding the decision.[30]

The skillful national leader necessarily becomes involved to some extent in duplicity, projecting one face to the national population and another to the center. This may explain why political diversion and financial corruption have been so common in the republics. People in this role apparently grow cynical. The national leaders often project an image of docility, posing as dutiful servants of the center. There are rational grounds for acting in this rather inconsistent way. If the national leaders show loyalty to the center, it may be from a "form of rational political calculation."[31]

The National Cadres and a "National Climate"

The structural relationships with the central organizations provide for direct channels of central control. However, the effectiveness of those channels is reduced by their very reliance upon the nativization policy within the republics. The nativization policies combine with the natural identification of the members of the native elite with their ethnic brethren, traditions, and homelands to produce a "national climate" among the leadership in the republics. How strong is this national climate? It differs from republic to republic and region to region. If one thinks in terms of a simple spectrum distinguishing "localists" from "centralists," at one end of the spectrum there are the groups which express the greatest resentment toward the union and toward the Russians in particular. These groups—prior to glasnost and the events of 1988—tended to be politically ineffectual. In this category are localists and nationalists. Members of these groups favor either political secession or some basic redefinition of autonomy within the union. They tend to champion the national languages as the "official" language of the republic, tend to favor economic self-sufficiency or, short of that, economic control exercised through the republic's capital. They lean toward an exclusivist nationality policy. If the option of separatism is not viable, many will favor economic and social encapsulation within the Soviet system as a means of excluding the "Soviet" influence.

There is a second category which includes groups whose main concerns emphasize the struggle for cultural autonomy in the region. These groups maintain that the logic of the situation dictates a certain amount of accommodation with the center. They tend to favor bilingualism, sometimes argue that independence will endanger national development, and often favor a socialist economy with local, that is enterprise-level, control rather than republican-level control.

Finally, a third category represents the more internationalized orientation. The members of this group are either Russians or Slavs themselves or members of a national minority who live outside their namesake republic or do not have a namesake republic. The movements for republican-level rights therefore threaten their rights in the multinational union. They often affirm the importance of Russian as the *lingua franca* of the realm and argue for "internationalist" protections from the center.

In addition to these ideological positions, among the native cadres in the borderlands there are three discernible strata. First, there is the broad working class. Second, there is the native managerial and political cadre, which we have described under the rubric of the "national leadership" of the republic. Finally, there is an increasingly active group which includes the members of the national intelligentsia who are active in the symbolic-analytic fields. These include the members of the scientific and cultural elite known in the USSR as the intelligentsia. It is another of the many ironies of Soviet socialism that this socialist "upper class" has grown so influential in forming and reinforcing national consciousness. In many cases the native intelligentsias are direct products of the Soviet period. The expansion of literacy and the elaboration of scientific and cultural institutes in Soviet Central Asia, for instance, have given momentum to the creation of a stratum of highly intelligent and sophisticated defenders of national traditions. As Martha Olcott has observed, Soviet policy has produced a "well educated and technologically sophisticated population and a new Kazakh Soviet elite to staff the party and state organizations." She pointed out that it is especially the members of the artistic and academic establishment which "wage constant battles with Moscow over the limits of Kazakh self-expression and the definition of cultural conformity."[32]

There is a great deal of variation in the roles of the groups among the different republics. For example, members of the creative intelligentsia have supplied the greatest organizational and public relations support for the development of popular fronts in the Baltic regions. Yet, even in this case, the pattern of party-state-front relations is quite varied. In Estonia the party elite is dominated by officials whose political backgrounds are tied to the Russian republic. The party elite was quickly discredited once the Estonian popular front acquired momentum. But, having been discredited, the elite quickly accepted the wisdom of acceding to the platform of the popular front. The party elite grasped the link between perestroika and political change in the republic. In contrast, the Latvian and Lithuanian parties were populated by coopted ideological conservatives who expected retaliation from Moscow. Both these parties refused to accommodate to local nationalist demands on principle. They were quickly branded as Moscow-centric and lost virtually all political credibility.

A reverence for symbolic traditions has been observed in the Russian movements of imaginative fiction and in the plastic arts. In the republics there is common approbation of national cultures, a sense of the urgency of defending these symbols, and a commitment to defining the traditions of the ethnic past. This explains why over the past several years the number of increasingly candid discussions of nationality relations in republican journals and newspapers has risen. Local journalists have succeeded in moving the dialogue away from the barren and abstract formulas characteristic of discussions in the 1970s toward real problems of national cultural autonomy.

Recent articles have begun to abandon the ritualistic recitations of the principles of Leninist nationality relations and the obligatory denunciations of Western "bourgeois falsifications" of ethnic processes in the USSR. They have begun to forthrightly address a wide array of questions previously considered sensitive. As a result of the sudden and sweeping abandonment of many censorship strictures, many of the "burning" questions of national relations have become fair play.[33] To name but a few, these include questions of intercultural contact; political indoctrination, agitation, and propaganda; workplace organization; national psychology, consciousness, and identification; manifestations of national exclusiveness; internationalist upbringing and training; religious practices associated with national cultures; the treatment of historical themes, figures, monuments, and shrines; and the development of the national cultural intelligentsia.[34] Some very tentative remarks have been made by way of criticism of the terms of trade which structure the national incomes of the republics. There has been a quickening of the pace of criticism about the growing disparity in the socio-occupational structure of the different republics.[35] There has been more candor in discussions of persistent economic problems such as the underutilization of regional labor reserves relative to occupational patterns in the other republics of the USSR.

A fuller appreciation of the implications of the national climate in the republics can be gained from a survey of some of the more important instances of nationalist resurgence.

Notes

1. The text of the law first appeared in *Pravda* (3 December 1988).

2. A translation of the 1919 version may be found in Leonard Schapiro, ed. *The USSR and the Future* (New York: Praeger, 1963), pp. 255–324. The 1961 version was published as *The Programme of the Communist Party of the Soviet Union* (Moscow: Foreign Languages Publishing House, 1961). A text of the 1986 version appeared in *Kommunist* No. 4 (March 1986).

3. *Pravda.* (5 June 1988).

4. Sidney Tarrow, *Between Center and Periphery* (Yale: Yale University Press, 1977), p. 29.

5. Grey Hodnett, *Leadership in the Soviet National Republics* (Oakville: Mosaic Press, 1978), p. 16.

6. Ibid.

7. Mary McAuley, "Party Recruitment and the Nationalities in the USSR: A Study in Center–Republican Relationships," *British Journal of Political Science* Vol. 10 (October 1980): p. 486.

8. John Soper, "Nationality Issues Under Review in Kirgizia," *Radio Liberty Bulletin* 49/88 (1988).

9. *Sovettik Kurguzstan* (5 December 1987).

10. Vernon Aspaturian, "The Non-Russian Nationalities," in Allen Kassof, ed., *Prospects for Soviet Society* (New York: Praeger, 1968), p. 196. Soviet discussions of cadres policies usually affirm proportional representation "in principle," but fall short of advocating a quota system. As a second secretary of the Kazakh Party organization in 1984 expressed it: "By means of the *nomenklatura* of the party committees, and the composition of the party, soviet, and ministerial *aktiv* the republican party organization strives on a daily basis to attain a more complete reflection of the social and national composition of the population, ensuring the wide representation of each nation and nationality in the leadership of socioeconomic and cultural processes." O.S. Miroshkhin, "Podbor, rasstanovka i vospitanie kadrov v usloviakh mnogonatsional'noi respubliki," in A.M. Korolev, ed., *Kadry–reshaiushchaia sila partiinogo rukovodstva* (Moscow: Politizdat, 1984), p. 51.

11. For the Council of Ministers statutes see *Pravda* (6 July 1978). For Gorbachev's remarks see *Pravda* (29 June 1988).

12. *Pravda vostoka* (23 December 1978).

13. This document was published in all the major Soviet newspapers on March 14, 1989.

14. V. Laptev, "Sil'nyi tsentr–sil'nye respubliki," *Ekonomicheskaia gazeta* No. 17 (April 1989): p. 17.

15. V. Golovachev, "Kakov apparat upravleniia?" *Trud* (11 March 1989): p. 1.

16. E. Dunaev, "Golosuem za kontserny," *Ekonomicheskaia gazeta* No. 17 (April 1989): p. 5.

17. G. Iastrebtsov, "Chernyi kvadrat: sokrashchaiut li shtaty v ministerstve?" *Pravda* (9 April 1989): p. 2.

18. Peter Vanneman, *The Supreme Soviet: Politics and the Legislative Process in the Soviet Political System* (Durham: Duke University Press, 1977), p. 52.

19. *Izvestiia* (12 February 1957).

20. O.I. Ivashchenko, "Deiatel'nost Ekonomicheskoi Komissii Verkhovnogo Soveta SSSR," *Sovetskoe gosudarstvo i pravo* No. 4 (April 1962): pp. 32–45.

21. See G.A. Ivanov, *Planovye organy v SSSR* (Moscow: Ekonomika, 1967), p. 159.

22. For a discussion of the Council see Ivanov. On its abolition see Michael Rywkin, *Moscow's Muslim Challenge* (New York: M.E. Sharpe, 1981) pp. 132–133.

23. See Gorbachev's remarks to the 19th Party Conference. *Pravda* (29 June 1988).

24. A definition of the role of a member of the national elite, in this case a hypothetical Kazakh, is offered by Olcott. "The Kazakh aspirant who wants

to rise in oblast, republic, or all-union politics must still be Russian-speaking (ideally, fluent) and must look and behave as a Russian does. He need not be assimilated but he should appear assimilated, so as not to "stick out" in Russian-dominated settings any more than his unusual facial characteristics make necessary. The Kazakh candidate must also work harder than his Russian competitor and prove himself even more loyal. He must demonstrate a commitment to Moscow's goals and endorse its development strategy as the only way that true Kazakh development could be achieved: on the Russian-paved road to communism." Martha Brill Olcott, *The Kazakhs* (Stanford: Hoover Institution press, 1987), pp. 248–249.

25. Donna Bahry, *Outside Moscow: Power, Politics, and Budgetary Policy in the Soviet Republics* (New York: Columbia University Press, 1987), p. 114.

26. This literature appeared so suddenly on the scene that western specialists have not had an opportunity to critically analyze it. An exception is James Critchlow, "Corruption, Nationalism, and the Native Elites in Soviet Central Asia," *The Journal of Communist Studies* Vol. 4, No. 2 (June 1988): pp. 142–161.

27. See A. Zharnikov, "Dialektika natsional'nykh protsessov," *Pravda* (27 September 1987).

28. Bohdan Nahaylo, "Shelest Confirms He Was Ousted for 'Nationalism'," *Report on the USSR* Vol. 1, No. 4 (27 January 1989): pp. 12–14.

29. For the observation that monolingualism among the national minorities is on the rise in some areas, see Iulii Bromlei, "Sovershenstvovanie natsional'nykh otnoshenii v SSSR," *Kommunist* 8 (May 1986): pp. 79–86.

30. See Kolbin's report to the Kazakh Party Central Committee, *Kazakhstanskaia pravda.*

31. T.H. Rigby argued that Stalin's answer of loyalty with loyalty to many of his close personal aides was not from a sense of Bolshevik or socialist fellow-feeling but from a "form of rational political calculation." See T.H. Rigby, "Was Stalin a Disloyal Patron?" *Soviet Studies* Vol. 38, No. 3 (1986): p. 322.

32. Olcott, *The Kazakhs*, p. 249.

33. Vladimir Solodin, a section chief of Glavlit, the Soviet censorship agency, recently reported that there were about 2,000 censors in the USSR and that Glavlit had intended to remove restrictions on about fifty percent of previously censored material but had wound up releasing close to ninety-five percent. See FBIS Daily Report, FBIS-SOV-89-007, (11 January 1989): p. 73.

34. See, for instance, V.P. Sherstobitov, "Aktual'nye problemy izucheniia natsional'nykh otnoshenii v SSSR na sovremennom etape," *Istoriia* No. 5 (1986): pp. 29–49; Zh.T. Tulenov, "Nekotorye voprosy dialektiki natsional'nykh otnosheniia," *Obshchestvennye nauki v Uzbekistane* No. 2 (1984): pp. 11–16; G. Shirmatova, "Intensifikatsiia vzaimodeistviia natsional'nykh kul'tur," *Kommunist Uzbekistana* No. 2 (1986): pp. 50–55.

35. See, for instance, the article by Rakhima Ubaidullaeva, director of the Economics Institute of the UzSSR Academy of Sciences (*Sel'skaia zhizn'* 25 March 1987) discussing unemployment in Central Asia. Ubaidullaeva asserted that there are 1,000,000 unemployed workers in Uzbekistan alone. Soviet writers are currently debating this issue of contrasting socio-occupational structures. The

national question is rapidly shifting to a question of socioeconomic competition. As one writer noted "Objectively, class and national interests are, above all, social in their content." S.A. Sadykov, "Edinstvo klassovykh i natsional'nykh interesov pri sotsializme," *Vestnik Moskovskogo universiteta: Teoriia nauchnogo kommunizma,*" No. 3 (1986): p. 33. Writing in Turkmenistan, the Slavic sociologist L.P. Verevkin recently concluded on the basis of sociological research in Central Asia that the dispersion of nationalities within occupational-class categories of workers, peasants, and intelligentsia was stabilizing and that nations were continuing to merge. However, the data he presents may cause some to draw different conclusions. See L.P. Verevkin, "Sblizhenie sotsialisticheskikh natsii po sotsial'no-klassovoi strukture," *Izvestiia Akademii Nauk Turkmenskoi SSR: Seriia obshchestvennykh nauk* No. 5 (1986): pp. 3–8.

6

Nationalism Resurgent

What is national culture under the dictatorship of the proletariat? A culture socialist in content and national in form, the aim of which is to educate the masses in the spirit of internationalism and to consolidate the dictatorship of the proletariat.

—Stalin

The Russian term *uglublenie* ("deepening") best describes the evolution over recent decades of cultural autonomy into bureaucratic nationalism. Pro-nativist sentiments in the republics continued to develop under the umbrella of "cultural autonomy." This was reinforced by the activities of the national elites and national intelligentsias. As this took place, it was accompanied by a gradual accretion of bureaucratic power in the republics. This was a limited form of power. It was not a positive power to formulate or to initiate policy. Rather, it was a negative power; the power to interpose, to divert, and, in some cases, to subvert the interests of the center. The accretion of power encouraged the roots of national sentiment to spread deeper. Resentments against central control produced what a Soviet commentator accurately referred to as a certain "allergy" to the *diktat* of the center.[1] As Gorbachev openly acknowledged, a deep and abiding suspicion toward the center lingered in the localities.[2] Certain republics became notorious for corrupt government. Crime statistics showed a ten percent greater rise in crime in cities under republican administration than under central administration.[3] The practice by local public officials of diverting public resources to ends other than those for which they were intended, embezzlement, protectionism, and the spread of mafia-like crime syndicates suggested that, in many respects, central control of the republican areas could be more apparent than real.

These developments in the republics fueled the fears among central government and party officials of the dangers of factionalism, regionalism, and national divisiveness. At the same time the central party officials, who had historically demonstrated their vigilance by being constantly on guard against any type of "nationalist" ideological subversion, openly applied a different standard toward pro-center nationalist sentiments. Such groups as Dmitrii Vasilev's xenophobic "Pamyat Patriotic Association" were allowed to lobby for exclusivist pro-Russian values. Literary champions of "Russite nationalism" such as Valentin Rasputin and Vasilii Belov not only were permitted to publish, but gained an influential following among disgruntled Russians who contended that "fraternal help" to the borderlands had imposed an unacceptable burden on Russia. Their complaints gave credence to the centrists' arguments for Great Russian "tutelage" (*shefstvo*)—for censorship, for secret police monitoring and surveillance, and for "pan-Soviet" policies. The "internationalist" character of pan-Soviet policies depended in large measure on who made the decisions. Since the policies were formulated in the center, they were viewed in the republics as expressions of "Great Russian chauvinism." Nevertheless, the authoritarian instruments of central control were limited. They could retard, but not reverse, the slow growth of fissiparous nationalisms.

In such circumstances, nationalist sentiment in the republics only awaited a spark to ignite the elemental processes of national consolidation. That spark was provided by the spirit of glasnost ushered in by Gorbachev. Not really a policy at first, glasnost was introduced by Gorbachev and his entourage merely as a new style. Perestroika supporters began speaking in terms of the importance of more open communication. They intentionally avoided their predecessors' hackneyed and politically empty cliche of "self-criticism." But what they espoused was not so different in theory. They sought a rationale for self-corrective analysis. Soviet political style required that they adopt a slogan to serve as a mobilizing concept. The slogan had to be one not tainted by the past. They struck upon the idea of "glasnost." Based on the old Russian word "*golos*" (voice) and closely related to the verb "*glasit'*," (to express) the word had an old Slavonic root which provided the right connotations of high literary style. The concept fit their purposes. We should not imagine that the adoption of this idea was not an element in a political agenda. Openness and public disclosure could embarrass many a political official. Gorbachev's bureaucratic opponents were the ones most likely to have skeletons in their closets and, accordingly, the ones most likely to suffer from public scrutiny. Nevertheless, openness eventually had a remarkable tonic effect upon a society so long unable to critically examine itself.

As might well be expected in a society accustomed to secrecy and indirection, the initial response to the sudden widening of the domain of legitimate political discourse was reticence and conservatism.[4] After progressivist journals such as *Oganek* took up the standard of Gorbachev's new openness theme, the wider populace gradually abandoned its reserve. At the center, glasnost produced mainly criticisms of the bureaucracy. In the republics, however, glasnost unleashed open dissension with Moscow's cultural, economic, and political policies. The ferment first broke out among members of the cultural intelligentsia in the republics. Soon complaints swept to areas other than the stifled atmosphere of the arts. Open expression of the resentments of broader population segments, notably industrial workers and tradespeople, followed not long afterwards. From Kaliningrad in the West, to Samarkand in the south, the psychological wounds of long standing political suppression of national symbols and causes became openly visible. The suddenness and depth of the nationalist resurgence surprised many central authorities and, as one would gather from individual accounts, many nationalists as well.

The profound upswelling of ethnic sentiment was especially visible in the republics of Central Asia, the Caucasus, and the Baltics. One of the first places in which open political conflict erupted was Central Asia. By the end of 1988, that remarkable "year of firsts" in the USSR, resurgent nationalist sentiment had precipitated a constitutional crisis. To illustrate the dynamics behind these events it is useful to follow, on a step-by-step basis, the evolution from nationalist climate, to politicized ethnicity, and, finally, to the constitutional crisis of 1988.

Central Asia

As a *Pravda* correspondent recently expressed it, the "cotton affair" in Central Asia "exploded loudly and unexpectedly like thunder from a clear blue sky."[5] Data published in the statistical handbook for 1987 provided figures disclosing that cotton production was overstated by nearly 6 million tons during the period 1976–1985.[6] The overstatement averaged about 385,000 tons annually during this period. Apparently, the overstatement in some years was much greater than in others.[7] For instance, one Soviet writer estimated the overstatement as nearly one million tons in Uzbekistan alone in the early 1980s.[8] The affair involved the embezzlement of more than twelve million rubles of state funds through a sophisticated network of "protection" extending from the farms of rural Uzbekistan to the offices of the USSR Ministry of Internal Affairs. Late in 1988 a military tribunal sentenced Iurii Churbanov, son-in-law of the late Leonid Brezhnev, to twelve years in a hard labor camp for his complicity in the affair during his tenure from 1980 to 1984 as the second highest law enforcement official in the USSR.[9]

The lurid revelations that accompanied the exposure of a patronage system worthy of a banana republic were no doubt in part motivated by the political objectives of central politicians intent on publicly embarrassing recalcitrant local officials. Nevertheless, for Soviet internal audiences, public exposure of such a litany of high and petty crimes was unprecedented. Accustomed by years of adulation of local officials in terms of paeans of "internationalism," "socialist selflessness," and "devotion to the party," the Soviet public was suddenly exposed to rather different epithets; prominent among them were charges of extortion, swindling, devotion to local bosses, exclusivist national fellow-feeling, sponsorship, dependency, tutelage, nepotism, toadyism, fawning, bribery, machinations, whitewash and protectionism. The seriousness of the charges was underscored by Gorbachev's observation that for years individuals and even "whole territories in Central Asia were outside government control."[10]

While the cotton affair gave impetus to dark ruminations about the implications of anti-Slavic sentiment in Central Asia, the partially repressed Slavic fears of the gradual "yellowing" of the union due to high Asian population growth rates eventually gave additional salience to concerns in the party with personnel policies. It was in this atmosphere that the "Alma-Ata events" erupted. As the capital of the Kazakh republic, Alma-Ata is a regional center of government, commerce, and industry in Central Asia. Over the years a gradual influx of Slavs has reduced the native proportion of the population of the republic and the capital until Kazakhs, while densely concentrated in the southern regions of the republic, nevertheless no longer constitute a majority in the republic as a whole nor in the city of Alma-Ata itself.

Traditionally, the head of the party organization in Kazakhstan was a native. While this had not always been true (Brezhnev, for instance, had headed the Kazakh Party organization briefly in the days of Khrushchev's "Virgin Lands" agricultural expansion campaign), the symbolic importance of a native as the head of republican party organizations had gradually grown to such an extent that it was assumed that the aging party head in the 1980s, Dinmukhamed Kunaev, would be replaced by a native Kazakh upon his death or retirement.

Gorbachev's personnel managers, however, had other ideas. In an effort to combat the insularity and secretiveness of local Asian officials, central managers decided to emphasize a policy of "internationalist" appointments. Accordingly, plans were made to name a Russian to the post to succeed Kunaev. Kunaev was either asked to resign or word was leaked to him that he soon would be asked. In an apparent attempt to outmaneuver the central party officials, Kunaev's supporters are said to have incited a public riot in hopes of impressing upon the central officials that only a native Kazakh would be able to suppress the rising tide of nationalism in the republic.[11] Central officials held to their course, appointing the ethnic Russian, Gennadii Kolbin, as Kunaev's successor.

Kolbin later explained to the Kazakh Party Central Committee that the participants in the Alma-Ata riots had been urged on by assertions that the center had appointed a non-Kazakh to head the party organization.[12]

The Kunaev–Kolbin case represents just one example of the political purge that took place throughout Central Asia, starting as early as 1983 under the short-lived Andropov administration.[13] The first sign of changes in the administration which had grown independent and corrupt under the years of Brezhnev's rule came with the transfer of the second secretary of the Communist Party of Uzbekistan (CPUz) in May 1983. In the next two months the heads of the Ministry of Internal Affairs and the republic KGB were removed. Just months later, in October 1983, CPUz first secretary Rashidov died and was immediately replaced by Inamzhon Usmankhodzhaev. Between winter and early summer the investigations quietly continued under the new leadership. As those who had been offering protection from above began to lose their influence, the local people were increasingly exposed. In June, a plenum of the CPUz Central Committee, addressed by Egor Ligachev, then the CPSU Central Committee secretary for organizational and party work, the second ranking secretary in the USSR, made allegations of widespread corruption in the lower party ranks. With the active participation of Usmankhodzhaev, the purge continued to gather momentum. Usmankhodzhaev appeared in both *Pravda* and *Izvestiia*, presenting revelations of corruption which provoked shock and outrage from citizens around the USSR.[14] In November the republic's Prime Minister, Narmokhonmadi Khudaiberdyev, was removed. Then the purge swept through the educational, financial, and agricultural bureaucracies. Especially hard hit was the cotton growing industry. The Minister of Cotton production, his first deputy minister, and another deputy minister were fired for graft and corruption.

By late 1984–early 1985 the purge had reached the local level. In one area of particularly flagrant corruption, officials removed the bulk of the administrative hierarchy. In Kashkadar oblast the first and second secretaries of the oblast party committee as well as at least six first secretaries of raion party committees were dismissed for various abuses. Nonetheless, early in September, the newly appointed officials had to be removed because they too had engaged in graft.[15] By this time the purge had no doubt developed its own dynamic as ideological enemies exploited the opportunities to settle old scores.

The purge then spread outside of Uzbekistan. In November the Kirgiz Party first secretary, Turdakun Usubaliev, was removed. In December, Rakhman Nabiev was removed as first secretary of the Tadzhik Party organization. Days later, Mukhamednazar Gapurov was removed as first secretary of the Turkmen Party organization. Boris Eltsin, addressing a conference of the Tashkent City Party organization late in 1985, explained in words that he could not know were prophetically self-referential that the renewal process in the republic had "just begun."[16] The statistics tell the story. In the period between the local party organization congresses (1981–1986), more than eighty-two percent of the secretaries of the raion and city party committees had been replaced in Kirgizia. As the Uzbek Party first secretary noted, more than half of the composition of the CPSU Central Committee and CPUz *nomenklatura* in Uzbekistan had been replaced.[17]

By 1986 the late Sharaf Rashidov, who as Uzbek Party secretary had managed to win a longer tenure than any other republican secretary (with twenty-four years of service), was being publicly ridiculed and denounced for having fostered the *"Sharafrashidovshchina."*[18] Ligachev, addressing the 27th CPSU Congress in Moscow noted the importance of maintaining the momentum of the program through a policy of regular rotation of circuit personnel.[19]

The provocative replacement of Dinmukhamed Kunaev with the ethnic Russian Genadii Kolbin as first secretary of Kazakhstan occurred in December 1986. By January 1988, with the replacement of Inamzhon Usmankhodzhaev as CPUz first secretary by Rafik Nishanov, the central administrative officials had moved full circle to establish a new generation of political leadership in the Central Asian and Asian republics. Between 1985 and 1988, all of the first secretaries of the Central Asian party organizations were changed. By the end of 1988, the Cotton Affair was officially brought to a close with the verdict against Churbanov and eight co-defendants.[20]

While central officials chose to concentrate on personnel policies to contain a drift toward "decolonization" in Central Asia, the response among the local political and administrative elite and intelligentsia was to champion causes which dramatized the center's lack of understanding and consequent mismanagement of local conditions and affairs. Chief among these affairs is the question of the terms of trade between Moscow central planners and the industry and agriculture of Central Asia. With slightly more visibility than in the past, local leaders continue to maintain this issue before the public; such economic questions often have failed to move public opinion or excite the passions of the public. For this reason, perhaps, the nationalists of Central Asia sought other causes to dramatize their concerns and to serve as a lobbying device with the public and with the central bureaucrats.

One example of this type of lobbying is the case of female self-immolation in Soviet Central Asia. Ever since Adil Iaqubov's expose about the self-immolation of women in Central Asia a debate has raged over the issue of culpability.[21] The controversy was exacerbated by the fact that the Slavic central authorities have used this as a pretext for attacking Islam as a religion justifing patriarchally dominated social institutions. Revelations in *Pravda* about as many as 270 such suicides in the two years previous were merely another salvo in this ideological conflict.[22] The local rationalization was that the Central Asian women who resorted to self-immolation did not do so out of despair over "vestiges of feudalistic social institutions"—the charge laveled by Moscow critics. In the view of the locals, to agree to this would be to assent to the expressions of reproach of Islamic traditions. Rather, the local response was that the suicides stemmed from oppressive working conditions, heavy physical labor, and a sense of entrapment, all of which, they suggested, are imposed on Central Asian women not by Islamic tradition but by government-enforced production targets.[23]

One of the more successful examples of the lobbying process in recent years is the case of the anguished and impassioned appeals that have been made in an effort to save the Aral Sea.[24] Although reports vary, the surface level of the Aral Sea has been dropping at a precipitous rate for nearly two decades. The two main feeder rivers of the Aral, the Syr Darya and the Amu Darya rivers, have ceased to replenish the Aral Sea. The reason for the desiccation of the sea is plainly linked to the type of agricultural expansion that has occurred in Soviet Central Asia in recent decades. For years, complaints have been heard from Central Asian figures regarding the high social and ecological costs of monocrop agriculture.[25] The "cotton first" strategy has resulted in extreme periodic labor demands disrupting Central Asia's schools and factories as young people are called out in brigades to bring in the harvest by hand.[26] The strategy has brought salinization to some of the best grazing and farm land and it has caused environmental decay resulting from heavy defoliant and pesticide use. In the 1980s, the local critics argued, it was threatening to turn Central Asia's major reservoir into a desert. The Central Asians had no illusions about the source of the problem. As a noted Uzbek figure explained: "the cotton plan has been increased to the heavens, new lands have been brought under cultivation, reservoirs have been poorly constructed, and many industrial enterprises have been erected on the banks of local rivers."[27]

The growth of nationalism in Central Asia has been a product of center-periphery disagreement and anti-colonial attitudes. It is important to remember that unlike the other republican borderlands of the USSR, none of the Central Asian republics existed as a separate state prior to Soviet control. Understandably, the national identity of the groups is linked to the Soviet period. This contrasts sharply with the situation in areas such as the Caucasus. While the Central Asian conflicts could be described as anti-center and perhaps anti-Slavic in character, the implications for federal change are still inchoate. Moreover, the emotional defense of Central Asian traditionalism—which was no doubt motivated by a desire to protect traditional culture from "Soviet" (read: Russian) semi-colonial encroachment—had the effect of defending underdevelopment. The defense of the periphery, in other words, threatened to do just that—strengthen peripheral underdevelopment and dependency of the area. The case was quite different in the Caucasus.

The Caucasus

The most vivid example of the transformation of cultural autonomy into nationalism is provided by the events in the Caucasus during 1988. The conflict in the Caucasus was not precipitated by anti-Russian or anti-Soviet attitudes nearly so much as by a historical conflict between Armenian irredentism and Azeri political control. Unlike the case of Central Asia, where territorially based nationalism is still illdefined, Armenian nationalism is a political value which is broadly based, historically established, and recognized by an active international community championing allegiance to Armenian ethnic identity. The sources of this identity are important. In many parts of the developing world of Africa and the Middle East, nationalism arises as a creation of a mobilizational elites' attempting to harness political dissatisfactions or resentments to their own political agendas. The Armenian brand of nationalism must be distinguished from such instrumental nationalisms. If Armenian national identity at some point in the past came into being by virtue of such a process, it was long ago; Armenians today see themselves with a long and heroic, if tragic, past. They anticipate a national future just as expansive.

The conflict between the Armenian and Azeri ethnic communities is only one of a great many historical conflicts among the ethnic groups inhabiting the Transcaucasian isthmus. Social conflicts erupted in the late 19th century as a result of the strains of rapid industrial development during an oil boom along the shores of the Caspian. These social conflicts resulted in a political confrontation between the primarily Turkophone and Muslim Azeri and the primarily Christian and Armenian-speaking Armenians. In the prevailing circumstances of social competition at the time, the better educated and skilled Armenian businessmen acquired a privileged commercial position. This drew the resentment of under skilled, under educated, and thus easily exploited Azeri workers. Antagonisms erupted in the "Tatar-Armenian War" in 1905 centered in Baku. After the Bolshevik Revolution a "Transcaucasian Federation" was created but was unmanageable. The isthmus was eventually split into three republics not so much as a technique of the Russians to divide and conquer as an instrument by which to separate the antagonistic groups from one another. Ever since the initial republican division took place, strong feelings have prevailed among many non-Armenian peoples of the region that the Armenians received special treatment from Moscow.

Today the region is divided among the three Soviet Socialist republics (SSRs) of Georgia, Armenia, and Azerbaidzhan. Contained within the Armenian republic is the "Nakhichevan Autonomous Soviet Socialist Republic" (NaASSR). This "autonomous republic" is administratively subordinated not to Armenia but to the Azerbaidzhan Republic. To make matters even less symmetrical, the Azeri Republic physically encloses the "Nagorno-Karabakh Autonomous Oblast" (NKAO). The explanations for this strange system of overlapping territories and jurisdictions has to do with both the physical dispersion of ethnic groups and the politics of the period of the consolidation of Soviet power. As constitutionally recognized political structures, however, these "autonomous" republics and oblasts enjoy their own political institutions, including ministerial (i.e., economic) structures, "soviet" (i.e., parliamentary) organizations, and communist party apparatuses. Consequently, each has various strata of local political leadership.

Armenians have long felt that the Nagorno-Karabakh Autonomous Oblast (NKAO), having a principally (about 75 percent) Armenian population, should be subordinated to the Armenian republic. Late in 1987, spurred on by the newly permissive atmosphere of Gorbachev's glasnost, a delegation from the NKAO traveled to Moscow to discuss redistricting with central officials. On January 8, 1988, a delegation of deputies armed with a petition containing some 80,000 signatures presented their demands to the USSR Supreme Soviet Commission for Nationalities. The cool reception in Moscow encouraged many of the deputies to turn back to the general population for further support. Petitions for unification of the NKAO with Armenia began to circulate in Stepanakert, the capital of the NKAO. Popular demonstrations spread in a number of days to the Armenian capital of Erevan. The soviet of the NKAO passed a resolution on February 20, 1988, demanding annexation of the NKAO to Armenia. On February 25, 1988, Red Army tanks took up positions in Erevan.

In response to the Armenian demands, anti-Armenian riots broke out in Azerbaidzhan late in February in a predominantly Armenian neighborhood just north of Baku in the city of Sumgait. Eyewitness reports say that the Sumgait events were particularly brutal. On March 4, 1988, TASS acknowledged that thirty-one people had been murdered. Many thousands of Armenians living in Azerbaidzhan were said to have left for fear of further violence. Tensions remained high throughout the summer and early fall until mid-September when a new crescendo was reached. A general strike and mass rallies in Erevan precipitated an announcement of a state of emergency by party officials in September 1988.[28]

Moral leadership of the Armenian irredentist movement was provided by an informal, ad hoc group known as the "Karabakh Committee." Formed from a mixture of official and unofficial figures, the "Committee" acted throughout the summer and fall almost as a parallel government. It should not seem surprising under the circumstances, that the Committee eventually fell prey to disagreements. One original member of the Committee, Silva Kaputikian, had established a reputation as a pro-native writer by publishing on such topics as local economic problems and the problems of minority language grammar schools. She noted in July that "many Armenian intellectuals had severed connections with the Committee because of the 'anti-Russian tone'" that the movement assumed.[29]

What is most striking about the Committee is its endurance over such a long period of time in an atmosphere of extreme tension. Despite the fact that the Committee was not official, it managed to gain considerable power. Official leaders not only acknowledged it but also met with its representatives. For instance, the special Moscow envoy sent to oversee policy initiatives in the NKAO, Arkadii Vol'skii, was reported to have met with members of the Committee in July 1988,[30] and the Armenian Party first secretary, Suren Arutunian, was said to have met with members of the Committee on September 19, 1988.[31]

The official stratum of political leaders in the two republics has also undergone change, but these republics have not seen anything resembling a wholesale purge as in Central Asia. Kyamran Bagirov, who had served as chief of the Azeri Party apparatus, was removed from that post on May 21, 1988. Bagirov, like the top party official in Armenia, Karen Demirchian, was removed not only because the disturbances occurred during his watch but also because he may have abetted the annexation movement. Demirchian's successor in Armenia, Suren Arutiunian, told the delegates to the 19th Party Conference in June that the mistakes of his predecessor had already been addressed in the plenums and meetings of the Armenian Party organizations. He noted that his comrades had directed "sharp criticism toward negative phenomena, the practice of protectionism, and the advancement of cadres on the basis of personal loyalty."[32]

Both of the new top party officials in the two republics shared the characteristic of having had substantial recent work experience outside of the republics. Abdul-Rakhman Khalil ogly Vezirov, the new first secretary of the Azeri Party apparatus, had worked for the past several years as a diplomat in Asia. Suren Arutiunian, the new party leader of

Armenia, worked for many years as a sector head in the Propaganda Department of the CPSU Central Committee and only returned to Armenia as recently as two years previously. Presumably, the long experience of both men outside their native republics serves to reassure Moscow officials that they will be less beholden to local interests than their predecessors.

It is difficult to foresee the long-term implications of the December 1988 earthquakes, which brought such a horrifying loss of life to Armenia. In light of the Armenian response to the vicissitudes of centuries of violent conflict and such travails as the 1915–1918 massacre of Armenians at the hands of the Turks, one has grounds, however, for expecting that the Armenian republic which emerges from the devastation of earthquake will be as nationalistic as the one which preceded it.

Unlike the anomic nationalist ferment of Central Asia, the recent events in the Caucasus raised theoretical questions of federal import. To the extent that the constitutional status of the national minorities derived from their ethnic identity, the irredentist claim of a "natural" overlap between ethnographic and politico-administrative boundaries in the Caucasus demanded more recognition from the center. Events in the Baltic republics posed the question to the center in yet more stark terms.

The Baltic Republics

Certainly the most remarkable challenge to Soviet central power in the past seven decades is the response to glasnost and perestroika that has emerged in the Baltic republics. In the period since Gorbachev's accession to power, the popular discontent in the Baltic regions of the USSR has given rise to a nationalist resurgence of unprecedented scope and virulence. Private political meetings, which began as early as the summer of 1986, paved the way for political organization and mobilization. By the summer of 1988 the meetings had become movements, already presenting overt political challenges to the central authorities. Crowds that numbered in the tens of thousands met in public rallies commemorating the 49th anniversary of the Soviet-German treaty that led to the occupation of the countries of Estonia, Latvia, and Lithuania. The political atmosphere was unparalleled in Soviet history; it constituted an open, direct, and unambiguous political challenge to the legitimacy of Soviet rule in the Baltic regions. What were the causes of these events? Why were they permitted to take place?

The nationalist resurgence in the Baltic regions was fueled by moral outrage at two things. First and most important was the way the Baltic countries fell under Soviet control in 1940. The second source of outrage was the persistent resentment felt by the native populations of the Baltics at the "Russification" policies of the central authorities and the resultant lack of control the local people had over their republican resources.

After wresting independence from Russia in the political turmoil of the Bolshevik Revolution, the three countries enjoyed political independence for just slightly over two decades before succumbing as pawns in great-power machinations between Hitler's Germany and Stalin's Soviet Union. The Molotov-Ribbentrop Agreement of August 23, 1939 included a secret protocol between Stalin and Hitler acknowledging spheres of influence in the center of Europe. According to the agreement, the Baltic countries fell within the suzerainty of the USSR. Using slightly different pretexts in each country but with one and the same objective in mind, Stalin transformed these nations into "Soviet republics." Bogus parliaments under Soviet control voted for admission to the USSR.

The secret protocols were discovered by Allied forces shortly before the end of the war in Nazi archives. The U.S. State Department published them in 1948. The Soviet Union, however, officially denied their existence, calling the documents falsified provocations. In August 1988, just weeks before the 49th anniversary of the Molotov-Ribbentrop agreement, Valentin Falin, the head of the Soviet press organization Novosti, announced at a news conference that an official commission to investigate the secret protocols concluded that the protocols were either destroyed or had never existed.[33]

The summer of 1988 witnessed an unprecedented level of public discussion over the circumstances of the Baltic states' "voluntary" reincorporation into the USSR. Empowered by the glasnost campaign, the nationalistic intelligentsia of the Baltic republics raised the question of the underlying principle of the "autonomy" of the Soviet republics with exceptional vigor. Soviet news sources reported with suprising candor the open challenges to central authority. At the public gatherings in August 1988 commemorating the loss of national independence, the existing communist governments were equated with Nazi rule. This is an extremely sensitive subject. Soviet central officials have historically considered this one of the most invidious comparisons possible. Official estimates of the crowds in Vilnius were 100,000. Unofficial estimates were twice that number.[34] In October, a Lithuanian "Sajudis" political group calling itself the "Movement in Support of Perestroika" drew over 200,000 people into the streets for a torchlit parade.[35] At the first congress of the organization, delegates issued a number of demands including the creation of a separate currency, the right to send Lithuanian missions abroad, the establishment of limits on in-migration to the republic, and the establishment of republican control over the Lithuanians serving in the Red Army. In a direct insult to central rule, Latvians, in a rally on

November 18, 1988, celebrated the republic's pre-Soviet "bourgeois" independence day.

By the summer of 1989, the defiant attitude of public demostrators had reached such a level that Soviet authorities in Moscow were no longer able or willing to maintain the fiction regarding the secret protocols. On August 23, 1989 hundreds of thousands of citizens of the Baltic republics linked hands in a massive protest of Soviet annexation of the Baltic areas. The protesters formed a human chain across 400 miles of territory from the capitals of Tallin to Riga, to Vilunius. Bowing to public pressure, Soviet authorities reversed course and acknowledged the existence of the secret protocols. But the authorities continued to insist that the protocols were irrelevant to questions of the contemporary legal status of the Baltic countries. On August 22, 1989 a commission of the Lithuanian Supreme Soviet became the first official body to openly challenge not just the morality but the *legal* legitimacy of Soviet rule by declaring that the annexation of the territory of Lithuania was illegal.

Although the terms of political incorporation into the Soviet Union were the main historical factor motivating the Baltic nationalist resurgence, the agenda for the future mainly concerned contemporary cultural, economic, and political problems.

The members of the creative intelligentsia have been among the most influential in organizing the Baltic popular fronts. The cultural issues, accordingly, received high priority on the agenda for change. The Lithuanian Party first secretary, installed in the fall of 1988, Algirdas Brazauskas, was quick to announce that Lithuania was "the first of the Baltic republics to have restored the historical national symbols and to have given the native tongue the status of an official language."[36] Those national symbols to which he was referring included the tricolor flag used after Lithuania joined the League of Nations, the state anthem, and the national coat of arms. Brazauskas championed the reopening of Vilnius Cathedral and St. Casimir's Church in Vilnius.

Perhaps out of fear that the window of opportunity provided by perestroika might close, the other Baltic republics were equally intent upon instituting protections of republican cultural rights. In September 1988 the Latvian SSR Supreme Soviet published a draft decree, "On the Status of the Latvian Language." The following month a resolution was issued on "national symbols" identifying Latvian as the official language of the republic. Estonia published a draft law in October 1988 aimed at making Estonian the official language of that republic. Later, in January 1989, the draft was passed into law. The law not only made Estonian the official medium of science, literature, and commerce in the republic but also, in an effort to mollify the insult of Russification of Estonian names, proclaimed that Estonians would no longer be required to supply a Russian-style patronymic (middle name). Early in 1989 the Lithuanian legislature passed a decree officially recognizing February 16, 1918 as a national holiday, commemorating Lithuanian independence. In an effort to secure the longevity of the restoration of cultural symbols, the republics began focusing on educational reform.[37]

Moscow was surprisingly accommodating on cultural questions. But cultural autonomy does not imply political autonomy. As many commentators have pointed out, the flowering of native dress, handicrafts, and songs will not make the republics strong. The key issue in gaining long term political rights is control over the direction of the economy. A Lithuanian economist posed the dilemma of local control bluntly: "How long" he asked, "will some Ivan Petrovich in Room 421 be the one deciding whether to build a toilet in some Lithuanian city, whose name he cannot even pronounce?"[38] Advocates of central planning will explain that a certain amount of absentee economic decision making is necessary to attain overarching social goals. In order to manage proportional development of the republics, these advocates maintain, subsidies and inter-republican transfers must be directed from the center. But the problem of resource transfers is: who decides how much and to where?

Conducting their own analyses, economists in the Baltic republics produced a report in 1988 concluding that the Baltic republics were suffering from the current terms of trade. They suggested an extension of the *khozraschet* accounting principle to the level of the republic to remedy the situation.[39] Central officials had long paid lip service to ideas of self-financing. The practice promised to relieve them of burdensome subsidies. But the principle had been applied exclusively to economic organizations—farms, offices, enterprises, and such—not to politico-administrative organs. The question of switching over to republican *khozraschet* and self-financing, as one official expressed it, "is now directly connected with the question of national economic sovereignty."[40] The 19th Party Conference responded positively if vaguely to the idea of republican-level self-financing. Later, central leaders admitted that they were not sure what the practical implications of such a principle would be. Aleksandr Yakovlev, for instance, told audiences in the Baltic republics that the 19th Party Conference had endorsed republican cost accounting in general terms but did not know precisely what was entailed in implementing it.[41]

The Presidium of the Council of Ministers promised in November 1988 to conduct a study on the subject. The following March the draft document summarizing the findings was published.[42] The proposals for change opened up an extremely lively debate centered on how to achieve the competing goals expressed in the slogan "a strong center and strong republics." On one side were the centrists, arguing that a "strong center cannot exist without a number of ministries, part of which, despite withering criticism, should be retained."[43] On the other side were those who were arguing that "the independence of the republic should be based on the unlimited right to manage the economic levers of all the enterprises and economic organizations situated on its territory."[44] Proponents of the federalist position insisted that "economic sovereignty is a compulsory precondition for the revival of a genuine federation."[45] In the middle of this debate are those who maintain that "economic decentralization should not lead us to economic chaos."[46]

The debate not only held implications for internal political functioning. It also implied changes in the relationship of the republics to other countries through commercial ties. During the discussion period preceding the political reform of 1988, many people in the Baltics hoped that the enticing prospects of developing a "Hong Kong in the Baltic" would encourage independent commercial ties between the Baltic republics and nearby European trading partners. Many argued that the Baltics could be a conduit for technology from the West. On December 2, 1988 the Council of Ministers passed a comprehensive decree on "External Economic Activity of the State, Cooperative, and other Public Enterprises, Associations and Organizations." It declared that after April 1989 the right to directly carry out export-import operations would be exercisable by all enterprises, associations, producer cooperatives and other organizations whose products were competitive on the foreign market. Moreover, the concept of "special economic zones" received serious discussion.[47] But the guidelines that the Council of Ministers eventually produced provided for "special economic zones" only in the far eastern reaches of the USSR, and not in the Baltic.[48] These questions of economic rights set the republics against the center and, on yet another level, the party against the society within the republics.

The people's fronts in the Baltic republics appeared first as support groups for perestroika. But their ranks soon swelled and their political agendas enlarged accordingly. Increasingly over the months of 1988 and early 1989, they came to resemble opposition political parties. They acquired official status as "approved independent groups," not as political organizations. In practice they have served as instruments of interest articulation. Moreover, they have demonstrated the kind of patience and maneuverability necessary for continued political existence. In the elections of 1989, for instance, Sajudis decided to withraw its election challenges to the Lithuanian Party leader, Algirdas Brazauskas, and to the party second secretary, Vladimir Berezov, out of a concern that a sweeping defeat for the party in Lithuania might invited central retaliation. By avoiding a rigid, confrontational stance of presenting non-negotiable demands, they invited recognition from the center as a negotiating partner.

The basic problem with their negotiating posture, however, was that they are, by definition, exclusivist. They tend to defend, for instance, "Lithuanian traditions" rather than the Lithuanian republic. Many of the inhabitants of Lithuania, not being of Lithuanian heritage themselves, are thus excluded. A response to this has been the formation of Russian-based counter organizations. The "Association of Unity," for instance, was formed as a counterbalance to Sajudis.

The surprising thing about the "Baltic summer" of 1988 was the central authorities' attitude of reserve. Authorities granted permits for public rallies. There were no arrests and no violence at the rallies. The central authorities saw changes in the center-periphery relationship as both inevitable and beneficial, if those changes were kept within certain bounds. A moderate spokesman for the center, Aleksandr Yakovlev, was sent in the late summer to mediate disputes with representatives of the Baltic political organizations. Yakovlev was a good choice. He had associated himself with opposition to Russian nationalism. And, in his speeches in the Baltic republics, he suggested that he appreciated the importance of developing national cultures, but was opposed to stridency and confrontation that might lead to reprisals or result in reversals for the greater goal of perestroika.[49] Central authorities seem to have taken the position that to defuse the situation they would let it continue to develop. The central Soviet press visibly played down the threat to all-union solidarity, while the local press in the Baltic republics conducted an essentially uncensored discussion of complaints.

The challenges posed by the Baltic republics held different implications for Soviet federalism than those posed by the Asian and Caucasian republics. As we have seen, the Central Asian case was characterized by a tendency of internal withdrawal. Separatist sentiment in Central Asia was still mainly utopian, glancing toward the heroic past toward "greater Turkestan." The feeling is strong, however, that Central Asians must not suffer the fate of their Afghan cousins in an attempt to "go it alone." Similarly, separatist sentiment was inconsequential in the Caucasus simply because the republics of the isthmus have nowhere to go. The experience of small states in the international system, especially small Middle-eastern states (e.g. Lebanon), stands as eloquent testimony to the dangers of independence. Armenia's immediate neighbors could not be expected to respond with civility to an independent Armenia. The Baltic republics, differ in this regard. More industrialized and socioeconomically advanced than the all-union average, these areas have roots in Europe which could easily, under conditions of independence, allow a blossoming of their economies in the European unified market.

While central leaders are loathe to forfeit the industriousness of these areas, they can nevertheless benefit from using the republics much in the way that they have used the East European countries in the past— as conduits for Western technology. Separatism from the Baltics, then, presents Moscow with a different set of problems; problems which were thrown into stark relief by the constitutional crisis of 1988.

The Constitutional Crisis

The two core questions of the constitutional crisis are summed up in the "Armenian challenge" and the "Estonian Clause." Respectively these are:

1. If the right to representation and recognition is based upon relatively enduring ethno-national identity, then should not the politico-administrative divisions and the ethnographic boundaries in the USSR coincide?
2. If political reform is acknowledged to be a necessary precondition of the rehabilitation of Soviet socialism, then what will be the definition of the "sovereign and independent" status which the central government formally accords the republics?

The Armenian challenge came to the fore in early summer 1988. As we have seen above, tensions over Azerbaidzhan political control of the NKAO had given rise to months of open conflict and violence. Finally, the Presidium of the Armenian SSR Supreme Soviet adopted a solution that only a short time before would have been widely viewed as extreme: on June 15, 1988, it responded to requests of the NKAO Supreme Soviet by passing a resolution calling for the annexation of the NKAO to Armenia. In retaliation, two days later the Azerbaidzhan Supreme Soviet Presidium responded in kind; it rejected the Armenian solution as "unconstitutional." The Azerbaidzhani response was on firm legal grounds. Article 78 of the USSR constitution stipulates that a union republic's territory may not be altered without the republic's consent.

The general strike in Stepanakert was brought to a close in July amid a mixture of promises of central government economic assistance and threats of reprisals. At the same time, the USSR Supreme Soviet, on July 18, 1988, officially rejected the irredentists' demands as a matter of constititutional principle.

Despite the fact that the Armenian nationalists were unsuccessful in achieving their goals and were condemned by central authorities as anti-Soviet, they did succeed in focusing all-union attention on the problems of the national minorities in legitimizing public discussion of those problems. More importantly, perhaps, the announcement of the economic development for the NKAO package suggested that, even in "losing," the nationalists had won some important gains. Moreover, these developments served as an example to others. In combination with the Caucasian events, the movements for Baltic independence created increasing pressure on Moscow for a reevaluation of the constitutional status of the republics.

In a surprise announcement at the 19th Party Conference in July, Gorbachev unveiled plans for a political reform. The reform would include a relatively minor redistribution of the representation of the republics in a newly constituted all-union legislative assembly called the Congress of People's Deputies. In the Baltic areas the formalistic representation granted the republics was quite openly regarded as a sham. As an Estonian Academy of Sciences economist expressed it in the Russian language daily, *Sovetskaia Estoniia*, "up till now neither Estonia nor any other union republic has enjoyed real sovereignty—that is a fact. But formally it has existed."[50] Nevertheless, sensing perhaps the historic opportunity provided by the constitutional revisions, defenders of republican rights were quick to criticize the proposed changes on the grounds, as one writer explained, that the amendments amounted to a "virtual denial . . . of sovereignty for the union republics and [the draft] treats the republics not as national states but as merely administrative territorial units."[51] Critics of the draft law saw it as removing the right of secession (also widely regarded as patently unenforceable), tightening Moscow's economic control, reducing union republic representation in the all-union legislature, and as being hurried through the deliberative process by Gorbachev to circumvent potential opposition.

Such principled objections as these to the proposed changes were reinforced by the outpouring of public sentiment in the Baltics. This persuaded the central officials of the need for negotiation. Three Central Committee secretaries were dispatched to the Baltic republics in early November to defuse the situation and explain the center's position on the proposed changes. Despite conciliatory efforts by Moscow's envoys, an extraordinary session of the Estonian Supreme Soviet on November 16, 1988 adopted changes in the Estonian Constitution which reserved for the republic the right to veto all-union legislation. The legislation declared the land, natural resources, industry, banks, and general capital located in the Estonian republic to be the property solely of the Estonian SSR. Finally, the changes appeared to legalize private property.[52] The measures of the Estonian legislature became known as the "Estonian Clause."

Responding with what was no doubt authentic surprise, central officials were quick to invalidate the "Estonian Clause." On November 18, 1988 the USSR Supreme Soviet Presidium found the Estonian Supreme Soviet's actions to be in violation of all-union law.[53] Nor was the Estonian clause adopted by the neighboring republics. On November 22, Latvia decided not to declare its sovereignty along these lines. Clearly pointing to the explosive potential of republican unilateralism, Gorbachev explained the center's position on the question to the USSR Supreme Soviet.

> We feel the concern of the workers over the state of things in our union. We have come across a situation in which resolutions of the supreme body of power of one of the republics run counter to the USSR Constitution. This does not only concern minor details, but problems that affect the destiny of our union as a whole. This is why they should be recognized as erroneous and invalid.[54]

Two days later, *Pravda* printed a USSR Supreme Soviet Presidium decree formally invalidating Articles 2, 3, 4, and 5 of the the Estonian constitutional amendments. This first phase of the constitutional crisis was resolved in favor of the center. But the events dramatized a principle: that disagreement over fundamental questions could be kept within manageable limits. This principle may survive as one of the most important lessons for political development in the Soviet Union in the period since de-Stalinization. Events also pointed to the need for a new approach to the nationalities question. The search for a new formula—one which combines federal reorganization with nationality policy—was commenced with the newly announced goal of achieving "harmonic relations" among the republics.

The dramatic process of political reform went forward during the spring of 1989 buoyed by the evident enthusiasm of members of the press and the electronic media. Under the new protocols of glasnost, the press offered the Soviet public remarkably more candid reportage of Soviet politics than had been possible for decades. Although the Estonian nationalists had failed in their first attempt to force a reinterpretation of Moscow's authority with respect to the republics, the meeting of the first Congress of Peoples Deputies offered a new opportunity to publicize the issue. In the March 1989 elections, Baltic nationalists won strong pluralities from the national electoral districts and found seats among the other two contingents—the "social organizations" and general electoral districts—such that Baltic delegations of deputies were resolved to carry out the mandate of the previous autumn.

While the center prevailed in the parliamentary contest of 1988, the public statements of the Baltic deputies in advance of the Congress made it clear that they approached the issue as a stalemate rather than a defeat. On May 18 1989, for instance, the Lithuanian Supreme Soviet passed a resolution "On Government Sovereignty in Latvia" which was intended to demonstrate the republic's resolve on the sovereignty issue, thereby strengthening the hand of the more nationalistically minded deputies when they arrived for the opening of the Congress in Moscow. When the first session of the Congress of People's Deputies convened, the Baltic deputies were among the most outspoken on the issue of center–republican relations. On the whole, the Congress deputies could be grouped into three separate ideological orientations. There were the "reformers," intent on carrying out the perestroika agenda. There were the members of the *apparat*, whose main concern appeared to be preventing change which would threaten the prevailing organizational structure and, presumably, their own privileges and perquisites. And there were the "localist" deputies—nationalists among them—who were arguing mainly local agendas and proposing what, judging from the press reportage, seemed to the majority of deputies to be rather idiosyncratic programs for change. The Congress was in session from May 25 until June 9, 1989. By the end of the Congress's first session, the USSR Supreme Soviet had already been formed and commenced its first session (which ran from June 3 until August 4, 1989). Sensing the need for an authoritative statement on the issue of republican juridical sovereignty, Gorbachev proposed the establishment of a constitutional review body. The Lithuanian delegates countered with a dramatic walkout in protest.[55] At the close of the Supreme Soviet session, the tensions between center and republic were no closer to a harmonious resolution than they had been twelve months before, when the Estonian clause was first proposed. Most commentators at this point looked forward to the promised Central Committee Plenum on nationalities and interethnic relations for the definitive statement of republican rights.[56]

Notes

1. V. Tomashkevich, "Kakoi zhe on—novyi oblik ministerstva?" *Ekonomicheskaia gazeta* Vol. 16 (1989): p. 12.

2. *Pravda* (2 December 1988).

3. This figure was reported by a first deputy minister of the Ministry of Internal Affairs, Iu. Astakhov. See the discussion in *Sovetskaia Latviia* (31 January 1989): p. 3.

4. For an analysis of the effect of intimidation on popular attitudes see Donna Bahry and Brian D. Silver, "Intimidation and The Symbolic Uses of Terror in the USSR," *American Political Science Review* Vol. 81, No. 4 (1987): pp. 1065–1098.

5. G. Ovcharenko, "Kobry nad zolotom," *Pravda* (23 January 1988).

6. *Narodnoe khoziaistvo SSSR 1917–1987.*

7. Estimates of the actual cotton production during the period 1976–1986 computed by the Central Intelligence Agency were reprinted in *Newsletter for Research on Soviet and East European Agriculture* Vol. 9, No. 4 (December 1987).

8. *Literaturnaia gazeta* (10 June 1987).

9. *The New York Times* (31 December 1988).

10. *Pravda* (13 January 1988).

11. This allegation was clearly made by Genadii Kolbin. In his report to the Central Committee of the Kazakh Party, he asserted that the participants in the anti-Russian riots in Alma-Ata had been informed that a Russian from outside the republic was about to be appointed party first secretary. "How did they know this? It was quietly whispered to them, an idea was presented to them which they publicly voiced in the square. The essence of this secret idea was this: If someone has to be promoted, then let it be someone who would be dependent on the former leadership caste." See Kolbin's address in *Kazakhstanskaia pravda* (15 March 1987).

12. See Kolbin's report to the Kazakh Party Central Committee, *Kazakhstanskaia pravda* (15 March 1987).

13. Two important recent discussions of the link between economic crime and the political elites in Central Asia are Dmitri Likhanov, "Organized Crime in Central Asia," *Telos* Vol. 75 (Spring 1988): pp. 90–101; and James Critchlow, "'Corruption,' Nationalism, and the Native Elites in Soviet Central Asia," *The Journal of Communist Studies* Vol. 4, No. 2 (June 1988): pp. 142–161.

14. See *Izvestiia* (4 November 1984) and *Pravda* (2 February 1986).

15. See *Pravda Vostoka* (27 September 1984).

16. *Pravda vostoka* (15 December 1985).

17. *Pravda* (28 February 1986).

18. The expression defies translation. It is a play on words on Rashidov's name and on the "Ezhovshchina." The "Ezhovshchina" refers to a period of the great purge during 1936–1938, bearing the name of the head of the NKVD, Nikolai Ezhov.

19. *Pravda* (28 February 1986).

20. *The New York Times* (31 December 1988).

21. Adil Iakubov, "Tragediia v kishlake," *Literaturnaia gazeta* (19 August 1987). Also see E. Gafarov, "Zhivye fakely," *Pravda* (21 April 1988).

22. See *Pravda* (5 February 1988).

23. The debate is reminiscent of the disputes over child labor in the agricultural fields of Central Asia. Central officials, scandalized by the practice, have used it in the campaign of atheistic propaganda against Islam, citing it as a holdover from the feudal past. Local officials have rationalized the practice as "socialist work training." The dispute continues. See the article by N. Gladkov and V. Somov, *Pravda* (6 March 1985).

24. See James Critchlow, "Desertification of the Aral Region: Economic and Human Damage," *Radio Liberty Bulletin* RL 392/87 (26 August 1987); Abdizhamil Nurneshov, "O sud'be arala," *Ogonek* No. 1 (January 1988): pp. 25–26.

25. The politics of Soviet Central Asian agriculture are explored in Grey Hodnett, "Technology and Social Change in Soviet Central Asia: The Politics

of Growing Cotton," in Henry R. Morton and Rudolf L. Tokes, eds., *Soviet Politics and Society* (New York: Free Press 1974), pp. 60–117, and in Gregory Gleason, "Ministries versus Territories: Evidence from Agricultural Administration in Soviet Central Asia," *Studies in Comparative Communism* Vol. 19, Nos. 3/4 (Autumn/Winter 1986): pp. 227–245.

26. Esther B. Fein, "In Land of Proletariat, Child Labor," *The New York Times* (10 November 1988).

27. Oktir Hashimov, "Avladlarga Nima Deymiz?," (What Shall We Say to Future Generations?), *Shark Iulduzi* (In Uzbek), No. 2 (1988): p. 153.

28. *New York Times* (23 September 1988).

29. Quoted in Elizabeth Fuller, "Recent Developments in the Nagorno–Karabakh Dispute," *Radio Liberty Research Bulletin* RL 312/88. (July 11 1988): p. 3.

30. *The Sun* (Baltimore) (17 September 1988).

31. See Elizabeth Fuller, "Further Fatality Reported as New Violence Flares Up in Nagorno–Karabakh," *Radio Liberty Research Bulletin* RL 428/88 (20 September 1988): p. 2.

32. *Pravda* (1 July 1988).

33. *New York Times* (17 August 1988).

34. Bill Keller, "The Baltic Gamble," *The New York Times* (25 August 1988): p. 6.

35. *The New York Times* (25 October 1988).

36. *Sovetskaia Litva* (21 December 1988).

37. See Kestutis Girnius, "Dispute over Education between Lithuania and Moscow," *Report on the USSR* Vol. 1, No. 6 (10 February 1989): pp. 13–16.

38. See the roundtable discussion "SSSR–Nash obshchii dom." *Pravda* (2 November 1988).

39. The conclusions of these studies were contained in the programs of the popular fronts in the Baltic republics. See, for instance, the "Program of the Estonian Popular Front," in *Molodoezh Estonii* (19 August 1988). Also see "A General Model for Restructuring Economic Management of the Latvian SSR." *Sovetskaia molodezh* (Riga) (7 September 1988).

40. See the roundtable discussion "SSSR–Nash obshchii dom," *Pravda* (2 November 1988).

41. *Sovetskaia Litva* (16 August 1988).

42. This was published in all the major newspapers in the USSR on 14 March 1989. It was titled "Obshchie printsipy perestroiki rukovodstva ekonomikoi i sotsial'noi sferoi v soiuznykh respublikakh na osnove rasshireniia ikh suverennykh prav, samoupravleniia i samofinansirovaniia."

43. V. Tomashkevich, "Kakoi zhe on–novyi oblik ministerstva?" *Ekonomicheskaia gazeta* No. 16 (1989): p. 12.

44. A. Kalnyn'sh, "Slyshat' drug druga," *Kommunist* No. 6 (April 1989): p. 62.

45. Viktoria V. Koroteeva, et al., "Ot biurokraticheskogo tsentralizma k ekonomicheskoi integratsii suverennykh respublik," *Kommunist* No. 8 (November 1988): pp. 22–33.

46. Boris V. Kravtsov, "Zakaz na zakon," *Ekonomicheskaia gazeta* No. 14 (March 1989): p. 2.

47. See I. Savelova, "Chto takoe spetsial'nye raiony," *Ekonomicheskaia gazeta* No. 9 (February 1989): p. 21. The proposal to set up enterprise zones in the Baltic regions has been, in fact, explicitly expressed as a possibility by Estonian officials. See "Conformist Communists Propose Turning Estonia into Closed Economic Zone," *Baltic Situation Report, Radio Free Europe Research* (28 October 1987).

48. See "O merakh gosudarstvennogo regulirovaniia vneshneekonomicheskoi deiatel'nosti" *Ekonomicheskaia gazeta* No. 13 (7 March 1989): p. 21.

49. Ann Sheehy, "Aleksandr Yakovlev Discusses Nationality Issues," *Radio Liberty Research Bulletin* RL 395/88 (31 August 1988).

50. Igor Griazin, as reported in *Daily Report: Soviet Union* (Washington, D.C.: Foreign Broadcast Information Service) FBIS-Sov-88-223.

51. *Sovetskaia Estoniia* (28 October 1988).

52. *Sovetksaia Estoniia* (17, 18, and 19 November 1988).

53. *Pravda* (18 November 1988).

54. *The New York Times* (28 November 1988).55. *The New York Times* (9 June 1989); *Izvestiia* (10 June 1989).

56. See, for instance, N. Mikhaleva and Sh. Papidze, "Federativnyi soiuz," *Pravda* (12 July 1989).

7

Epilogue

Show me a country without national problems and I will go there.
—Gorbachev

There is a certain historical irony in the fact that the flagship country of communism proclaims a federal order. Marx was critical of federal arrangements, insisting that the interests of the proletariat could best be served through a unitary government structure. Throughout most of his life, Lenin too was stridently opposed to federal arrangements, fearing their potential for abetting nationalism. After the dramatic events of 1917, however, Lenin's views on the subject changed rather remarkably. Political expediency convinced Lenin to reinterpret the principles of Marxism. He came to believe that only a federal solution for Russia's problems could prevent the dismemberment of the Tsarist empire. At Lenin's insistence, a form of federalism—socialist federalism—was adopted as one of the basic organizational principles of the union. That form of federalism endures until the present day.

Even when it is only a facade, a country's form of government is important. In the intellectual ferment of contemporary political reform in the USSR, articulate proponents of national minority groups are industriously striving to restore their national legacies and traditions, to fill in the amnesiac "blank spots" of Soviet history, to rekindle visions of their national futures, and to compel, insofar as that is possible, Soviet leaders to publicly and explicitly state the principles of "Leninist nationality policy," which are said to guide public policy in the Soviet multinational state. In this atmosphere of political change, proponents of republican rights often appeal to the doctrinal sources of Soviet socialist federalism. The formal constitutional guarantees—so long meaningless in practice—have become charged with symbolic significance. Beyond the symbolism, one senses an expectation that promises repeated frequently and loudly enough eventually will be honored. It is, after all, a tenet of Marxist thought that incremental quantitative changes combine, ultimately, to produce a qualitative change.

For these reasons, contemporary discussions of nationality policy in the USSR repeatedly return to Leninism, to the formative period of the Soviet federal state, and to an analysis of what went wrong. Understandably, the interested parties in these discussions often have a favored interpretation of why the ethnic groups of the USSR are officially recognized as "nations," of what "national statehood" should imply, or of the extent to which local political institutions should be empowered. An accurate reading of the current contest over republican rights in the USSR requires a knowledge of Soviet federal development. Such is the motivation of this book. It offers an analysis of the original terms of the "federal contract" in the USSR and an interpretation of the changes that have taken place in doctrine and practice regarding the status and function of the Soviet republics throughout the Soviet period.

The argument of the book is straightforward. The federal structure of the USSR arose out of an attempt by Lenin to satisfy two opposing goals. He sought to grant symbolic concessions to nationalist sentiment in the former Tsarist colonies while simultaneously establishing the conditions for the creation of a strong, centralized state apparatus. The federal structure adopted in 1918 was seen by Lenin as a "transitional" form of government, one which would ultimately give way to a unitary political organization. Local leaders naturally favored an arrangement which appeared to offer them local control. Hence, a tactical alliance of local and central officials, each with quite different objectives, coalesced in support of the creation of a socialist federal state.

Given the divergence of interests in the original compromise of the Soviet federal order, there were many possibilities. Which way would it go? Would the system follow Lenin's logic toward greater unity, or would the nationality-based territorial units overwhelm the center with demands for recognition of the Soviet state's multinational and regionally disparate heterogeneity? As we have seen in the preceding chapters of this book, by the latter part of the century both groups could claim partial success. The Soviet central government created a tightly centralized party-government structure. At the same time, the "national-territorial" principle, adopted as a temporary compromise, proved enduring. Despite the centralizing influence of the planned economy, the politically centralizing influence of the monoparty state, and the practice of more than seven decades of socialism, national identity remained strong in the USSR. The grouping of ethnically compact groups into territorial entities called union republics gave sanction to the feelings of national statehood. Efforts to "nativize" the political and administrative mechanisms of the republics further reinforced the proprietary sense of republican identity.

Political leaders drawn from the national groups saw it in their interest to encourage a "national climate" in the republics. National identity, ethno-national compactness, nativized administrative institutions, and national leadership sustained the vitality of national statehood in the contemporary USSR. These are the ingredients in the struggle for republican rights in the USSR.

By the early 1980s, with the end of the Brezhnev *zastoi* period, the bureaucratic structures within the fifteen national republics of the USSR had developed an unprecedented basis of internal political resourceful-ness. The intensity and breadth of these local political resources varied widely from republic to republic, region to region, and national minority to national minority. Despite variations, it was by means of these resources that the formal bureaucratic organizations of the national constituent republics gradually altered the terms of the federal contract in the USSR. In a system as highly bureaucratized as that of the USSR, control over the implementation of policy *is* control over policy. In the national minority areas, policy is implemented by national minorities. The efforts of the minority populations, working within the nativized bureaucracies, to develop self-protective tactical responses to central policy have grad-ually had the cumulative effect of reinforcing the segmented "federal" nature of the Soviet state. Federalism and nationalism in the USSR are mutually reinforcing.

This book argues that, considered cumulatively, these self-protective and self-promoting strategies on the part of local elites, intelligentsias, and indigenous bureaucracies have combined with social and economic changes—and now have been given additional momentum by *peres-troika*—to augment the *de jure* federalism proclaimed in the Soviet constitutional order. Manifestations of "bureaucratic nationalism" have produced a form of federalism based in the numerous disjunctions between central administrative institutions and the subordinate branches in the national federal republics. The proprietary attitude of local officials within the national minority republics has resulted in what may be termed "national federalism." Only a few years ago such an interpretation of Soviet internal political development was dismissed by many if not most Western observers. After the events of 1988, including an Armenian uprising, an open constitutional challenge from Estonia, and a political reform introduced by central officials, the existence of bureaucratic nationalism can no longer be seriously questioned. But to understand the dynamics of the contest for republican rights in the USSR, we must understand the unusual etiology of "Soviet federalism."

Of the major countries in the Communist world, only two, the USSR and Yugoslavia, are constitutionally organized in accordance with the federal principle. The USSR and Yugoslavia are quite different cases and we should not draw too heavily on circumstantial similarities. Yet, since Yugoslavia has been less resistant to change than the USSR, its political development may suggest some of the underlying dynamics of multinational socialist federalism and point toward challenges that the USSR eventually must confront. In recent years the relations among Yugoslavia's component republics have evolved in the direction of increased regional autonomy and power. As Milovan Djilas observed, the republics have, to all intents and purposes, acquired "confederation status." The party retained a monopoly on symbolic power, but in terms of the rough-and-tumble of everyday politics, "most political decision-making is now taking place in the republics' capitals."[1]

Is the emergence of a "Soviet confederation" even possible? What tendencies does Soviet style federalism hold for the future? Trend is not destiny. But, if the stages of political maturation through which other societies have passed are any guide to the Soviet future, a few observations may be made. The contest over republican rights in the USSR has moved out of its "symbolic" phase. These battles have largely been won and lost. In the coming stages of conflict we can expect the disagreements and compromises to center on two things: (1) financial control of the republican economies and (2) the adoption of a new formula for the advancement of the national minorities. Recent dialogue in the Soviet press has focused precisely on these issues.[2]

The struggle over republican rights in the USSR is part of a larger, perhaps universal, struggle for control over financial resources between center and periphery. The contest involves not only the structurally determined dynamics of heartland and hinterland, but also a specific mix of historical and cultural factors in the very unique Soviet case. When we speak of republican "sovereignty" we are dealing with a concept which is comparative in scope and must be understood in terms of the peculiar features of the Soviet system. In that system, sovereignty is defined in terms of the ability of the republic to exercise its prerogatives by means of generating its own sources of revenue. All-union ministries have historically controlled a preponderant share of economic activity in the republics and, accordingly, have had a proportional influence over republican budgetary incomes and expenditures. State revenues were provided through a "turnover tax" on the production of goods and services. Built into the pricing system itself, these turnover taxes left the establishment of the terms of trade among republics in the hands of Moscow officials.

Control over incomes was a key "lever" of Soviet nationality policy. Brezhnev, for instance, was fond of speaking of "Leninist nationality policy" as being carried out in the language of economics. Given the regime's commitment to ethnic egalitarianism, however, questions of fiscal federalism were seldom directly addressed for fear of "sowing enmity" among nations of the "Soviet fraternity." For decades the protectors of vested bureaucratic interests at the center chilled any meaningful public discussion of the valuation of "material balances" between and among republics. Subdued discussion which did take place within the bureaucracies was dominated by imprecision and uncertainty. In the days before glasnost, accurate assessments of the actual terms of trade in the administered economy, with its disguised scarcities and valuations, were easily concealed. As an article in the Communist party theoretical journal *Kommunist* noted, "at the present time there is no information as to what and how much the republics contribute to the all-union fund and what and how much they receive from it."[3] Only in 1988 did the issue of terms of trade emerge dramatically from behind the cloak of censorship to become one of the most contentious issues in contemporary Soviet politics. Placed on the public agenda thanks to a study of economists from the Estonian Academy of Sciences in the summer of 1988, the notion of republic level *"khozraschet"* (financial accountability) quickly became one of the more politically charged issues of open debate in the USSR. The issue resonated in many of the presentations to the Congress of People's Deputies in 1989. The Soviet of Nationalities of the USSR Supreme Soviet later established a number of special commissions which took up the questions of *"khozraschet."* The chairman of the commission on social and economic development, Eduardas Vilkas, noted that he intended to concentrate the attention of the commission on the problem of republican level *khozraschet.*[4]

It is an axiom of comparative political studies that the process of nation building is a process of assimilation of peripheral groups into the political culture of the dominant group. Cultural assimilation takes place through centralization. The increasing capacity of states in the nineteenth and twentieth centuries to carry out centralization is the result of the technological changes which have reduced the historical barriers to transportation and communication. The process of techno-logical change is naturally regarded as placing greater power in the hands of those who manage the centralized state. Samuel Beer has proposed a "modernization hypothesis," noting that, while the balance of power in federal situations shifts over time, the drift of power accumulation is toward the political culture of the center. Beer noted that "In the United States, as in the other modernizing societies, the general historical record has spelled centralization. . . . The main reasons for this change are . . . to be found . . . in the new forces produced by an advanced modernity."[5]

If states are engaged in this historic "drift toward the center," how will the national minorities maintain their identity? Is there a formula for national self-advancement which does not entail, ultimately, the dissolution and disappearance of the national minority communities? As we have seen, Soviet leaders from Lenin to Gorbachev have proclaimed themselves to be in favor, if only temporarily, of the continued development of the national minority communities. Yet, Soviet leaders have never publicly adopted a principle of coalition politics, affirmed meaningful autonomy on the part of a constituent republic, proclaimed a policy of "arithmetic" proportional representation, or granted veto power to a national minority. What is known as "Leninist nationality policy" is essentially a policy of cultural assimilationism: it is a conscious attempt to institutionalize Beer's "logic of modernity." The comparison is sometimes made with the dominant ethos of the United States. But in the USSR there is none of the overarching "melting pot" sentiment, no impersonal economic forces to facelessly deprive people of their cultural traditions, no huddled multitude of immigrants willing, even anxious, to forget the travail of the Old World in favor of the promises of the new. In the USSR, the national minorities do not want to abandon their old identities.

A century ago, Russia was the last European country to support autocratic rule. When social and economic changes had undermined all support for that rule, the solution Russia found was not to liberalize but to create a new form of authoritarian rule. In similar fashion, the fissiparous pressures of multinationalism may engender a new and more resilient centrism rather than a polycultural federalism. But this does not have to happen. Much will depend upon the skill of political leaders at the center and in the peripheries as the new formula for nationality policy emerges. As it does, the centralizing policies radiating from Moscow will no doubt continue to be cast in the form of a "Leninist nationality policy." When the long-awaited outlines of the "Nationality Policy of the Party in Contemporary Circumstances" appeared on the pages of *Pravda* in August 1989, the document spoke of "revolutionary renewal" but relied upon the principles articulated in the resolution on interethnic relations passed by the 19th Party Conference.[6] Would these old formulas meet the challenges of the times ahead? Many within the USSR believed that they would not.[7]

The CPSU Central Committee approved the party "platform" on nationality policy the following September. The platform spoke of the legacy of the Stalin and Brezhnev periods in terms of "deformations" in Soviet society. It accused the "administrative-command" system of ushering in extreme centralization, of creating a hierarchical "branch" form of bureaucratism, and of eventually neutralizing the rights of the republics. Without legal and institutional protection, many minority peoples could not defend themselves against the inroads of the center.

They became victims of repression, deportation, and Russification. Migration brought on new problems, exacerbating the inevitable conflict between the maintenance of national self-identity and the process of modernization. The platform pledged changes to rectify the situation through strengthening the federal principle, expanding the rights of republics, defending the rights of the nationalities without republican status, protecting all the indigenous languages, providing new legal protections against discrimination, renewing public education and ideological efforts, and emphasizing the principle of mutual respect among nationalities.

The platform is to be applauded for its candid and realistic acknowledgment of the problems of the past. Of course, the current leadership has an interest in discrediting its predecessors. For this reason alone, the document cannot be isolated from this political context. Nevertheless, such candor must be the first step in shaping new policies. Will it provide a successful formula for the future? The verdict of this book is that Soviet national federalism has not produced a mobilizational conduit for political loyalties, shifting them first from ethnic group to republic, then from republic to the union, then from union to the larger internationalist community of man. On the contrary, Soviet national federalism has resulted in divided loyalties. In precisely this way, Soviet federalism has become an instrument by which ethnic identities are reinforced, aspirations for collective ethnic advancement are encouraged, and the visions of minority national futures are legitimized. Since it is the Soviet system which has created it, this process will also no doubt continue. As it does, the formula for achieving "unity in diversity" will be increasingly complex. When the latent forces of nationalism coalesce as they recently have in violent outbreaks around the USSR, they do so at least in part as a consequence of conditions which Soviet socialism itself has created and encouraged.

Notes

1. *New York Times* (23 November 1983).
2. See N. Mikhaleva and Sh. Papidze, "Federativnyi soiuz," *Pravda* (12 July 1989) and Iulii Bromlei "Federatsiia ili konfederatsiia?" *Pravda* (7 August 1989).
3. Viktoria Koroteeva, et al., "Ot biurokraticheskogo tsentralizma k ekonomicheskoi integratsii suverennykh respublik," *Kommunist* No. 15 (1988): p. 26. In 1989, *Kommunist* began a series of articles on the subject of regional *khozraschet* under the rubric "Toward the CC CPSU Plenum on the Strengthening of Interethnic Relations in the USSR." See especially S. Cheshko, "Ekonomicheskii suverenitet i natsional'nyi vopros," *Kommunist*, No. 2 (1989): pp. 97–105; M. Bronshtein , "Regional'nyi khozraschet: nuzhny trezvost' i dokazatel'nost'," *Kommunist* No. 5 (1989), pp. 60–64.

4. Andrei Borodenkov, "Priority—Republican Cost Accounting," *Moscow News* No. 26 (July 1989): p. 9.

5. Samuel Beer, "The Modernization of American Federalism," *Publius* Vol. 3 (February 1973): p. 73.

6. "Natsional'naia politika partii v sovremennykh usloviiakh," *Pravda* (17 August 1989).

7. M. Marchenko, "Nuzhen zakon o federatsii," *Pravda* (20 August 1989).

Appendix

Table 1
Population and Territory of the USSR and the National Republics, January 1989

	Population	Territory (1000 square kilometers)
USSR	286,717	22,402
RSFSR	147,386	17,075
Ukrainian SSRR	51,704	603
Belorussian SSR	10,200	207
Uzbek SSR	19,906	447
Kazakh SSR	1,653	2,717
Georgian SSR	5,449	69
Azerbaidzhan SSR	7,029	86
Lithuanian SSR	3,690	65
Moldavian SSR	4,341	33
Latvian SSR	2,681	63
Kirgiz SSR	4,291	198
Tadzhik SSR	5,112	143
Armenian SSR	3,283	29
Turkmen SSR	3,534	488
Estonian SSR	1,573	45

Source: *Narodnoe khoziaistvo SSSR v 1985*, pp. 12-17. The 1989 population figures are from *Trud* (30 April 1989).

Table 2
Rate of Growth of Population by Republic, 1913-1989
(selected years; percent change)

	1913-87	1950-59	1959-70	1970-79	1979-89
USSR	65	17	16	9	9
RSFSR	53	16	11	6	7
Ukrainian SSR	41	15	13	6	4
Belorussian SSR	39	5	12	6	7
Uzbek SSR	255	30	45	30	29
Kazakh SSR	162	43	40	3	13
Georgian SSR	93	16	16	7	9
Azerbaidzhan SSR	158	30	39	18	17
Lithuanian SSR	20	5	15	9	9
Moldavian SSR	92	26	24	11	10
Latvian SSR	1	8	13	7	6
Kirgiz SSR	308	20	42	20	22
Tadzhik SSR	268	31	46	31	34
Armenian SSR	203	31	41	21	8
Turkmen SSR	165	27	42	28	28
Estonian SSR	54	10	13	8	7

Sources: Viktor I. Kozlov. *Natsional'nosti SSSR: Etnodemograficheskii obzor*, 2nd ed. (Moscow: Finansy, 1982), p. 65, and *Narodnoe khoziaistvo SSSR v 1986* (Moscow: Finansy i statistiki, 1987).

Table 3
First Secretaries of the Republican Party Organizations, November 1988

	Name	Date of Appointment
RSFSR	n/a	n/a
Ukrainian SSR	Vladimir V. Shcherbitskii	2/72
Belorussian SSR	Efrem E. Sokolov	2/87
Uzbek SSR	Rafik N. Nishanov	1/88
Kazakh SSR	Gennadii V. Kolbin	12/86
Georgian SSR	Dzhumber I. Patiashvili	6/85
Azerbaidzhan SSR	Abdul-Rakhman K. Vezirov	6/88
Lithuanian SSR	Al'girdas M. Brazauskas	10/88
Moldavian SSR	Semen K. Grossu	12/80
Latvian SSR	Ian Ia. Vagris	10/88
Kirgiz SSR	Absamat M. Masaliev	11/85
Tadzhik SSR	Kakhar Makhkamov	12/85
Armenian SSR	Suren G. Arutiunian	6/88
Turkmen SSR	Saparmurad A. Niazov	12/85
Estonian SSR	Vaino I. Vialias	2/87

Source: Author's files.

Table 4
Chairmen of the Presidia of the Councils of Ministers of the Republics, November 1988

	Name	Date of Appointment
RSFSR	Aleksandr V. Vlasov	10/88
Ukrainian SSR	Vitalii A. Masol	7/87
Belorussian SSR	Mikhail V. Kovalev	2/82
Uzbek SSR	Gairat Kh. Kadyrov	11/84
Kazakh SSR	Nursultan A. Nazarbaev	3/84
Georgian SSR	Otar E. Cherkeziia	4/86
Azerbaidzhan SSR	Hasan N. Seidov-ogly	1/81
Lithuanian SSR	Vitautas V. Sakalauskas	11/85
Moldavian SSR	Ivan P. Kalin	12/85
Latvian SSR	Vilnis-Edvins Bresis	6/88
Kirgiz SSR	Apas Dzh. Dzhumagulov	5/86
Tadzhik SSR	Izatullo Kh. Khaeev	1/86
Armenian SSR	Fadei T. Sarkisian	1/77
Turkmen SSR	Annamurad Kh. Khodzhamuradov	1/86
Estonian SSR	Bruno E. Saul	1/84

Source: Author's files.

Table 5
Proportion of Urban Population by Republic, 1913-1989
(selected years)

	1913	1939	1959	1970	1979	1989
USSR	18	32	48	56	62	66
RSFSR	17	33	52	62	69	74
Ukrainian SSR	19	34	46	55	61	67
Belorussian SSR	14	21	31	43	55	65
Uzbek SSR	24	23	34	37	41	41
Kazakh SSR	10	28	44	50	54	57
Georgian SSR	26	30	42	48	52	56
Azerbaidzhan SSR	24	36	48	50	53	54
Lithuanian SSR	13	23	39	50	61	68
Moldavian SSR	13	13	22	32	39	47
Latvian SSR	38	35	56	62	68	71
Kirgiz SSR	12	19	34	37	39	38
Tadzhik SSR	9	17	33	37	35	33
Armenian SSR	10	29	50	59	66	68
Turkmen SSR	11	33	46	48	48	45
Estonian SSR	19	34	56	65	70	72

Sources: Viktor I. Kozlov, *Natsional'nosti SSSR: Etnodemograficheskii obzor,* 2nd ed. (Moscow: Finansy, 1982), p. 80, and *Narodnoe khoziaistvo SSSR v 1986* (Moscow: Finansy i statistiki, 1987).

Table 6
Average Annual Number of Industrial and Service Workers by Republic,
1940-1985 (selected years; in thousands)

	1940	1960	1970	1980	1985
USSR	33,926	62,032	90,186	112,498	117,798
RSFSR	22,173	39,505	54,376	65,612	67,641
Ukrainian SSR	6,578	10,659	16,200	20,042	20,679
Belorussian SSR	1,136	1,887	3,075	4,046	4,271
Uzbek SSR	756	1,530	2,642	4,169	4,834
Kazakh SSR	917	2,977	4,692	6,043	6,500
Georgian SSR	494	940	1,490	1,978	2,178
Azerbaidzhan SSR	486	748	1,273	1,802	2,058
Lithuanian SSR	179	674	1,166	1,461	1,563
Moldavian SSR	101	439	944	1,511	1,610
Latvian SSR	262	725	1,033	1,202	1,231
Kirgiz SSR	175	434	780	1,102	1,239
Tadzhik SSR	149	320	586	927	1,101
Armenian SSR	156	427	838	1,192	1,355
Turkmen SSR	188	314	478	711	811
Estonian SSR	176	453	613	700	718

Source: *Narodnoe khoziaistvo SSSR v 1985*, p. 393.

Table 7
Labor Force* and Administrative Cadres (Apparat)** by Republic, 1960-1984 (selected years; in thousands)

	1960	1970	1975	1980	1984
USSR	62,032.0	90,186.0	n/a	112,498.0	117,798.0
RSFSR	n/a	n/a	n/a	n/a	n/a
Ukrainian SSR	10,659.0	16,200.0	18,356.0	20,042.0	20,540.0
apparat	n/a	1.9	2.1	2.3	2.4
Belorussian SSR	3,156.0	4,103.0	4,505.0	4,826.0	4,974.0
apparat	n/a	n/a	n/a	n/a	n/a
Uzbek SSR	1,529.8.0	2.641.5	3,343.0	4,168.7	4,759.7
apparat	1.8.0	2.1	2.1	2.2	2.1
Kazakh SSR	2,977.0	4,692.0	5,375.0	6,043.0	6,424.0
apparat	2.6	2.8	2.9	2.9	2.9
Georgian SSR	940.0	1,490.0	1,733.0	1,978.0	2,130.0
apparat	2.0	2.0	2.0	3.0	3.0
Azerbaidzhan SSR	n/a	n/a	1,798.0	2,090.0	2,306.0
apparat	n/a	n/a	n/a	n/a	n/a
Lithuanian SSR	179.0	674.0	1,166.0	1,461.0	1,563.0
apparat	n/a	n/a	3.8	4.3	4.6
Moldavian SSR	439.0	944.0	1,251.0	1,511.0	1,610.0
apparat	1.2	1.7	1.9	2.0	2.1
Latvian SSR	725.0	1,033.0	1,127.0	1,202.0	n/a
apparat	2.0	3.0	3.0	3.0	n/a
Kirgiz SSR	n/a	n/a	n/a	1,101.6	1,215.2
apparat	n/a	3.2	n/a	3.2	3.2
Tadzhik SSR	320.0	586.0	n/a	927.0	1,063.0
apparat	3.0	3.0	n/a	3.0	3.0
Armenian SSR	426.7	837.9	991.4	11,191.7	1,310.0
apparat	n/a	n/a	n/a	n/a	n/a
Turkmen SSR	313.5	478.3	574.0	711.6	797.0
apparat	n/a	2.9	3.1	3.1	3.0
Estonian SSR	453.1	613.3	658.6	699.8	716.1
apparat	2.7	2.8	n/a	3.1	3.1

* "Labor" is defined as workers (rabochie) and service personnel (sluzhashchie).

** "Administrative cadres" (apparat) are defined as: "numbers of persons in the apparatus of organs of goverment management, organs of management of the cooperative and social organizations, in credit and government insurance." It is not possible to determine from Soviet sources whether this is intended to include Party personnel who hold dual positions in government and party organizations.

Sources: *Narodnoe khoziaistvo SSSR v 1985*, p. 393 (see table 4); *Narodnoe khoziaistvo Ukrainskoi SSR, 1984*, pp. 252-254; *Narodnoe khoziaistvo Belorusskoi SSR, 1985*, p. 137; *Narodnoe khoziaistvo Uzbekskoi SSR, 1985*, pp. 224-226; *Narodnoe khoziaistvo Kazakhskoi SSR, 1984*, pp. 172-175; *Narodnoe khoziaistvo Gruzinskoi SSR, 1984*, pp. 163-165; *Narodnoe khoziaistvo Azerbaidzhanskoi SSR, 1984*, pp. 143-145; *Narodnoe khoziaistvo Litovskoi SSR, 1984*, pp. 141-143; *Narodnoe khoziaistvo Moldavskoi SSR, 1984*, pp. 182-184; *Narodnoe khoziaistvo Latvizhskoi SSR, 1984*, pp. 208-210; *Narodnoe khoziaistvo Kirgizskoi SSR, 1984*, pp. 142-144; *Narodnoe khoziaistvo Tadzhikskoi SSR, 1984*, pp. 184-185; *Narodnoe khoziaistvo Armianskoi SSR, 1984*, pp. 211-213; *Turkmenistan v tsifrakh, 1984*, pp. 57-70: *Narodnoe khoziaistvo Estonskoi SSR, 1984*, pp. 143-144.

Table 8
Scientific Cadres in the USSR and Union Republics, 1985
(In thousands)

	Total	Ph.D. Cand.	Ph.D.
USSR	1,491.3	44.3	463.5
RSFSR	1,019.1	30.2	299.0
Ukrainian SSR	210.3	5.9	68.5
Belorussian SSR	42.4	1.0	13.2
Uzbek SSR	38.1	1.2	15.7
Kazakh SSR	40.4	0.9	1.8
Georgian SSR	27.6	1.4	10.7
Azerbaidzahn SSR	27.6	1.4	10.7
Lithuanian SSR	23.2	1.0	9.3
Moldavian SSR	14.8	0.5	6.0
Latvian SSR	13.5	0.4	4.7
Kirgiz SSR	9.1	0.2	3.1
Tadzhik SSR	8.4	0.2	3.1
Armenian SSR	21.5	0.7	6.7
Turkmen SSR	5.6	0.1	2.4
Estonian SSR	7.0	0.3	3.0

Source: *Narodnoe khoziaistvo SSSR v 1985*, p. 65.

Select Bibliography

Abramovich, A.M. *Konstitutsiia SSSR–voploshchenie leninskoi natsional'noi politiki*. Moscow: Nauka i Tekhnika, 1987.

Agamkhodzhaev, A. *Obrazovanie i razvitie Uzbekskoi SSR*. Tashkent: Fan, 1971.

Agamkhodzhaev, A. and Sh. Urazaev. *SSSR–sotsialisticheskoe gosudarstvo sovetskikh narodov*. Tashkent: Fan, 1972.

———. "Natsional'no-gosudarstvennomu razmezhevaniiu respublik Sovetskoi Srednei Azii—60 let." *Sovetskoe gosudarstvo i pravo* No. 10 (1984): 25–33.

Aivazian, N.A. *Kompetentsiia soiuznoi respubliki i konstitutsionnyi mekhanizm*. Erevan: Erevanskogo Universiteta, 1985.

Agursky, Mikhail. *The Third Rome: National Bolshevism in the USSR*. Boulder, Westview, 1987.

Alekhin, A.P. *Pravovoe polozhenie ministerstv SSSR*. Moscow: Iuridicheskaia literatura, 1971.

Alexeyeva, Ludmilla. *Soviet Dissent: Contemporary Movements for National, Religious, and Human Rights*. Middletown, CT: Wesleyan University Press, 1985.

Allworth, Edward, ed., *Soviet Nationality Problems*. New York: Columbia University Press, 1971.

———. *The Nationality Question in Soviet Central Asia*. New York: Praeger, 1973.

———, ed., *Ethnic Russia in the USSR: the Dilemma of Dominance*. New York: Pergamon, 1980.

Ananov, I.N. *Sistema organov gosudarstvennogo upravleniia v sovetskoi sotsialisticheskoi federatsii*. Moscow, 1951.

———. *Ministerstva v SSSR*. Moscow: Gosiurizdat, 1960.

Anderson, Barbara A. and Brian D. Silver. "Equality, Efficiency, and Politics in Soviet Bilingual Education Policy." *American Political Science Review* 78, No. 4 (1984): 1019–1039.

Armstrong, John A. *Ukrainian nationalism, 1939–1945*. New York: Columbia University Press, 1955.

———. "Federalism in the USSR: Ethnic and Territorial Aspects." *Publius* 7, No. 4 (1977): 89–105.

———. *Nations before Nationalism*, Chapel Hill: The University of North Carolina Press, 1982.

Arutiunian, Iu.V. "Natsional'nye osobennosti sotsial'nogo razvitiia." *Sotsiologicheskie issledovaniia* No. 2 (1985): 28–35.

Arzhanov, M.A. *Teoriia gosudarstva i prava*. Moscow: Gosiurizdat, 1949.

Aspaturian, Vernon V. "Theory and Practice of Soviet Federalism." *Journal of Politics* 12, No. 1 (1950): 20–51.

_____. *Process and Power in Soviet Foreign Policy.* Boston: Little, Brown and Company, 1971.

Aver'ianov, V.B. *Organazatsiia apparata gosudarstvennogo upravleniia (strukturno-funktsional'nye aspekt).* Kiev: Naukova Dumka, 1985.

Azrael, Jeremy R., ed., *Soviet Nationality Policies and Practices.* New York: Praeger, 1978.

Bachilo, I.L. *Sluzhashchii sovestskogo gosudarstvennogo apparata.* Moscow: Iurizdat, 1970.

Bahry, Donna. *Outside Moscow: Power, Politics, and Budgetary Policy in the Soviet Republics.* New York: Columbia University Press, 1987.

Baimakhanov, M.T. *Konstitutsionnye osnovy statusa soiuznoi respubliki.* Alma-Ata: Nauka, 1985.

Bairiev, B.S.and A.V. Abal'ian. "Nauchnye osnovy razvitiia i sovershenstvovaniia organizatsionnoi struktury upravleniia narodnym khoziaistvom soiuznoi respubliki." *Izvestiia AN TuSSR20* No. 1 (1986): 19–25.

Banac, Ivo. *The National Question in Yugoslavia: Origins, History, Politics.* Ithaca: Cornell University Press, 1984.

Bandera, V.N. and Z.L. Melnyk, eds., *The Soviet Economy in Regional Perspective.* New York: Preager, 1973.

Barabashev, G.V. and K.F. Sheremet. "KPSS i sovety." *Sovetskoe gosudarstvo i pravo* No. 11 (1967): 31–41.

Barghoorn, Frederick C. *Soviet Russian Nationalism.* Westport, Connecticut, 1976.

Barry, Donald D., F.J.M. Feldbrugge, George Ginsburgs, and Peter Maggs, eds. *Soviet Law After Stalin: Part III, Soviet Institutions and the Administration of Law.* Alphen aan den Rijn, The Netherlands: Sijthoff and Noordhoff, 1979.

Bauer, O. *Natsional'nyi vopros i sotsial-demokratiia.* Petrograd, 1918.

Belousov, I.I. *Osnovy ucheniia ob ekonomicheskom raionirovanii.* Moscow: Izdatelstvo Moskovskogo Universiteta, 1976.

Bennigsen, Alexandre and S. Quelquejay. *The Evolution of the Muslim Nationalities of the USSR and their Linguistic Problems.* London: Central Asian Research Centre, 1961.

_____ and S. Enders Wimbush. *Muslim National Communism in the Soviet Union: A Revolutionary Strategy for the Colonial World.* Chicago: The University of Chicago Press, 1979.

Berger, Ia.M. and E.V. Tadevosian. *Sovetskii narod–novaia istoricheskaia obshchnost liudei.* Moscow: Akademiia Nauk SSSR, 1980.

von Beyme, Klaus. *Federalism in the Soviet Union* Heidelberg: Quelle & Meyer, 1964.

Bialer, Seweryn. *Stalin's Successors: Leadership, Stability, and Change in the Soviet Union.* New York: Cambridge University Press, 1980.

_____, ed., *Politics, Society, and Nationality Inside Gorbachev's Russia.* Boulder: Westview Press, 1989.

Biddulph, Howard. "Local Interest Articulation at CPSU Congresses." *World Politics* 36, No. 1 (1983): 28–52.

Bielasiak, Jack. "Policy Choices and Regional Equality Aming Soviet Republics." *American Political Science Review* 74, No. 2 (1980).

Bilmanis, Alfred. *A History of Latvia*. Westport, CN: Greenwood Press, 1970.

Bisher, I.D. "Ministerstva soiuznykh respublik: Nazrevshie problemy." *Sovetskoe gosudarstvo i pravo* No. 5 (1973): 28–35.

Blaustein, Albert P. and Gisbert H. Flanz. *Constitutions of the Countries of the World*. Dobbs Ferry, NY: Oceana Publications, date varies.

Bloembergen, Samuel. "The Union Republics: How Much Autonomy." *Problems of Communism* No. 16 (1967): 27–35.

Blough, Roger A. and Philip D. Stewart. "Political Obstacles to Reform and Innovation in Soviet Economic Policy." *Comparative Political Studies* 20, No. 1 (1987): 72–97.

Bondarskaia, Galina, A. *Rozhdaemost' v SSSR: Etnodemograficheskii aspekt*. Moscow: Statistika, 1977.

Boroshchevskii, L.M. "Prerdacha prav vyshestoiashchikh organov upravleniia nizhestoiashchim." *Sovetskoe gosudarstvo i pravo* No. 8 (1969): 58–63.

Borys, Jurij. *The Sovietization of Ukraine, 1917–1923*. Edmonton: The Canadian Institute of Ukrainian Studies, 1989.

Breslauer, George. *Khrushchev and Brezhnev as Leaders: Building Authority in Soviet Politics*. London: Allen and Unwin, 1982.

_____ . "Is There a Generation Gap in the Soviet Political Establishment? Demand Articulation by RSFSR Provincial Party First Secretaries." *Soviet Studies* 36, No. 1 (1984): 1–25.

Breuilly, John. *Nationalism and the State*. New York: St. Martin's Press, 1984.

Brezhnev, L.I. *Ob osnovnykh voprosakh ekonomicheskoi politiki KPSS na sovremenom etape*. Moscow: Politizdat, 1979.

_____ . *Aktual'nye voprosy ideologicheskoi raboty*. 2 Vols. Moscow: Politizdat, 1979.

Bromlei, Iulii. *Sovremennye etnicheskie protsessy v SSSR*. Moscow: Nauka, 1975.

_____ . "Sovershenstvovanie natsional'nykh otnoshenii v SSSR." *Kommunist* No. 8 (1986): 79–86.

Brown, Archie. "The Soviet Leadership and the Struggle for Political Reform." *The Harriman Institute Forum* 1, No. 4 (April), 1988.

Bruchis, Michael. *The USSR: Language and Realities* Boulder: East European Monographs, 1988.

Bunce, Valerie. 1979. "Leadership Succession and Policy Innovation in the Soviet Republics." *Comparative Politics* 11, No. 4 (1979): 379–402.

Burg, Steven L. "Muslim Cadres and Soviet Political Development." *World Politics* 37, No. 1 (1984): 24–47.

Burkhanova, L.M. "Voprosy federatsii i sovetskogo natsional'no-gosudarstvennogo stroitel'stva v programmakh KPSS." *Obshchestvennye nauki v Uzbekistane* No. 5 (1986): 3–14.

Burlatskii, Fedor. "Razgovor nachistotu." *Literaturnaia gazeta* 40 (1986).

Carr, Edward H. *The Future of Nations: Independence or Interdependence*. London: Macmillan, 1941.

_____ . *Nationalism and After*. London: Macmillan, 1945.

_____ . *The Bolshevik Revolution, 1917–1923*. 3 Vols. London: Penguin, 1971.

Cattell, David. "Local Government and the Sovnarkhoz Reform in the USSR." *Soviet Studies* 15, No. 4 (1964): 430–442.

Chikhvadze, V.M. *Natsional'nye otnosheniia i gosudarstvo v sovremennyi period.* Moscow: Nauka, 1972.

Chirkin, V.E. *Forma sotsialisticheskogo gosudarstva.* Moscow: Iuridicheskaia literatura, 1973.

Chistiakov, O.I. "Razvitie federativnykh otnoshenii mezhdu USSR i RSFSR (1917–1922 gg)." *Sovetskoe gosudarstvo i pravo* No. 2 (1954): 14–25.

———. *Stanovlenie rossiiskoi federatsii (1917–1922).* Moscow: Izdatelstvo Moskovskogo universiteta, 1966.

Chotiner, Barbara Ann. *Khrushchev's Party Reform.* Westport: Greenwood Press, 1984.

Chugaev, D.A. *Obrazovanie soiuza sovetskikh sotsialisticheskikh respublik.* Moscow, 1951.

———. *Lenin–osnovatel' Sovetskogo mnogonatsional'nogo gosudarstva.* Moscow, 1960.

Clem, Ralph S. *Research Guide to the Russian and Soviet Censuses.* Ithaca: Cornell University Press, 1988.

Colton, Timothy. "Approaches to the Politics of Systemic Economic Reform in the Soviet Union." *Soviet Economy* 3, No. 2 (1987): 145–170.

Connor, Walker. "Eco- or Ethno-nationalism?." *Ethnic and Racial Studies* 7, No. 3 (1984): 342–359.

———. *The National Question in Marxist-Leninist Theory and Strategy.* Princeton: Princeton University Press, 1984.

Conquest, Robert. *Soviet Nationality Policy in Practice.* New York: Frederick A. Praeger, 1967.

Crozier, Michael. *The Bureaucratic Phenomenon.* Chicago: University of Chicago Press, 1966.

Davies, R.W. *The Development of the Soviet Budgetary System.* Cambridge: Cambridge University Press, 1958.

Davis, Horace B. *Nationalism and Socialism: Marxist and Labor Theories of Nationalism to 1917.* New York: Monthly Review Press, 1967.

———, ed., *The National Question: Selected Writings by Rosa Luxemburg.* New York: Monthly Review, 1969.

Davitnidze, I.L. *Kolegii Ministerstv.* Moscow: Iuridicheskaia literatura, 1972.

Dekrety Sovetskoi vlasti. Moscow: Politizdat, 1957.

Dellenbrandt, Jan Ake. *Soviet Regional Policy.* Stockholm: Almqvist and Wiksell, 1980.

D'Encausse, Hélène Carrère. "Party and Federation in the USSR: the Problem of the Nationalities and Power." *Government and Opposition* 13, No. 2 (1978): 133–150.

———. *Decline of an Empire: The Soviet Socialist Republics in Revolt.* New York: Newsweek, 1979.

Deutsch, Karl W. *Nationalism and Social Communication: An Inquiry into the Foundations of Nationality.* Cambridge: M.I.T. Press, 1966.

Diablo, V.K. "Otnoshenii suvereniteta Soiuza SSR i suverenitetov soiuznykh respublik." *Sovetskoe gosudarstvo i pravo* No. 2 (1987): 119–123.

Duchachek, Ivo. *Comparative Federalism: The Territorial Dimension of Politics.* New York: Holt, Rinehart and Winston, 1970.

Dunlop, John B. *The Faces of Contemporary Russian Nationalism*. Princeton: Princeton University Press, 1983.

————. "The Russian Nationalist Spectrum Today: Trends and Movements." *Canadian Review of Studies in Nationalism* 11, No. 1 (1984): 63–70.

————. *The New Russian Nationalism*. New York: Praeger, 1985.

Dyker, David. *The Process of Investment in the Soviet Union*. Cabridge: Cambridge University Press, 1983.

Dzhunusov, M.S. *Dve tendentsii sotsializma v natsional'nykh otnosheniiakh*. Tashkent: Fan, 1975.

Dzuba, Ivan. *Internationalism or Russification? A Study in the Soviet Nationalities Problem*. London: Weidenfeld and Nicolson, 1968).

Evdokimov, V. *Finansirovanie ministerstv, vedomstv, i sovnarkhozov*. Moscow: Gosfinizdat, 1962.

Farberov, N.P. "O nekotorykh spornykh voprosokh v teorii sovetskogo gosudarstvennogo prava." *Sovetskoe gosudarstvo i pravo* No. 9 (1961).

Fedorenko, N.P. *Kompleksnoe narodnokhoziaistvennoe planirovanie*. Moscow: Ekonomika, 1974.

————. *Nekotorye voprosy teorii i praktiki planirovaniia i upravleniia*. Moscow: Nauka, 1979.

Fedoseev, P.N. *Leninizm i natsional'nyi vopros v sovremennykh usloviiakh*. Moscow: Izdatelstvo politicheskoi literatury, 1974.

Feldbrugge, F.J.M., ed., *Encyclopedia of Soviet Law* 2 vols. Dobbs Ferry, NY: Oceana Publications, 1973.

————, ed., *The Distinctiveness of Soviet Law*. Boston: Kluwer Academic, 1988.

Feshbach, Murray. "Prospects for Outmigration from Central Asia and Kazakhstan in the Next Decade." *Soviet Economy in a Time of Change*. Washington, D.C.: US Government Printing Office. No. 1 (1979): 656–709.

————. "The Soviet Union: Population Trends and Dilemmas." *Population Bulletin* 37, No. 19 (1982).

Friedgut, Theodore, A. *Political Participation in the USSR*. Princeton: Princeton University Press, 1979.

Friedrich, Carl and Zbigniew Brzezinski. *Totalitarian Dictatorship and Autocracy*. Cambridge: Harvard University Press. revised edition, 1965.

Gabrizhidze. B.N. *Konstitutsionnyi status organov sovetskogo gosudarstva*. Moscow: Iuridicheskaia literatura, 1982.

Galilov, S.S. "Razrabotka V.I. Leninym printsipov stroitel'stva Sovetskogo mnogonatsional'nogo gosudarstv." In *O deiatel'nosti V.I. Lenina v 1917–1922 gg*. Moscow, 1958.

Gellner, Ernest. *Nations and Nationalism*. Ithaca: Cornell University Press.

Genkina, E.B. *Obrazovanie SSSR: Sbornik dokumentov* Moscow: Izdatelstvo Akademii Nauk, 1949.

Gill, Graeme. "The Single Party as an Agent of Development: Lessons from the Soviet Experience." *World Politics* 39, No. 4 (1987): 566–578.

Gillulla, James. "The Economic Interdependence of Soviet Republics." *The Soviet Economy in a Time of Change*. 1 (1979): 618–655.

Gitelman, Zvi. "Are Nations Merging in the USSR?" *Problems of Communism* 32 (1983): 35–47.

Gitlin, S.I. *Natsional'naia politika KPSS v usloviakh razvitogo sotsializma.* Tashkent: Fan, 1983.

Gleason, Gregory. "Between Moscow and Tashkent." Unpublished Ph.D. dissertation, University of California, Davis, 1984.

———. "Educating for Underdevelopment: The Soviet Vocational Education System and its Central Asian Critics." *Central Asian Survey* 4, No. 1 (1985): 59–81.

———. "Sharaf Rashidov and the Dilemmas of National Leadership." *Central Asian Survey* 5, No. 3/4 (1986): 133–160.

———. "Ministries Versus Territories: Branch and Territorial Principles in Soviet Agricultural Administration." *Studies in Comparative Communism* 19, No. 3/4 (1987): 227–245.

Glezerman, G.E. *Klassy i natsii.* Moscow: Politizdat, 1977.

Gorbachev, Mikhail S. *Korennoi vopros ekonomicheskoi politiki partii.* Moscow: Politizdat, 1985.

———. *Perestroika: New Thinking for Our Country and the World.* New York: Harper and Row, 1987.

Gosudarstvennyi biudzhet SSSR i biudzhety soiuznykh respublik, 1981–1985. Moscow: Finansy i statistika, 1987.

Gurvich, Georgii Semenovich. *Osnovy Sovetskoi Konstitutsii.* Moscow: Gosudarstvennoe izdatelstvo, 1922.

———. *Istoriia Sovetskoi Konstitutsii.* Moscow, 1923.

———. *Printsip avtonomizma i federalizma v sovetskoi sisteme.* Moscow, 1924.

Gustafson, Thane. *Reform in Soviet Politics: The Lessons of Recent Policies on Land and Water.* New York: Cambridge University Press, 1981.

Hammer, Darrell. "Alternative Visions of the Russian Future: Religious and Nationalist Alternatives." *Studies in Comparative Communism* 20, No. 3/4 (1987): 265–275.

Harasymiw, Bohdan. *Political Elite Recruitment in the Soviet Union.* London: Macmillan Press, 1984.

Hauslohner, Peter. "Gorbachev's Social Contract." *Soviet Economy* 3, No. 1 (1987): 54–89.

Hazard, John N. *Communists and their Law.* Chicago: University of Chicago Press, 1969.

———. *The Soviet System of Government.* Chicago: The University of Chicago Press, 1980.

———. *Managing Change in the USSR.* Cambridge: Cambridge University Press, 1983.

Heilbroner, Robert. *Marxism: For and Against.* New York: W.W. Norton, 1980.

Heinemeier, Meredith M. *Bibliography of Regional Statistical Handbooks in the USSR.* Washington, D.C.: US Bureau of the Census, Center for International Research Revised May, 1987.

Hodnett, Grey. "The Debate over Soviet Federalism." *Soviet Studies* 18, No. 4 (1967): 458–481.

———. "Technology and Social Change in Soviet Central Asia: The Politics of Cotton Growing." *Soviet Politics and Society in the 1970s.* Eds. Henry Morton and Rudolf Tokes, New York: Free Press, 1974. pp. 60–117.

———. *Leadership in the Soviet National Repulics: A Quantitative Study of Recruitment Policy.* Oakville, Ontario: Mosaic Press, 1978.

Hodnett, Grey and Val Ogareff. *Leaders of the Soviet Republics, 1955–1972.* Canberra: Australian National University, 1973.

Hohmann, Hans-Hermann; Alec Nove; and Heinrich Vogel, eds. *Economics and Politics in the USSR: Problems of Interdependence.*, Boulder, CO: Westview, 1986.

Holzman, Franklyn D. *Soviet Taxation.* Cambridge: Harvard University Press, 1955.

Hough, Jerry F. *The Soviet Prefects: The Role of Local Party Organs in Industrial Decision Making.* Cambridge: Harvard University Press, 1969.

Hough, Jerry F. and Merle Fainsod. *How the Soviet Union is Governed.* Cambridge: Harvard University Press, 1979.

Hutchings, Raymond. *The Soviet Budget.* Albany: State University of New York Press, 1983.

Iakubovskaia, S.I. *Stroitel'stvo soiuznogo sovetskogo sotsialisticheskogo gosudarstva 1922–1925.* Moscow: Izdatelstvo AN SSSR, 1960.

———. *Obrazovanie i razvitie Sovetskogo mnogonatsional'nogo gosudarstva.* Moscow, 1966.

Ibragimov, S.I. and V.I. Lysenko. "Vsaimootnosheniia ministerstv soiuznoi respubliki s mestnymi Sovetami po kompleksnomy razvitiiu territorii." *Sovetskoe gosudarstvo i pravo* No. 8 (1986): 28–34.

Ilinskii, I and B.V. Shchetinin. *Gosudarstvennoe pravo stran narodnoi demokratii.* Moscow: Izdatelstvo IMO, 1964.

Information Department of the Royal Institute of International Affairs. *The Baltic States: A Survey of the Political and Economic Structure and the Foreign Relations of Estonia, Latvia, and Lithuania.* London: Oxford University Press, 1938.

Iurchenko, O. *Priroda i funktsii sovetskikh federatyvnykh form.* Munich, 1956.

Iusupov, V.A. *Sochetanie otraslevogo i territorial'nogo upravleniia promyshlennost'iu v SSSR.* Kazan, 1973.

Ivanov, Georgii, Alekseevich. *Planovye organy v SSSR.* Moscow: Ekonomiki, 1967.

Ivashchenko, O. I. "Deitel'nost' ekonomicheskoi komissii soveta natsional'nostei Verkhovnogo Soveta SSSR i ee dal'neishee sovershenstvovanie v svete programmy KPSS." *Sovetskoe gosudarstvo i pravo* No. 4 (1962): 39–48.

Jones, Ellen and Fred W. Grupp. "Modernization and Traditionality in a Multiethnic Society: The Soviet Case." *American Political Science Review* 79, No. 2 (1985): 1019–1039.

Kaltakhchian, Surgen Tigranovich. *Leninizm o sushchnosti natsii i puti obrazovaniia internatsional'noi obshchnosti liudei.* Moscow: Izdatelstvo Moskovskogo universiteta, 1969.

Kamenetsky, Ihor, ed., *Nationalism and Human Rights: Processes of Modernization in the USSR.* Littleton, CO: Libraries Unlimited, 1977.

Kamshibaev, R.A. "Sbalansirovannost' i proportsii vosproizvodstva ekonomiki respubliki." *Izvestiia AN KazSSR: Seriia obshchestvennykh nauk* No. 4 (1986): 54–61.

Karklins, Rasma. "Ethnic Politics and Access to Higher Education: The Soviet Case." *Comparative Politics* 16, No. 3 (1984): 277–294.

_____ . Ethnic Relations in the USSR. Boston: Allen and Unwin, 1986.

Karpat, Kemal. "Moscow and the 'Muslim Question'." Problems of Communism (1983): 71–79.

Katsenelinboigen, Aron. Soviet Economic Thought and Political Power in the USSR. New York: Pergamon Press, 1980.

Kauppi, Mark V. "The Resurgence of Ethno-nationalism and Perspectives on State–society Relations." Canadian Review of Studies in Nationalism 11, No. 1 (1984): 119–132.

Kautsky, Karl. The Dictatorship of the Proletariat. Ann Arbor: University of Michigan Press, 1964.

Kelley, Donald R. The Politics of Developed Socialism: The Soviet Union as a Post-Industrial State. Westport, CT: Greenwood Press, 1986.

Khakimov, M. Kh. "K voprosu o predmete nauki sovetskogo konstitutsionnogo prava." Obshchestvennye nauki v Uzbekistane No. 1 (1961): 36–41.

_____ . Razvitie natsional'noi sovetskoi gosudarstvennosti v Uzbekistane. Tashkent: Fan, 1965.

_____ . Novaia konstitutsiia SSSR i upravlenie narodnym khoziaistvom: uchet otraslevogo i territorial'nogo printsipov. Tashkent: Fan, 1979.

Khalilov, A.M. "Novyi etap natsional'no-gosudarstvennogo stroitel'stva v SSSR." Sovetskoe gosudarstvo i pravo No. 12 (1979): 3–10.

Khanazarov, K. "Sovershenstvovanie sotsializma i natsional'nye otnosheniia." Partiinaia zhizn' No. 6 (1986): 91–95.

Khidoiatov, G.A. Leninskaia natsional'naia programma i sovremennaia ideologicheskaia bor'ba. Tashkent: Uzbekistan, 1977.

Kim, Maksim Pavlovich. Sovetskii narod–novaia istoricheskaia obshchnost'. Moscow: Politizdat, 1972.

Kirin, V.A. "Kompetentsiia soiuza SSR i soiuznykh respublik v oblasti zakonodatel'stva." Sovetskoe gosudarstvo i pravo No. 5 (1970): 5–6.

Kis, Theofil. Le Federalisme Sovietique. Ottawa: Editions de L'Universite D'Ottawa, 1973.

Kislitsin, I.M. Voprosy teorii i praktiki federativnogo stroitel'stva Soiuza SSR. Perm, 1969.

Kochumov, Ia.Kh. Konstitutsiia SSSR i problemy upravleniia ekonomicheskim i sotsial'nym razvitiem soiuznoi respubliki. Ashkhabad, 1982.

Kohn, Hans. The Idea of Nationalism: A Study in its Origins and Background. New York: Macmillan, 1944.

_____ . Nationalism: its Meaning and History. Princeton, NJ: Van Nostrand, 1965.

Kokoshkin, F.F. Avtonomiia i federatsiia. Petrograd, 1917.

Kolarz, Walter. Russia and Her Colonies. New York: Praeger, 1955.

_____ . Communism and Colonialism. London: Macmillan, 1964.

Kolibab, K.E. "O pravovom polozhenii ministerstv SSSR." Sovetskoe gosudarstvo i pravo 1 (1968).

Kolosovskii, N.N. Teoriia ekonomicheskogo raionirovaniia. Moscow: Mysl, 1969.

Konstantinov, F.V. Filosofskaia entsiklopediia 5 Vol. Moscow: Sovetskaia entsiklopediia, 1960–1970.

Konstantinov, F.T. Kommunizm i natsii. Moscow: Nauka, 1985.

Kopeichikov, V.V. *Mekhanizm gosudarstva v Sovetskoi federatsii.* Moscow: Iuridicheskaia literatura, 1973.

Koropeckyj, Iwan. "Equalization of Regional Development in Socialist Countries: An Empirical Study." *Economic Development and Cultural Change* 21, No. 1 (1972): 68–86.

Koropeckyj, Iwan and Gertrude E. Schroeder. *Economics of Soviet Regions.* New York: Praeger, 1981.

Koroteeva, Viktoria, L. Perepelkin and O. Shkaratan. "Ot biurokraticheskogo tsentralizma k ekonomicheskoi integratsii suverennykh respublik." *Kommunist* No. 15 (1988): 22–33.

Koshanov, A.K. and A.Kh. Attapkhanov. "Problema vyravnirovaniia etnosotsial'noi struktury rabochego klassa soiuznykh respublik." *Vestnik AN KazSSR* No. 11 (1985): 56–63.

Kovalenko, A. "Vsemernoe uprochnenie i razvitie SSSR kak edinogo soiuznogo mnogonatsional'nogo gosudarstva." *Sotsialisticheskaia zakonnost'* No. 7 (1986): 42–45.

Kozlov, Iu.M. *Koordinatsiia v upravlenii narodnym khoziaistvom SSSR.* Moscow, 1976.

Kozlov, Viktor Ivanovich. *Soiuz svobodnykh i ravnykh.* Moscow, 1964.

————. *National'nosti SSR: Etnodemograficheskii obzor.* Moscow: Statistika, 1975.

Kress, John H. "Representation of Position on the CPSU Politburo." *Slavic Review* 39, No. 2 (1980): 218–238.

Kukushkin, Iu. and O. Chistiakov. *Ocherk istorii Sovetskoi Konstitutsii.* Moscow: Politizdat, 1987.

Kulichenko, M.I. "V.I. Lenin o federatsii i ee roli v stroitel'stve Sovetskogo mnogonatsional'nogo gosudarstva." *Voprosy istorii KPSS* No. 5 (1961).

————. *Natsional'nye otnosheniia v SSSR i tendentsii ikh razvitiia.* Moscow: Izdatelstvo Mysl, 1972.

————. *Natsional'nye otnosheniia v razvitom sotsialisticheskom obshchestve.* Moscow: Mysl, 1977.

————. *Rastsvet i sblizhenie natsii.* Moscow, 1981.

Lane, David. *Politics and Society in the USSR.* London: Martin Robertson, 1978.

Lapidus, Gail Warshofsky. "Ethnonationalism and Political Stability: The Soviet Case." *World Politics* 36, No. 4 (1984): 555–580.

Lashin, A.G. *Vozniknovenie i razvitie form sotsialisticheskogo gosudarstva.* Moscow: Izdatelstvo MGU, 1965.

Latvian Legation. *Latvia in 1939–1942.* Washington, D.C.: Press Bureau of the Latvian Legation, 1942.

Lazarev. B.M. *Kompetentsiia organov upravlenia.* Moscow: Iurizdat, 1972.

————. *Grazhdanin i apparat upraveleniia v SSSR.* Moscow: Izdat Nauka, 1982.

Lenin, V.I. *Polnoe sobranie sochinenii.* 5th ed. 55 Vols. Moscow: Izdatelstvo politicheskoi literatury, 1960–65.

Lepeshkin, A.I, ed., *Soiuz SSR–sodruzhestvo ravnopravnykh narodov.* Moscow: Iuridicheskaia literatura, 1972.

————. "Sovetskii federalizm v period razvitogo sotsializma." *Sovetskoe gosudarstvo i pravo* 8: 3–12, 1975.

_____ . *Sovetskii federalizm.* Moscow: Iuridicheskaia literatura, 1977.

Levin, I.D. and I.M Vail'. eds. *Sovremennyi burzhuaznyi federalizm.* Moscow, 1978.

Lewin, Moshe. *The Making of the Soviet System.* New York: Pantheon Books, 1985.

Lewis, Robert A. and Richard H. Rowland. *Population Redistribution in the USSR.* New York: Praeger, 1979.

Lewis, Robert A., Richard H. Rowland, and Ralph S. Clem. *Nationality and Population Change in Russia and the USSR.* New York: Praeger, 1976.

Lubin, Nancy. *Labor and Nationality in Soviet Central Asia.* Princeton: Princeton University Press, 1984.

Lustick, Ian. "Stability in Deeply Divided Societies: Consociationalism versus Control." *World Politics* 31: (1979): 325–344.

Lychagin, V.A. *Ekonomicheskie problemy razvitiia natsiei i natsional'nykh otnoshenii v SSSR na stadii razvitogo sotsializma* Saransk: Modovskoe Knizhnoe Izdatelstvo, 1975.

Macartney, C.A. *National States and National Minorities.* London, 1934.

McAuley, Mary. "Party Recruitment and the Nationalities in the USSR: A Study in Center-Republican Relationships." *British Journal of Political Science* 10 (1980): 461–487.

McGrath, W.J. "The Politics of Soviet Federalism." Unpublished Ph.D. Dissertation, Carleton University, 1981.

Manning, Clarence A. *The Forgotten Republics.* New York: Philosophical Library, 1952.

Manokhin, V.M. ". . . S uchetom otraslevogo i territorial'nogo printsipov.." *Sovetskoe gosudarstvo i pravo* No. 10 (1978): 21–30.

Marx, Karl and Frederick Engels. *Collected Works.* London: Lawrence and Wishart, 1975.

Meissner, Boris. "Entstehung, Fortentwicklung und ideologische Grundlagen des sowjetischen Bundesstaates." *Osteuropa* 22, No. 12 (1972): 869–907.

Meyer, Alfred G. *Leninism.* Cambridge: Harvard University Press, 1957.

Millar, James R. and Donna Bahry. "Financing Development and Tax Structure Change in the USSR." *Canadian Slavonic Papers* 21, No. 2 (1979): 166–174.

Minagawa, Shugo. *Supreme Soviet Organs.* Nagoya: University of Nagoya Press, 1985.

Mochalov, B., ed., *Territorial'no-otraslevoi printsip planirovaniia: Teoriia i praktika.* Moscow: Mysl', 1980.

Moses, Joel C. *Regional Party Leadership and Policy-Making in the USSR.* New York: Praeger, 1974.

_____ . "Regionalism in Soviet Politics: Continuity as a Source of Change, 1953–1982." *Soviet Studies* 37, No. 2 (1985): 184–211.

Motyl, Alexander. *Will the Non-Russians Revolt?* Ithaca: Cornell University Press, 1987.

Nahaylo, Bohdan. *The Soviet Disunion* New York: Unwin Hyman, 1989.

Narkiewicz, Olga A. *The Making of the Soviet State Apparatus.* Manchester: The University of Manchester Press, 1970.

Narodnoe khoziaistvo SSSR. (annual) Moscow.

Nechemias, Carol. "Regional Differentiation of Living Standards in the RSFSR: The Issue of Inequality." *Slavic Review* 32, No. 3 (1980): 366–378.

Nekrasov, N.I. *Regional'naia ekonomika: Teoriia, problemy, metody.* Moscow, 1975.

Nelson, Daniel N. "Dilemmas of Local Politics in Communist States." *Journal of Politics* No. 41 (1979): 23–54.

Nissman, David B. *The Soviet Union and Iranian Azerbaijan.* Boulder: Westview Press, 1987.

Nordlinger, Eric. *Conflict Regulation in Deeply Divided Societies.* Cambridge: Center for International Affairs, Harvard University, Occasional Paper No. 29, 1971.

Nove, Alec and J.A. Newth. *The Soviet Middle East.* New York: Praeger, 1967.

Nuykin, Andrei. "Idealy ili interesy." *Novy mir* No. 1 (1988): 20–211.

Ogareff, Val. *Leaders of the Soviet Republics, 1971–1980.* Canberra: Australian National University, 1980.

Olcott, Martha Brill. "Yuri Andropov and the 'National Question'." *Soviet Studies* 37, No. 1 (1985): 103–117.

––––––. *The Kazaks.* Stanford: Hoover Institution Press, 1988.

Page, Stanley W. *The Formation of the Baltic States: A Study of the effects of Great Power Politics upon the Emergence of Lithuania, Lativa, and Estonia.* New York: Howard Fertig, 1970.

Pavlenko, V.F. *Territorial'noe planirovanie v SSSR.* Moscow, 1975.

Petro, Nicolai N. "The Project of the Century: A Case Study of Russian National Dissent." *Studies in Comparative Communism* 20, No. 3/4 (1987): 235–252.

Petrov, A.S. "Ekonomicheskaia reforma: tendentsii organizatsii otraslevogo upravleniia promyshlennost'iu." *Sovetskoe gosudarstvo i pravo* No. 3 (1971): 12–30.

Petrov, V.S. *Sushchnost, soderzhanie i formy gosudarstva.* Leningrad: Nauka, 1971.

Pinkus, Benjamin. *The Jews of the Soviet Union.* Cambridge: Cambridge University Press, 1988.

Pipes, Richard. *The Formation of the Soviet Union: Communism and Nationalism, 1917–1923.* rev. ed. Cambridge: Harvard University Press, 1964.

Piskotin, M.I. "Demokraticheskii tsentralizm i problemy sochetaniia tsentralizatsii i detsentralizatsii." *Sovetskoe gosudarstvo i pravo* No. 5 (1981): 39–49.

Ponomareva, B.N. *Konstitutsiia SSSR.* Moscow: Izdatelstvo politicheskoi literatury, 1982.

Potichnyj, Peter. "Permanent Representatives (Postpredstva) of Union Republics in Moscow." in Peter Potichnyj and Jane Shapiro Zacek, eds., *Politics and Participation Under Communist Rule.* New York: Praeger, 1983. Pp. 50–83.

Raiabov, S.A. "Geographical Factors and Certain Problems of Federalism in the USSR." *International Social Science Journal* 30, No. 1 (1978): 88–97.

Rakowska-Harmstone, Teresa. *Russia and Nationalism in Central Asia: the Case of Tadzhikistan.* Baltimore: Johns Hopkins Press, 1971.

––––––, ed., *Perspectives for Change in Communist Societies.* Boulder: Westview, 1979.

Ramet, Pedro. *Nationalism and Federalism in Yugoslavia, 1963–1983.* Bloomington: Indiana University Press.

Raun, Toivo U. *Estonia and the Estonians.* Stanford: Hoover Institution Press, 1988.

Ravin, S.M. *Razvitie gosudarstvennogo prava na osnove Konstitutsii SSSR 1936.* Leningrad: Izdatelstvo LGU, 1957.

―――. "Sozdanie teorii sovetskogo federalizma." *Uchenye zapiski LGU.* No. 255, Vyp. 10 (1958).

―――. "Sozdanie teorii sovetskogo federalizma." *Voprosy gosudarstvo i pravo* (1958): 36–48.

Reikhel, M.O., ed., *Sovetskii federalizm.* Moscow, 1930.

Remington, Thomas. "Federalism and Segmented Communications in the USSR." *Publius* No. 15 (1985): 113–132.

Report on the USSR (known until 1989 as *Radio Liberty Research Bulletin*) (biweekly).

Reshetar, John S, Jr. *The Ukrainian Revolution, 1917–1920: A Study in Nationalism.* Princeton: Princeton University Press, 1952.

Rianzhin, V.A. *Problemy territorial'noi organizatsii Sovetskogo gosudarstva.* Leningrad: Izdatelstvo LGU, 1973.

Riege, G. "Sowjetfoderation und nationale Frage." *Staat und Recht* 21, No. 12 (1972): 1881–1892.

Rigby, T.H. and Bohdan Harasymiw, eds. *Leadership Selection and Patron-Client Relations in the USSR and Yugoslavia.* New York: Pergamon Press, 1983.

Rothschild, Joseph. *Ethnopolitics: A Conceptual Framework.* New York: Columbia University Press, 1981.

Rowland, Richard H. "Regional Population Redistribution in the USSR: 1979–84." *Soviet Geography* 28, No. 3 (1986): 158–181.

Rozenbaum, Iu.A. "Sistema raboty s kadrami v usloviiakh perestroiki." *Sovetskoe gosudarstvo i pravo* No. 12 (1986): 11–20.

Rumer, Boris. *Soviet Central Asia.* Boston: Unwin Hyman, 1989.

Rusinova, S.I. "Sotsialisticheskoe unitarnoe gosudarstvennogo ustroistva natsii." *Vestnik Leningradskogo universiteta* No. 11 (1957).

Sabaliunas, Leonas. *Lithuania in Crisis: Nationalism to Communism, 1939–1940.* Bloomington: Indiana University Press, 1971.

Saidbaev, T.S. *Islam: istoriia i sovremennost'.* Moscow: Znanie, 1985.

Schapiro, Leonard. *The Communist Party of the Soviet Union* New York: Random House, 1959.

Schlesinger, Rudolf. *Federalism in Central and Eastern Europe.* New York: Oxford University Press, 1945.

―――. *The Nationalities Problem and Soviet Administration.* London: Routledge and Kegan Paul, 1956.

Seers, Dudley. *The Political Economy of Nationalism.* Oxford: Oxford University Press, 1983.

Semenkov, V.I. and V.I. Shabailov. *Ministerstva, gosudarstvennye komitety i vedomstva soiuznoi respubliki.* Minsk: Nauka i tekhnika, 1984.

Semenov, P.G. "Programma KPSS o razvitii sovetskikh natsional'no-gosudarstvennykh otnoshenii." *Sovetskoe gosudarstvo i pravo* No. 12, (1961).

―――. "Natsiia i natsional'naia gosudarstvennost' v SSSR." *Voprosy istorii* No. 7 (1966): 72–81.

Seton-Watson, Hugh. *Nationalism and Communism: Essays, 1946–1963.* New York: Praeger, 1964.

_____ . *Nations and States: an Enquiry into the Origins of Nations and the Politics of Nationalism.* Boulder, CO: Westview Press, 1977.

Shafir, M.A. *Kompetentsiia SSSR i soiuznykh respublik.* Moscow, 1968.

Shaibalov, V.I. "Soiuzno-respublikanskie ministerstva soiuznykh respublik (nazrevshie problemy)." *Sovetskoe gosudarstvo i pravo* No. 2 (1984): 65–70.

Sharlet, Robert. *The New Soviet Constitution of 1977: Analysis and Text* Brunswick, OH: King's Court Communications, 1978.

Shaumian, S.G. *O natsional'no-kul'turnoi avtonomii* Moscow, 1959.

Sherstobitov, V.P. "Aktual'nye problemy izucheniia natsional'nykh otnoshenii v SSSR na sovremennom etape." *Istoriia SSSR* No. 5 (1986): 29–49.

Shii, B.G. *Ekonomicheskoe vyravnirovanie soiuznykh respublik (Na opyte respublik Srednei Azii)* Dushanbe, 1973.

Shafir, M.A. *Kompetentsiia SSSR i soiuznykh respublik.* Moscow, 1968.

Shirkevich, N.A. *Rol' biudzheta v razvitii ekonomiki i kul'tury soiuznykh respublik* Moscow: Finansy, 1972.

Shmatov, I.I. "Osobennosti internatsionalizatsii obshchestvennoi zhizni v usloviiakh razvitogo sotsializma." *Voprosy filosofii* No. 12 (1984): 32–31.

Shtromas, Alexander. "The Legal Position of Soviet Nationalities and Their Territorial Units According to the 1977 Constitution of the USSR." *Russian Review* No. 37 (1978): 269–270.

_____ . "Dissent, Nationalism, and the Soviet Future." *Studies in Comparative Communism* 20, No. 3/4 (1987): 277–287.

_____ . *The Soviet Method of Conquest of the Baltic States* Washington, D.C.: Washington Institute Monograph, 1987.

Siegler, Robert W. *The Standing Commissions of the Supreme Soviet: Effective Co-optation* New York: Praeger, 1982.

Sigov, I. "Sochetanie otraslevogo i territorial'nogo upravleniia." *Voprosy ekonomiki* No. 9 (1984): 24–30.

Slider, Darrell. "More Power to the Soviets?" *British Journal of Political Science* 16, No. 4 (1986): 495–511.

Smal-Stocki, Roman. *The Nationality Problem of the Soviet Union and Russian Communist Imperialism.* Milwaukee: Bruce Publishing Company, 1952.

_____ . *The Captive Nations: Nationalism of the non-Russian Nations in the Soviet Union.* New York: Bookman Associates, 1960.

Smirtiukov, M.S. *Sovestskii gosudarstvennyi apparat upravleniia.* Moscow: Izdatelstvo politicheskoi literatury, 1982.

Smith, Anthony D. *The Ethnic Revival* Cambridge: Cambridge University Press, 1981.

_____ . "Nationalism and Classic Social Theory." *British Journal of Sociology* 34, No. 1 (1983): 19–38.

Snyder, Louis Leo. *The New Nationalism* Ithaca, NY: Cornell University Press, 1968.

Soderzhanie i struktura edinogo narodnokhoiaistvennogo kompleksa SSSR Moscow: Nauka, 1987.

Solchanyk, Roman. "Russian Language and Soviet Politics." *Soviet Studies* 34, No. 1 (1982): 23–42.

SSSR: Administrativno-territorial'noe delenie soiuznykh respublik, 1987 Moscow, 1987.

SSSR i soiuznye respubliki v 1984 Moscow: Finansy i statistika, 1985.

Stalin, Joseph. *Sochineniia* 13 Vols. Moscow, 1946–1952.

_____ . *Marxism and the National and Colonial Question* London: Lawrence and Wishart, 1947.

_____ . *Sochineniia* 3 Vols. Stanford: Hoover Institution Press, 1967.

Steiner, Jurg. "The Consociational Theory and Beyond." *Comparative Politics* No. 13 (1981): 339–360.

Stuchka, P. *Uchenie o Sovetskom gosudarstve i ego Konstitutsii* Moscow: Gosizdat, 1929.

Suny, Ronald Grigor. *The Making of the Georgian Nation* Bloomington: Indiana University Press, 1987.

Tadevosian, E.V. "V.I. Lenin o gosudarstvennoi federatsii." *Voprosy istorii KPSS* No. 2 (1961): 43–59.

_____ . *Lenin o gosudarstvennykh formakh resheniia natsional'nogo voprosa v SSSR* Moscow: Izdatelstvo MGU, 1970.

_____ . *Sovetskaia natsional'naia gosudarstvennost'* Moscow, 1972.

Tarrow, Sidney. *Between Center and Periphery* New Haven: Yale University Press, 1977.

Tarulis, Albert N. *Soviet Policy Toward the Baltic States, 1918–1940* Notre Dame, Indiana: University of Notre Dame Press, 1959.

Taubman, William. *Governing Soviet Cities: Bureaucratic Politics and Urban Development in the USSR* New York: Praeger, 1973.

Thotappa, K.B.Y. and Y.R. Ahmed. "In Defence of Soviet Federalism." *Journal of Political Studies* 4, No. 1 (1971): 23–34.

Todorskii, Iu. V. "Vzaimootnosheniia kraevykh, oblastnkykh sovetov s nepodvedomstvennymi ob"edineniiami." *Sovetskoe gosudarstvo i pravo* No. 9 (reprinted as "Relations of Territorial and Regional Soviets with Associations Not Subordinate to Them." in *Soviet Geography: Review and Translation* No. 18 (1979): 61–78.

Topornin, B.N. *Novaia Konstitutsiia SSSR* Moscow: Progress, 1980.

Towster, Julian. *Political Power in the USSR* New York: Oxford University Press, 1948.

Trainin, I.P. "Sovetskoe mnogonatsional'noe gosudarstvo." *Sovetskoe gosudarstvo i pravo* No. 10 (1947).

Triska, Jan F., ed., *Soviet Communism: Programs and Rules* San Francisco: Chandler Publishing Company, 1962.

_____ , ed., *Constitutions of the Communist Party States* Stanford: The Hoover Institution Press, 1968.

Tsvetkova, V.V. *Sovershenstvovanie apparata gosudarstvennogo upravleniia.* Kiev: Naukova Dumka, 1982.

Tucker, Robert C. *Stalin as Revolutionary, 1879–1929: A Study in History and Personality* New York: W.W. Norton and Co, 1973.

Tulenov, Zh.T. "Nekotorye voprosy dialektiki natsional'nykh otnoshenii." *Obshchestvennye nauki v Uzbekistane* No. 2 (1984): 10–16.

Uibopuu, Henn-Juri. "International Legal Personality of Union Republics of the USSR." *International and Comparative Law Quarterly* No. 24 (1975): 811–845.

Ulam, Adam B. *Stalin: the Man and his Era* New York: Viking Press, 1973.

Urazaev, Sh.Z. "Uzbekskoi sovetskoi natsional'noi gosudarstvennosti–60 let." *Obshchestvennye nauki v Uzbekistane* No. 5 (1984): 3–8.

Vanneman, Peter. *The Supreme Soviet* Durham: Duke University Press, 1977.

Vardys, Stanley V. *Lithuania Under the Soviets: A Portrait of a Nation, 1940–1965* New York: Praeger, 1965.

Vardys, Stanley V. and Romuald J. Misiunas. *The Baltic States in Peace and War, 1917–1945* University Park: The Pennsylvania State University Press, 1978.

Vasilenkov, P. and L. Voevodin. "Obrazovanie i razvitie RSFSR kak federativnogo gosudarstva." *Sovetskaia iustitsiia* No. 11 (1958): 7–10.

Vasil'ev V. *Federal'nyi biudzhet i natsional'nye prioretety SShA* Moscow: Nauka, 1987.

Vikharev, S.R. *Lenin o suverenitete soiuznykh respublik* Minsk, 1969.

Vishniakov, V.G. *Struktura i staty organov sovetskogo gosudarstvennogo upravleniia.* Moscow: Iuridicheskaia literatura, 1972.

_____ . *Dvoinoe podchinenie organov upravleniia narodnym khoziaistvom* Moscow, 1967.

_____ . "Otraslevoe i territorial'noe upravlenie: opyt i problemy." *Izvestie vyshikh uchebnykh zavedenii: Pravovedenie* No. 3 (1986): 13–22.

Volkov, N.A. *Vysshie i tsentral'nye organy gosudarstvennogo upravleniia SSSR i soiuznykh respublik v sovremennyi period* Kazan: Izdatelstvo Kazan'skogo Universiteta, 1971.

Voprosy ekonomicheskogo raionirovaniia Moscow: Gospolitizdat, 1957.

Voslensky, Michael. *Nomenklatura.* New York: Doubleday and Company, 1984.

Waldron, Arthur N. "Theories of Nationalism and Historical Explanation." *World Politics* 37,3 (1985): 416–433.

Weeks, Albert, L., compiler. *The Soviet Nomenklatura: A Comprehensive Roster of Soviet Civilian and Military Officials* Washington, D.C.: Washington Institute Press, 1987.

Wheare, K.C. *Federal Government* Oxford: Clarendon, 1946.

Wheeler, Geoffrey. *The Modern History of Soviet Central Asia* New York: Praeger, 1964.

White, Stephen. "The Supreme Soviet and Budgetary Politics in the USSR." *British Journal of Political Science* No. 12 (1982): 75–94.

Willerton, John Jr. "Clientelism in the Soviet Union: An Initial Examination." *Studies in Comparative Communism* 12, No. 2/3 (1979): 159-183.

_____ . "Patronage Networks and Coalition Building in the Brezhnev Era." *Soviet Studies* 39,2 (1987): 175–204.

Wimbush, Enders S. *Soviet Nationalities in Strategic Perspective* New York: St. Martin's Press, 1985.

Wolfe, Bertram D. "Nationalism and Internationalism in Marx and Engels." *American Slavonic and East European Review* 9, No. 3 (1950): 169–79.

_____ . *Three Who Made a Revolution* New York: Time–Life Books, 1964.

Yanov, Alexander. "The New Russian Right: Right-Wing Ideologies in the USSR." University of California, Berkeley Institute of International Studies, Research Series. No. 35. 1978.

————. *The Russian Challenge* New York: Basil Blackwell, 1987.

Zaslavsky, Victor. *The Neo-Stalinist State: Class, Ethnicity, and Consensus in Soviet Society* Armonk, N.Y.: Sharpe, 1982.

Zemtsov, Ilya. *Stuggle for Power in the Kremlin: Part I Andropov* Fairfax, VA: Hero Books, 1984.

————. "Andropov and the Non-Russian Nationalities: Attitudes and Policies." *Nationalities Papers* No. 8 (1985): 5–23.

Zenchenko, N.S. *Sochetanie territorial'nogo i otraslevogo planirovaniia* Moscow: Ekonomika, 1979.

Zenkovsky, Serge. *Pan-Turkism and Islam in Russia* Cambridge: Harvard University Press, 1960.

Zharnikov, A. "Dialektika natsional'nykh protsessov." *Pravda* 27 September 1987.

Zimanov, S.Z and I.K. Reitor. *Sovetskaia natsional'naia gosudarstvennost' i sblizhenie natsii* Alma-Ata: Nauka, 1983.

Zlatopol'skii, D.L. *Gosudarstvennoe ustroistvo SSSR* Moscow: Gosiurizdat, 1960.

Zwick, Peter. "Ethnoregional Socio-economic Fragmentation and Soviet Budgetary Policy." *Soviet Studies* No. 31 (1979): 380–400.

————. *National Communism* Boulder, Co: Westview, 1983.

Index